Revolving Doors:

Sex Segregation and

Women's Careers

REVOLVING DOORS

Sex Segregation and

Women's Careers

Jerry A. Jacobs

Stanford University Press   1989
Stanford, California

Stanford University Press
Stanford, California
© 1989 by the Board of Trustees of the
Leland Stanford Junior University
Printed in the United States of America

CIP data appear at the end of the book

Preface

My interest in sex segregation was sparked by earlier research with Brian Powell on sex differences in occupational prestige. The research reported in this book began as an attempt to statistically test the boundaries of women's labor market. The underlying assumption was that distinct barriers to mobility would emerge from this analysis. As evidence of mobility between male-dominated and female-dominated occupations accumulated with remarkable consistency from one data set to the next, my initial formulation had to be revised. Not content to provide an empirical critique of conventional approaches, I sought to develop an alternative framework. The social control / revolving door model emerged from this effort.

This project has lived several lives. As a dissertation in the Harvard University Sociology Department, the research benefited from the advice of Ronald Breiger, Lee Rainwater, Steven Rytina, and Harrison White. Chapters have been circulated, presented at conferences, and published as articles, and have profited from the comments of discussants and reviewers. Douglas Massey provided guidance on the measurement of segregation. Fred Block, Paula England, Arne Kalleberg, Phillip Morgan, and Myra Strober read the entire manuscript, and each had useful suggestions. In the final stages of this work, the research assistance of Tahmina Ferdousi and Alexis Lieberman aided in bringing this project to its conclusion. Grants from the Harvard Sociology Department and a Faculty Research Grant from the University of Pennsylvania provided time for and defrayed the computer expenses of this research. I owe a special debt to my wife, Sharon, for her patience, support, and confidence.

In this book I draw on some of my previous writings. I would like to thank the publishers of these works for allowing me to reuse portions of them. Chapter 5 draws selectively from my article "The Sex Typing of Aspirations and Occupations: Instability During the Careers of Young Women," published by the University of Texas Press in *Social Science Quarterly*, 68(1): 122–37. Table 6.2 and the discussion preceding it were first published in my essay "Sex Segregation in American Higher Education," pp. 191–214 in Laurie Larwood, Ann H. Stromberg, and Barbara Gutek, eds., *Women and Work: An Annual Review*, copyright © 1985 by Sage Publications; reprinted by permission of Sage Publications, Inc. Tables 6.3–6.5 are from my article "The Sex-Segregation of Fields of Study: Trends During the College Years," published in *The Journal of Higher Education*, 57(2): 134–54; reprinted by permission, © 1986 by the Ohio State University Press, all rights reserved. Portions of Chapter 7 and Tables 7.1–7.5 draw from my essay "The Sex Segregation of Occupations as a Circulating System," forthcoming in Ronald L. Breiger, ed., *Social Mobility and Social Structure*, © 1989 by Cambridge University Press; used with the permission of Cambridge University Press.

J.A.J.

Contents

Tables

Revolving Doors:

Sex Segregation and

Women's Careers

1

Introduction

This book is an effort to understand why women do "women's work." In 1985, over two-thirds of the women in the U.S. civilian labor force worked in occupations that were 70 percent or more female.[1] The study of women's work has attracted scholars from many disciplines, from psychology (Gutek, 1985) to history (Kessler-Harris, 1982) to anthropology (Sanday, 1981) to economics (Bergmann, 1986) to sociology (Reskin, 1984). A flurry of recent papers has addressed such topics as trends in occupational segregation (Bianchi and Rytina, 1986; Jacobs, 1986a), sex segregation among teenagers in the workplace (Greenberger and Steinberg, 1983), and sex segregation within voluntary organizations (McPherson and Smith-Lovin, 1986), between industries (Tienda, Smith, and Ortiz, 1987), across cities (Abrahamson and Sigelman, 1987), and within firms (Bielby and Baron, 1986). (See Reskin and Hartmann, 1985, for discussion of sex segregation in the workplace.)

This interest has undoubtedly been spurred by the growth in women's labor force participation (Goldin, 1983; Smith and Ward, 1984). Over 70 percent of women between the ages of 20 and 44 worked for pay in 1985, including nearly half of those with children under one year old. The overall rate of women's labor force participation has grown from 33.9 percent in 1950 to 54.5 percent in 1985 (U.S. Bureau of the Census, 1986). The women's movement has also heightened interest in working women. Legislative policies such as affirmative action, as well as the entry of feminist scholars into academia, have generated research on the disadvantaged position of working women. Most recently, calls for equal pay for work of comparable value have brought public and research attention to the concentration of women in low-paid, female-dominated occupations (Remick, 1984).

This book investigates the way women's careers intersect with the sexual division of labor in the workplace. We follow women's (and men's) life histories in order to understand the gender tracking system. We ask whether there is a decisive moment during women's lives when they are channeled into female-dominated occupations, or whether the process is more gradual. Is sex segregation principally due to a single life-course event, such as meeting with a guidance counselor in high school or becoming a parent, or is it the result of a cumulative process extending throughout much of the women's (and men's) lives?

In studying the lives of individual women, we examine stability and change in the development of occupational goals, the choice of fields of study in higher education, and the attainment of jobs. Are women locked into female-dominated occupations during their socialization as children and teenagers, or as a result of their choice of major in college? Do women get stuck in "female ghettos" if their first jobs are in traditionally female fields? Do women who aspire to careers in male-dominated occupations maintain these aspirations, obtain the appropriate education, and find and hold on to the jobs they desire? We are interested in the reproduction of segregation and examine the career patterns of women for evidence of the process of reproduction. (The term "career" is used to refer to a sequence of jobs, not to imply that all woman are "career women" [Shaw, 1983] or that women's work experiences can be characterized as being on a "career path" [Spilerman, 1977].)

A recent National Research Council committee has placed these questions high on its research agenda (Hartmann, Roos, and Treiman, 1985). The NRC Committee has urged research on the relationship between the sex typing of occupational aspirations and subsequent attainments as well as research on how occupational aspirations and expectations change over time. The committee has also called for research on whether "women who have moved into traditionally male jobs remain in these jobs" or "shift into traditionally female jobs" (1985: 26). While our research was begun before the delineation of this agenda, our work fits into this broad research program.

The questions we address are also similar to those being addressed by poverty researchers. Evidence has accumulated to show that while the size of the population in poverty changes slowly, the individuals in poverty change with much greater frequency (G. Duncan, 1984). We ask whether a similar pattern—aggregate stability with individual mobility—is evident for the sex segregation of occupations.

As the title of this book suggests, we find surprising rates of mobility for women among male-dominated, sex-neutral, and female-dominated occupations. This pattern of change is also evident when the dynamics of sex segregation of career aspirations and college majors are analyzed. Individual mobility is common, yet change in the structure of sex segregation is quite slow. This paradox is the central puzzle of this book.

The mobility described here does not imply the existence of equal opportunity for women. Quite the contrary. The rates of mobility we document are roughly proportionate to the distribution of *women* across occupations; they do not imply that women have the same chances as men. For example, the probability of a woman starting her career in a male-dominated occupation is approximately one in three for recent cohorts of women entering the labor force. Our data indicate that, for a woman who changes her occupation, the probability of moving into a male-dominated occupation is close to one in three, no matter whether her previous occupation was in a female-dominated, sex-neutral, or male-dominated field. This pattern suggests that women in female-dominated occupations who are able to change occupations stand a good chance of moving into a male-dominated occupation. Yet by the same token, women in male-dominated fields who change occupations also stand a good chance of moving to a sex-neutral or female-dominated occupation. Indeed, one of the more disturbing findings documented here is a startling rate of attrition of women in male-dominated occupations, even as these occupations appear to be opening their doors to them.

The revolving-door metaphor does not imply that women are getting nowhere. Rather, it suggests that gross mobility far exceeds the overall net change in opportunities for women. In recent years, for every 100 women in male-dominated occupations who were employed in two consecutive years, 90 remained in a male-dominated occupation, while 10 left for either a sex-neutral or female-dominated occupation. At the same time, 11 entered a male-dominated occupation from one of these other occupation groups. Thus, the revolving door sends 10 out for every 11 it lets in.[2] There has been a slow net accumulation of women in male-dominated occupations, but the net change is small compared to the size of the flows in both directions. If there were less attrition of women from male-dominated occupations, there would be more progress toward integrating men and women in the workplace.

This analysis also tracks the important changes observed over the last few decades in aspirations, education, and occupations. It examines the changes in sex segregation across cohorts and also considers the adaptability of individuals over time. In the terminology of mobility tables, the aggregate analysis tracks changes in the marginal distributions of the table, while the individual analysis examines the patterns of movement within the table. We examine whether women's aspirations and educational decisions respond to changes in opportunity in the workplace. We develop a theory of sex segregation that we call a "social control" perspective and test propositions about recent changes in sex segregation derived from this theory.

Occupational Sex Segregation and Gender Inequality

Students of society have long puzzled over the sexual division of labor. The definition of "masculine" and "feminine" in different cultures and the enforcement of the boundary between the two are long-standing concerns of social anthropologists (see Rogers, 1978, for a review of early studies in this area) and sociological theorists (Parsons and Bales, 1955). Thus, we are addressing classical social science questions in a new context, questions whose inherent interest may endure long after the current public policy debate has ended.

Yet it is the lively controversy over affirmative action hiring plans and comparable worth pay schemes that has drawn renewed attention to sex segregation as one of the causes of income inequality between men and women. In 1986, women working full-time brought home 64 percent of what men earned. While the sex gap in wages has narrowed somewhat in recent years, the annual earnings of women in 1986 constituted the same fraction of men's earnings as in 1955.[3] Women earn less than men in part because they work in female-dominated occupations. Earnings are lower in female-dominated occupations than in male-dominated occupations with similar educational requirements. Analyzing occupational data, Treiman and Hartmann (1981) estimate that from 35 to 39 percent of the gender gap in wages is due to the sex segregation of occupations. Individual-level analyses show smaller but still substantial effects of sex segregation on women's wages. Sorensen (1987) reviews studies reporting that between 9 and 38 percent of the earnings gap is attributable to sex segregation (averaging 25 percent), and she finds 27 percent so attributable in her own study, which controls for many individual characteristics as well as for industry. A U.S. Bureau of the Census report (1987) indicates that from 17 to 30 percent of the wage gap between men and women is due to women's concentration in female-dominated occupations.[4]

Comparable worth studies are also relevant in judging how much of the gender gap in wages is caused by sex segregation. One strategy for comparable worth research begins by estimating an earnings equation for male-dominated occupations in an organization that predicts wages from the attributes of these jobs as measured by the firm or by a survey. The next step is to estimate the wages women's jobs would receive if these jobs were compensated according to the same attributes as the men's jobs. This procedure accords to women's occupations the same incremental wages for such factors as education, experience, and supervisory responsibility as in men's occupations. Such studies have found that correcting for differences in the valuation of measurable traits reduces the within-firm sex gap in wages by approximately 50 percent (Sorensen, 1986; R. Steinberg, pers. comm.). This figure is close to the 43 percent estimate Blau (1984) reported for within-firm sex disparities due to sex differences in job classification.[5] This procedure is conservative in that it embodies male-based standards for judging female-dominated work and ignores other job attributes that perhaps should be valued. It should also be noted that comparable worth studies address within-firm inequality and do not correct the often substantial sex gap in wages between firms (Blau, 1977).

Studies such as those cited above attempt to measure the direct effect of sex segregation on wages. But there are indirect effects as well. For example, sex differences in education and experience are usually seen as voluntary, the result of the free choices of women. Yet if women's educational choices partly reflect their view of the limited occupational choices available to them, an estimate of the total wage consequences of sex segregation should include a portion of the education effect. Similarly, if women leave the labor force because their jobs are not sufficiently rewarding, this experience gap reflects an additional indirect effect of sex segregation. Adding these indirect effects of discrimination to the unexplained residual typically attributed to discrimination pushes the portion of the wage gap due to discrimination well above the conventional 50 percent estimate (Madden, 1985).

The differences in earnings between men and women are important to our understanding of the components of inequality in our society. But the earnings gap takes on special significance in light of the high proportion of women in poverty and high divorce rates. In 1984, 34.5 percent of families headed by women lived in poverty, and these families constituted 48 percent of poor families (U.S. Bureau of the Census, 1986). The feminization of poverty is principally due to the reduction in family income resulting from marital dissolution (Garfinkel and McLanahan, 1986). Approximately half of all marriages can be expected to end in divorce. Women with children are less likely to remarry, and they do so less quickly and securely (Furstenberg and Spanier, 1984; Cherlin, 1981; Jacobs and Furstenberg, 1986; Duncan and Hoffman, 1985). Ironically, a woman's obligations to her children heighten her financial need to remarry but make remarriage less likely.

A woman's earnings affect not only the standard of living for her family but also the very structure of that family. Among married couples, the relative earnings of husband and wife influence the distribution of power in the home. Studies have shown a direct association between the income of working women and their influence in family affairs, although researchers continue to argue over the magnitude of this relationship (England and Farkas, 1986). For example, when women join the paid labor force and their incomes increase, they do less housework, although men do not appear to take over the chores (Spitze, 1986, but see also Pleck, 1985). Thus, the segregation of women into a few low-paid occupations contributes to the inequality in power between men and women.

As we will see in Chapter 2, the allocation of tasks to men and women varies substantially over time and among societies. Consequently, researchers have explored the origins of the sexual definitions of particular occupations in our society. Davies (1982), for example, has examined the transformation of secretarial work from men's work to women's work in the late nineteenth century (see also Cohn, 1985). The rise of social work and teaching as part of women's sphere has also attracted a great deal of interest (Strober and Tyack, 1980; Rothman, 1978). And social historians have investigated the hiring of women during the two World Wars for jobs previously and subsequently reserved for men (Milkman, 1987; Greenwald, 1980; Anderson, 1981). Reskin and Roos (forthcoming) are presently studying a set of occupations whose sex composition has changed markedly in recent years.

In this book, we are not asking why one job is performed by women and another by men. Rather, we explore how these distinctions are maintained. We focus on the transmission of sex-role attitudes and the maintenance of sexual differentiation in the labor force, and ask how women are tracked into some occupations and are deterred from entering others. The sociological problem of matching individuals with positions while maintaining an elaborate sexual division of labor is the focus of this book. How do particular women, and men, end up in their respective occupations? As we will see in Chapter 2, the level of sex segregation in the U.S. labor force has declined slowly since the 1960's after remaining stable for most of the century. How does this structure persist? How is the sex-segregated structure of occupations maintained?

Sex Segregation and Social Control

To maintain any sexual division of labor, a society has to develop mechanisms for slotting men into male-dominated positions and women into female-dominated positions. Once positions or tasks are defined as masculine or feminine, societies must enforce these definitions. Sociologists refer to mechanisms by which societies bring about these results as mechanisms of social control.

The earliest stage of social control is socialization, during which society imbues the young with its prevailing values and beliefs. Central to our interest is vocational socialization, the development of gender identity that bears on the pursuit of careers. While the reproduction of social values may seem a simple matter in preindustrial societies, socialization is problematic in our own society. We argue that social control continues well beyond early socialization, involving the educational system, the decisions and behavior of employees and employers in the labor market, and the influences of family and friends throughout life. We raise questions about the efficacy of various gender-tracking mechanisms that are often assumed to be responsible for the maintenance of sex segregation.

The central thesis of this book is that the maintenance of sex segregation depends on a lifelong system of social control. While sex-role socialization is important, since it instills values and goals, it is inadequate by itself to maintain the system of sex segregation. Vocational aspirations have short life-expectancies, and young women frequently aspire to female-dominated occupations at one point in time and male-dominated jobs at another. Further, the relationship between the sex type of young women's vocational goals and the sex type of the jobs they obtain is weak. These patterns suggest that the influence of sex-role socialization is limited. Thus, sex-role socialization can be viewed as a system of social control for the early years, necessary but not sufficient to account for the persistence of occupational sex segregation.

For those men and women who attend college, social control continues during higher education. Many consider the educational system to be the realm of universalism, the paramount social institution in our society for promoting opportunities for all. Indeed, the declines in sex segregation in higher education have surpassed those in the labor force. Yet, as we will see, important gender differences persist in America's colleges. Men and women pursue different majors, and informal social control plays a prominent role on campus.

The field of study in college is an important but not decisive component of gender tracking. Segregation remains fluid during the college years as many students move among male-dominated, sex-neutral, and female-dominated majors. Further, the link between a person's major in college and subsequent occupational pursuits is far from direct for many fields. Thus, the sex segregation of college majors resembles in both structure and process the segregation of aspirations and the segregation of occupations. Like sex-role socialization, sex segregation in the educational system is a necessary but not sufficient cause of gender inequality in the labor force.

Sex segregation in the labor force is the most durable of any context we will consider, yet sex-role assignments are not fixed when women and men enter the labor force. Many women move among male-dominated, sex-neutral, and female-dominated occupations. The entry of women into male-dominated fields often does not immediately follow schooling, but instead may follow a period of employment in a female-dominated field or a spell as a homemaker. The patterns of stability and change in sex segregation are strikingly similar in aspirations, college majors, and careers, at both the aggregate and the individual level.

The problem, then, is accounting for the persistence of sex segregation at the societal or macro level despite its instability or permeability at the individual or micro level. Our resolution of this paradox is that sex roles are subject to continual, systematic, but imperfect control throughout life. Individuals move, but the system remains segregated, owing to the cumulative force of social pressures.

Data Sources

We examine data from a range of sources. Our aggregate analyses, which examine trends over time, employ the most comprehensive time-series data available. The essential element for the individual analyses is that the data contain information on the same individuals over time, allowing us to study stability and change in the lives of women and men. The principal sources of data about individuals are two National Longitudinal Surveys (NLS) of Labor Market Experience.

NLS Young Women and Mature Women. The National Longitudinal Survey of Young Women includes a representative national sample of 5,189 women aged 14–24 in 1968, who were surveyed ten times between 1968 and 1980. Nearly 75 percent of the women in the original sample remained in the survey by 1980. These data have been extensively analyzed in studies of young women's life experiences. Data on occupational aspirations are available for each of the survey years. Detailed descriptions of the data and the sample characteristics have been provided by the Center for Human Resource Research at Ohio State University (1981; see also Mott, 1978). At appropriate points we compare this group to the NLS Young Men, a national sample of men followed since 1966. These data allow us to examine the stability of aspirations over time and the connection between aspirations and occupational choices.

The National Longitudinal Survey of Mature Women contains data on a representative national sample of 5,083 women who were aged 30–44 in 1967 (Parnes, Jusenius, and Shortlidge, 1973). The NLS women were interviewed eight times between 1967 and 1977. The persistence rate in the NLS study has been high: 78 percent of the respondents remained in the sample in 1977. Data on a wide range of variables were collected and are employed in the analysis of the stability and change of women's employment patterns.

Current Population Survey. The Current Population Survey (CPS) includes information on large samples of individuals for a short span of time (U.S. Bureau of Labor Statistics, 1976). In its March survey, the CPS includes a limited set of questions about the respondents' major activities during the survey month and during the previous year. The data thus provide two measures of the occupation of employed individuals. This information can elucidate short-term changes in occupation and employment status. We analyze the March 1981 CPS data, which provide information about occupational changes between 1980 and 1981. The CPS data have several attractive features. The large sample (85,000 households providing information on nearly 100,000 employed individuals) enables one to generalize with confidence. The 1981 CPS data employ the 1970 U.S. Census occupational classification scheme; the NLS data are coded with the less detailed and more error-prone 1960 census occupational classification scheme. In addition, the CPS data include women of all ages, while the NLS data are restricted to two age cohorts of women. Finally, the CPS data allow comparisons of the short-term mobility patterns of men and women. The CPS data complement the NLS data in our analysis of the dynamics of women's employment. CPS data from 1971 provide a baseline for the examination of trends between 1971 and 1981, and 1986 CPS data are used to bring trends up-to-date.

Educational data. To examine trends in postsecondary degrees received, we use data from the National Center for Educational Statistics (NCES). The NCES publishes an annual series, *Earned Degrees Conferred in Higher Education*, which is reprinted in the annual *Digest of Educational Statistics*. We analyze the data from 1952 to 1984, modifying the list of fields when necessary to ensure comparability over time. The NCES data are based on complete or virtually complete reports from all colleges and universities in the United States.

These degree data are supplemented with data on trends in educational aspirations. The Cooperative Institutional Research Program (CIRP) at the University of California, Los Angeles, collects data on the goals and plans of nearly 250,000 freshmen annually in over 500 colleges and universities for the American Council on Education (ACE). The ACE-CIRP sample results are weighted to be representative of the national freshman class. Details of the surveys are presented in the annual reports of freshman norms (American Council on Education, 1966–72; Cooperative Institutional Research Program, 1974–80) and other publications (Astin, Panos, and Creager, 1966). To follow individuals over time, longitudinal studies of college students are explored. Data on intended majors and degrees received are compared with four national longitudinal surveys, including those of the college class of 1961 (Davis, 1965) and the high school class of 1972 (National Center for Educational Statistics, 1976). The other two longitudinal surveys are ACE-CIRP four-year follow-ups of college freshmen. The data on the 1967–71 cohort and the 1978–82 cohort are examined here (Bayer, Royer, and Webb, 1973; Green, Astin, Korn, and McNamara, 1983). These four studies are all large national samples of students with high response rates for follow-up interviews. These studies are richer in detail about college majors than the NLS data, and consequently allow for more detailed measurement of the sex segregation of fields of study.

Census data. Data from the 1900, 1910, 1970, and 1980 censuses are used to study trends in sex segregation. The 1900 and 1910 census data consist of samples of approximately 100,000 and 200,000 individuals drawn respectively from the 1900 and 1910 manuscript censuses. These data have been compiled for social science research by Samuel H. Preston and his colleagues, initially at the University of Washington and subsequently at the University of Pennsylvania (Graham, 1980; Strong, 1988). The analysis of the 1980 census draws primarily on published tabulations of the sex composition of detailed occupational categories. We pay particular attention to the comparability over time in occupational coding.

A range of statistics is employed to analyze these data. A measure is explained the first time it is used, and this explanation is referred to in subsequent chapters. Measures of segregation, employed in the aggregated analyses in Chapters 2, 4, and 6 are introduced in Chapter 2. Approaches to mobility, employed in the individual analyses in Chapters 5, 6, and 8, are developed in Chapter 5 and extended in Chapter 8.

The Plan of the Book

Chapter 2 reviews comparative data on the sexual division of labor. New data on long-term trends in occupational segregation by sex in the United States are presented. The discussion emphasizes the multidimensional nature of sex segregation and compares the focus on sex segregation with the more traditional sociological focus on socioeconomic inequality.

Chapter 3 lays out the theoretical perspective. We highlight the similarity between the educational levels of men and women in the labor force and suggest that it may be due to the companionate marriage system in our society. Since gender inequality in the workplace is not buttressed by the institutional support of the educational system, sex segregation must consequently rely on less formal, lifelong social controls. The discussion is placed in the context of sociological approaches to deviance and social control. We summarize the workings of social control during the early years of socialization, the college years, and the years in the labor force. Viewing sex segregation as the result of lifelong social control reveals the limitations of standard approaches while allowing us to incorporate many of their insights.

Theories have not paid sufficient attention to questions of

stability and change for individual women and men. While most theories assume that individual women and men remain in occupations with the same sex type throughout their lives, we place the ubiquity of change at the center of the analysis. Further, we show that the recent declines in sex segregation have affected women in many age groups, not only new entrants into the labor market. If sex segregation depends on social controls that extend throughout life, the weakening of these controls will allow women of all ages to make progress.

The presentation of results follows the stages of women's lives: aspirations, higher education, and careers. Aggregate trends are presented first. We pay particular attention to the age distribution of recent changes in order to assess the overall stability of women's aspirations, college majors, and careers. We then turn to an analysis of individual-level mobility for each of these phenomena.

Chapters 4 and 5 examine the occupational aspirations of young women and test the predictive power of the socialization perspective. First, data on the recent increase of women's choices of male-dominated occupations are presented. The data indicate substantial adaptability in women's aspirations: there is roughly as much net change over time in the aspirations of one cohort of women as there is across cohorts. We then explore the remarkable instability of individuals' aspirations. The evidence indicates that women often change their aspirations from female-dominated occupations to male-dominated occupations, and vice versa, and that the connection between aspirations and careers is weak. Data on the cumulative probability of aspiring to male-dominated, sex-neutral, and female-dominated occupations are also presented.

Chapter 6 examines analogous issues in the context of higher education, initially considering declines in the sex segregation of college majors. The data indicate that students in college are sensitive to contemporaneous social trends; changes in sex segregation among college students reflect trends outside the academy. Finally, we consider mobility among male-dominated, sex-neutral, and female-dominated majors. The patterns of sex-type mobility in college parallel those found in young women's aspirations.

Chapter 7 considers women's career patterns. The utility of labor market segmentation theory in explaining occupational sex segregation is examined. The sex segregation of occupations is the most stable over time of the three forms of segregation considered, but, again, individuals are far more mobile than the aggregate picture suggests. We note the extent of delayed entry of women into male-dominated fields and present brief case studies of women lawyers and doctors that reveal surprising evidence consistent with the social control perspective.

Chapter 8 outlines a theory of labor markets that is compatible with persistent occupational segregation by sex. If society arbitrarily assigns particular jobs to one sex or the other, as the anthropological data suggest, how does this system persist in a society constantly striving to maximize efficiency? The question of efficiency leads us inevitably to the economics of labor markets. The logic of labor markets is not inconsistent with the persistence of sex segregated work. Our theory draws upon and extends recent developments in labor market economics. We also consider an economic role for the women's movement not often discussed in economic analysis. The economic theory is separated from the central theoretical material in Chapter 3 because it is a lengthy analysis that does not predict specific mobility patterns, but rather suggests how discriminatory behavior is not inconsistent with the normal operation of the labor market.

Chapter 9 summarizes the social control perspective and the evidence that supports it. The chapter concludes with a discussion of the implications of this perspective for additional research, for policies relating to improving opportunities for women, and for the future of sex segregation.

2

Comparative and

Historical Perspectives

The sexual division of labor is a social construct. The work performed by men and women reflects the cultural definition of roles more than biological necessity. One source of evidence for this thesis comes from cross-national comparisons of the work done by men and women. Anthropologists have documented wide variations in the work men and women do. Data from the Human Research Area Files (HRAF) indicate that work performed by men in one place is often performed by women in other places. For example, Murdock and Provost (1973) present data on the sexual allocation of 50 tasks in 185 societies (see Table 2.1). Forty of these 50 tasks are performed exclusively by men in some societies and exclusively by women in others. All but five are allocated to men and women equally by some societies. Activities that require great physical strength, brief bursts of energy, or exposure to danger are performed exclusively by men in many societies, but exceptions to this pattern exist for most tasks. Women have been known to participate in stoneworking, fishing, lumbering, mining, butchering, tending large animals, clearing land, and building houses. Other tasks frequently performed by women require great strength: carrying water, bearing burdens, and farming are often, if not typically, performed by women. There is undoubtedly both error and bias in these data, as they some-

TABLE 2.1

Sex Allocation of 50 Activities in 185 Societies

Task	M	M−	N	F−	F	Index[a]
1. Hunting large aquatic fauna	48	0	0	0	0	100.0
2. Smelting of ores	37	0	0	0	0	100.0
3. Metalworking	85	1	0	0	0	99.8
4. Lumbering	135	4	0	0	0	99.4
5. Hunting large land fauna	139	5	0	0	0	99.3
6. Work in wood	159	3	1	1	0	98.8
7. Fowling	132	4	3	0	0	98.3
8. Manufacture of musical instruments	83	3	1	0	1	97.6
9. Trapping of small land fauna	136	12	1	1	0	97.5
10. Boatbuilding	84	3	3	0	1	96.6
11. Stoneworking	67	0	6	0	0	95.9
12. Work in bone, horn, and shell	71	7	2	0	2	94.6
13. Mining and quarrying	31	1	2	0	1	93.7
14. Bonesetting and other surgery	34	6	4	0	0	92.7
15. Butchering	122	9	4	4	4	92.3
16. Collection of wild honey	39	5	2	0	2	91.7
17. Land clearance	95	34	6	3	1	90.5
18. Fishing	83	45	8	5	2	86.7
19. Tending large animals	54	24	14	3	3	82.4
20. Housebuilding	105	30	14	9	20	77.4
21. Soil preparation	66	27	14	17	10	73.1
22. Netmaking	42	2	5	1	15	71.2
23. Making of rope or cordage	62	7	18	5	19	69.9
24. Generation of fire	40	6	16	4	20	62.3
25. Bodily mutilation	36	4	48	6	12	60.8
26. Preparation of skins	39	4	2	5	31	54.6
27. Gathering of small land fauna	27	3	9	13	15	54.5
28. Crop planting	27	35	33	26	20	54.4
29. Manufacture of leather products	35	3	2	5	29	53.2
30. Harvesting	10	37	34	34	26	45.0
31. Crop tending	22	23	24	30	32	44.6
32. Milking	15	2	8	2	21	43.8
33. Basketmaking	37	9	15	18	51	42.5
34. Burden carrying	18	12	46	34	36	39.3
35. Matmaking	30	4	9	5	55	37.6
36. Care of small animals	19	8	14	12	44	35.9
37. Preservation of meat and fish	18	2	3	3	40	32.9
38. Loom weaving	24	0	6	8	50	32.5
39. Gathering small aquatic fauna	11	4	1	12	27	31.1
40. Fuel gathering	25	12	12	23	94	27.2
41. Manufacture of clothing	16	4	11	13	78	22.4
42. Preparation of drinks	15	3	4	4	65	22.2
43. Potterymaking	14	5	6	6	74	21.1
44. Gathering wild vegetal foods	6	4	18	42	65	19.7
45. Dairy production	4	0	0	0	24	14.3
46. Spinning	7	3	4	5	72	13.6
47. Laundering	5	0	4	8	49	13.0
48. Water fetching	4	4	8	13	131	8.6
49. Cooking	0	2	2	63	117	8.3
50. Preparation of vegetal foods	3	1	4	21	145	5.7

SOURCE: Murdock and Provost, 1973. (Reprinted with permission of the publisher.)
ABBREVIATIONS: M, exclusively male; M−, predominantly male; N, sex-neutral; F−, predominantly female; F, exclusively female.
[a] "Index" is a measure of male representation.

times rely on the field notes of one anthropologist who may not have had interest in or access to women's work, but the bias probably consists of understating the range of work done by women (Rogers, 1978).[1]

The conclusion seems inescapable: for the preponderance of tasks, anthropologists have documented the entire gamut of possibilities, from male-exclusive through sex-neutral to female-exclusive. This is true despite the high fertility rates and low life expectancies in many of these societies, where women can expect to spend the majority of their adult lives caring for children. This diversity makes broad generalizations about the biological basis of the sexual division of labor subject to dispute (Rogers, 1978; Friedl, 1975; Whyte, 1978; Sanday, 1981).

Boserup (1970) demonstrates that the sexual division of labor remains highly varied as the countries of the developing world move toward more urban and industrialized economies. She documents wide variations across Africa, Asia, and Latin America in the representation of women in agriculture, trading, clerical work, and administration. Boulding et al. (1976) present data on the division of labor in 86 countries and report indices of segregation that vary from less than 5 to nearly 80 across eight broad occupational groups.

Table 2.2 presents a brief summary of recent data of the kind Boserup and Boulding examine. Statistics on the sexual division of labor in 42 countries were derived from data compiled by the International Labor Organization (1986). Wide variations are evident in the proportion of women in such broad groupings as professional, administrative, clerical, service, and agricultural work. Clerical work, for example, was performed almost exclusively by men in Morocco but mostly by women in the United States; service work is a male preserve in Turkey but employs many women in Bangladesh. Table 2.1 also presents a measure indicating women's over- or underrepresentation in each occupational group, which adjusts for national differences in women's labor force participation rate. For each of the seven occupational groups for which there are comparative data, women are substantially underrepresented in

TABLE 2.2

Representation of Women in Major Occupations
in 42 Countries, ca. 1980

Occupational grouping	Pct. women in occupation		Ratio of women in occupation to women in labor force	
	Lowest	Highest	Lowest	Highest
Professional, technical	11% Bangladesh	65% Philippines	.84 Turkey	4.05 United Arab Emirates
Administrative	1% United Arab Emirates	45% Canada	.10 S. Korea	1.12 Guatemala
Clerical	4% Morocco	80% United States	.20 Morocco	2.84 Guatemala
Sales	1% United Arab Emirates	69% Philippines	.12 Turkey	2.28 Guatemala
Service	7% Turkey	77% Norway	.20 Turkey	6.18 Bangladesh
Agriculture	1% Bangladesh	54% Turkey	.01 United Arab Emirates	2.18 Iraq
Production, transport	5% Luxembourg	39% Thailand	.02 United Arab Emirates	1.90 Bangladesh

SOURCE: International Labor Organization, 1986.
NOTE: Countries included in the analysis: Australia, Austria, Bangladesh, Barbados, Botswana, Canada, Chile, Costa Rica, Denmark, Dominican Republic, Ecuador, Egypt, W. Germany, Greece, Guatemala, Indonesia, Iraq, Ireland, Israel, Japan, S. Korea, Luxembourg, Malaysia, Morocco, Netherlands, New Zealand, Norway, Panama, Paraguay, Philippines, São Tomé, Singapore, Spain, Sri Lanka, San Marino, Sweden, Thailand, Turkey, United Arab Emirates, United States, Venezuela, Yugoslavia.

some countries and substantially overrepresented in others. Similarly, Roos (1985) reports variation in the representation of women across 14 broad occupational categories for 12 industrial societies and indicates that there are significant differences in the level of occupational segregation by sex among these countries. More detailed occupational measures would presumably show even greater variation, although detailed comparable occupational data are difficult to obtain. This comparative evidence demonstrates that a wide range of tasks can be performed by men or women and have been so performed in societies known to contemporary research. This evidence also suggests that a task considered to be perfectly natural and appropriate for women in one society is perfectly natural and appropriate for men in another society. No universal level of sex segregation exists across all forms of social organization. This evidence should make one skeptical of claims that the present sexual division of labor is natural or inevitable, and should put the burden of proof on those who claim that men are unable to perform certain roles in our society or that women are unable to perform others.

Three Dimensions of Segregation

Readily available occupational data in the United States enable us to compute detailed measures of segregation for the labor force. Most research on occupational segregation by sex has employed one measure of segregation: the index of dissimilarity (D). This index measures the main dimension of segregation—the degree to which two groups are unevenly distributed over a set of categories. The index of dissimilarity has a convenient interpretation: it represents the proportion of women who would have to change occupations to be distributed in the same manner as men. D is symmetrical; the same proportion of men would have to change occupations to be distributed in the same manner as women.[2]

While uniform reliance on this measure has been helpful in comparing the results of different studies, we examine other dimensions of segregation as well. Massey and Denton (forthcoming) have surveyed a wide range of measures of segregation and suggest that *concentration* and *isolation* are dimensions of segregation that complement the dimension of *unevenness* represented by the index of dissimilarity.

Two occupational distributions may be equal in their levels of unevenness but differ in the extent to which women are concentrated in a small number of occupations. Several studies have noted that young women's aspirations are concentrated in a limited set of choices (Marini and Brinton, 1984) and that working women are clustered in a small number of occupations (U.S. Department of Labor, 1975). Even if men and women remain segregated, the expansion in the absolute number of areas of opportunity for women should be considered evidence of progress.

The degree of concentration is measured in two complementary ways. The proportion of individuals in the 20 most populous occupations (out of 400-odd detailed occupations) is an easily interpretable indicator of concentration. A second measure, which includes the entire distribution rather than simply the top few categories, is analogous to the index of dissimilarity. The concentration index (C) indicates the proportion of a particular group of individuals who would have to change occupations to be evenly distributed across all occupations. Instead of comparing the distribution of women to that of men, as D does, C compares the actual distribution of women to an equal distribution. We also present results for a measure of relative concentration (RC), which indicates the extent to which women are more concentrated across occupations than men.[3]

The isolating effect of segregation depends on the relative size of groups in which men and women find themselves working, as well as the level of segregation. Lieberson (1980) has fruitfully employed an index of the probability of intergroup contact ($P*$) in recent studies of residential segregation (Lieberson and Carter, 1982; Massey and Mullan, 1984). This index supplements the standard index of dissimilarity by indicating the way in which each group experiences segregation. Two different settings with equal levels of segregation but different proportions of women will have different probabilities of contact, a feature of segregation revealed by $P*$. Another important property of this measure is that the probability of intergroup contact is different from the perspective of each group. When experiencing a given level of segregation, the majority group will always have a lower chance of encountering the minority; the minority is less isolated from the majority.[4]

Consider the hypothetical example displayed in Table 2.3. For the sake of simplicity, the labor force consists of five oc-

TABLE 2.3

Hypothetical Employment Patterns in Five Occupations

Occupation	No. of men	No. of women	Pct. women
Lawyer	20	5	20%
Teacher	10	15	60
Secretary	0	20	100
Carpenter	50	0	0
Bus driver	20	10	33
TOTAL	100	50	33

INDICES:

D (index of dissimilarity)	60	P^*WW (women's proba-		
C (concentration) for women	30	bility of sharing an oc-		
C (concentration) for men	30	cupation with women)	.67	
RC (concentration of		P^*MW (men's probability		
women − concentration		of sharing an occupation		
of men)	0	with women)	.17	
P^*WM (women's probability		P^*MM (men's probability		
of sharing an occupation		of sharing an occupation		
with men)	.33	with men)	.83	

cupations: lawyer, teacher, secretary, carpenter, and bus driver. The carpenters are all men, the lawyers and bus drivers are mostly men, the teachers are mostly women, and the secretaries are all women. For this hypothetical example, D (dissimilarity) is 60, indicating that 60 percent of men (or women) would have to change occupations to be equally distributed. C (concentration) for women is 30, as it is for men. In this example, there is no tendency for women to be more concentrated in a limited subset of occupations than men. The P^* (contact) figures reflect the disparity in the sex composition of the labor force. Because twice as many men are working as women in our example, women have twice as great a chance of sharing an occupation with men ($P^*WM = .33$) as men do with women ($P^*MW = .17$).

We add a discussion of concentration and group contact to the standard discussion of segregation in examining long-term trends in occupational sex segregation. We refer to segregation as the degree of unevenness, measured by the familiar index of dissimilarity, D; concentration as the relative degree of clustering, measured by RC; and isolation as the probability of intergroup contact, measured by P^*.[5]

Long-Term Trends in Segregation

Gross (1968) documents the stability of occupational sex segregation between 1900 and 1960. He analyzes changes in sex
segregation for each decennial census from 1900 to 1960. In
1900, more than 60 percent of employed women would have
had to change occupations to be distributed across occupations
in the same manner as men. Gross finds that in 1960 this level
remained above 60 percent. As we will see, in 1980 this figure
was only a shade under 60 percent. Thus, despite vast changes
in the economy, the technology of production, and the mix of
employment in the transition from an agricultural to a postindustrial society, fundamental differences in the work performed by men and women have persisted.

Williams (1979) criticizes Gross for failing to standardize
categories across censuses. Because census occupation codes
change each decade, Williams suggests that Gross's comparisons between censuses are likely to be flawed. The occupational categories in recent censuses have become increasingly
detailed, inflating the measures of segregation and suppressing
evidence of increased integration. Williams groups occupations
into larger categories that are consistent across censuses and
finds slow but consistent declines in sex segregation over time.
England (1981), however, notes that Williams's approach exaggerates the decline because it ignores any real differentiation
among occupations that has occurred. Williams's reliance on
aggregated categories ignores the emergence of new, segregated
occupations, a consideration that is especially important over
extended periods. England maintains that while Gross's approach understates change, Williams's exaggerates change. She
concludes that changes have occurred in this century, but their
precise extent is hard to estimate. While most students of sex
segregation have agreed that the changes have been small, the
evidence for this conclusion has not been entirely satisfactory.

Fortunately, data from the 1900 and 1910 censuses enable us
to reexamine this conclusion. A public use sample of the 1900
census double-codes occupations, once with the classifications
in use in 1900 and once with the 1950 census system (Graham,

1980). Data from the 1910 census double-codes occupations with the 1910 and 1980 occupational categories (Strong, 1988). The double-coding strategy circumvents the problem of changing classifications. The effect of different occupational classifications can be estimated by calculating indices of segregation for 1900 using both the detailed 1900 and the detailed 1950 census categories. If one obtains essentially the same results using the more recent, more detailed classification scheme as were obtained with the contemporaneous occupational codes, then one can be reasonably sure that the results are not artifacts of the coding employed. We compare temporally distant years with the more recent coding system, providing comparability without sacrificing detail in measurement. We compare 1900 and 1950 using the 1950 coding system for both years and compare 1910, 1970, and 1980 using the 1980 coding system for each year.[6] This procedure allows for the best possible assessment of long-term trends. It answers Williams's concern by relying on the same categories for both years, and England's concern by using the most detailed and most recent categories; newly developed occupations simply appear as empty cells in the earlier census.

Gross reported that the level of occupational segregation between men and women in 1900 was 66.9, using published data from the 1900 census. The comparable figure for the 1900 public use sample using the 1900 coding scheme is 64.9. The difference between these figures may be due to sampling, and it may also reflect small differences in the application of the 1900 classification rules. As measured by the 1950 coding scheme, the level of sex segregation in 1900 was 65.0. The difference between the 1900 and 1950 coding schemes' measurements of sex segregation in 1900 is less than one percentage point. The level of sex segregation in 1950 was 67.3, indicating virtually no change over this 50-year period.[7] Thus, Gross's reports of historical trends are almost exactly correct, despite the problem of classifying occupations. This analysis indicates that changes in occupational categories do not substantially change the long term picture.

Table 2.4 compares indices of segregation for 1910 and 1970,

TABLE 2.4
Indices of Segregation, 1910 and 1970

	Entire labor force		Nonfarm labor force	
Index	1910	1970	1910	1970
D	63.7	67.6	74.0	67.5
Size-standardized D	76.0	61.3	75.9	61.2
C women	81.7	68.4	80.0	68.9
C men	69.0	53.3	62.9	53.4
RC	12.7	15.1	16.9	15.5
Pct. women in top 20 occupations	73.5%	54.3%	72.4%	56.3%
Pct. men in top 20 occupations	48.2%	36.0%	48.5%	35.7%
P^*WM	.41	.29	.30	.29
P^*WW	.59	.71	.70	.71
P^*MW	.11	.18	.10	.19
P^*MM	.89	.82	.90	.81
Pct. women in labor force	21.7%	38.0%	24.9%	39.2%

SOURCES: Data were obtained from the 1910 Census Public Use Sample and from the 1970 census data reclassified by 1980 occupational codes.
NOTE: The indices are based on 1980 census occupational classifications.

with both years employing the 1980 census occupational classifications. The index of segregation was 63.7 in 1910, compared with 67.6 in 1970. These figures again confirm Gross's conclusion regarding the long term stability of occupational sex segregation.

One important consideration when examining occupational segregation at the turn of the century is the size of the agricultural sector. In 1910, 32.7 percent of the labor force was employed in farming. One might choose to exclude agriculture from an analysis of long-term trends for several reasons. First, the classification of men and women in farming may be more prone to error than in other types of occupations. Economists have long debated the labor force participation rate of farm women (Oppenheimer, 1970). Further, occupational distinctions between farm men and women may be artificial, since census coders may classify women as unpaid family farmers while classifying men as self-employed farmers, even when the work on the farm is actually shared.

Second, our theories about trends in occupational segregation apply most specifically to competition in the burgeoning industrial society, and they may not apply with equal force to the shrinking agricultural sector. The view that industrial society promotes standards of universalism over particularism applies most forcefully to the industrial economy, not to the vestiges of preindustrial social organization found on the farm. The competitive forces that drive employers to find the lowest-wage worker for a given job also apply primarily to the industrial economy, since women on the farm are mostly in the role of unpaid family worker and thus outside the cash nexus of the broader economy.[8] Sex segregation on family farms is more a matter of the division of household labor than an indicator of the differentiation of occupations. Third, even if farms were theoretically salient, the rapid decline of agricultural employment suggests a test of a compositional effect on long-term trends. If nonfarm sex segregation were to decline, we might conclude that this decline in sex segregation was masked by the rapid decline of the relatively integrated farm sector.

Removing the agricultural sector from our analysis, we see that occupational segregation by sex has in fact been declining slowly. In 1910, D was 74.0 for the nonfarm population, a figure that declines to 67.5 in the 1970 nonfarm population (see Table 2.4). Thus, while Gross's conclusion that there has been no significant change over the long term is approximately correct, the analysis of the nonfarm population gives a more optimistic picture. Sex segregation in the nonagricultural economy declined by roughly one point per decade between 1910 and 1970.

The size-standardized measure of segregation also shows a decline over this period. The size-standardized trend indicates the degree to which segregation would have changed had all occupations remained a constant size. A decline in size of a relatively integrated occupation, such as farming, would cause this measure to fall. This indicator points in the same direction as our analysis of nonfarming occupations.

Our measures of concentration show change in the absolute, but not the relative, position of women. The concentration of women in a limited number of occupations declined between 1910 and 1970. In 1910, the top 20 occupations employed 73.5 percent of working women; by 1970, this figure had dropped to 54.3 percent. For men, the comparable indicators were 48.2 percent in 1900 and 36.0 percent in 1970. Yet women's concentration did not decline more rapidly than men's; the index of relative concentration rose from 12.7 in 1910 to 15.1 in 1970. If the analysis is restricted to nonfarm employment, women's relative position improved slightly (RC declines from 16.9 to 15.5).

Our measure of isolation provides a dramatic indicator of the experience of change, despite the relatively slow decline in the level of segregation. The P^* measure may help to explain the appearance of change, despite the underlying durability of segregation. Comparing the probability of sharing an occupation in 1910 to that in 1970 reveals dramatic changes in the way men and women experience segregation. In 1910, men had a one-in-ten chance of sharing an occupation with a woman ($P^*MW = .11$); women had a two-in-five chance of sharing an occupation with a man ($P^*WM = .41$). In 1970, men's probability of sharing an occupation with women rose to .18, whereas women's probability of sharing an occupation with men dropped to .29. The level of segregation was close to identical for these two years, but the extent of women's labor force participation had substantially increased in the interim.[9]

The increase in women's labor force participation had dramatically divergent consequences for men and women. Men's chances of encountering women in a given occupation rose from less than one in ten to nearly one in five, despite slow changes in occupational segregation. But women's chances of sharing a job with men actually declined over this period, from two in five to less than one in three. The entry of women into the labor force may lead men to the conclusion that women are making major strides, even though women are seeing fewer men at work. Even as men are astonished at the extent of women's advances, women may be increasingly convinced that their situation is deteriorating, that they are increasingly concentrated in female ghettos. These complementary indices at once reveal the underlying continuity in segregation while suggesting an explanation for differing views on the extent of change.

Trends in Sex Segregation Since 1970

The broad sweep shows gradual change throughout the century. We now turn to a more detailed appraisal of changes since 1970. A number of studies have examined changes in the level of sex segregation since World War II (Blau and Hendricks, 1979; Burriss and Wharton, 1982; England, 1981; Treiman and Terrell, 1975; U.S. Commission on Civil Rights, 1978). All find modest declines in the level of occupational segregation by sex over this period. The 1960's and 1940's showed declines in the level of segregation, while the 1950's showed a slight increase.

Recent years have seen sustained, gradual downward movement in the level of occupational sex segregation. Table 2.5 summarizes recent trends in sex segregation. Results are drawn from published tabulations of census and Current Population Survey (CPS) data by Beller (1984a), Blau and Hendricks (1979), Bianchi and Rytina (1986), and Jacobs (1986a), as well as new tabulations of CPS data. The CPS comparison of 1971 and 1981 employing the 1970 occupational classification system shows a drop of nearly 7 points in the index of dissimilarity, from 69.5 to 63.0. Another comparison, using CPS annual average data, showed a 7.4-point drop between 1972 and 1982. Analysis employing the 1980 census occupational codes shows a 7.8-point decline between 1970 and 1980. These declines have continued into the 1980's. CPS annual average data show that the level of sex segregation has declined from 59.6 in 1983 to 57.3 in 1986. The rate of change has not been dramatic, but the pattern of decline that commenced in the 1960's has continued through the 1970's and 1980's. The size-standardized measures track the unstandardized measures closely, indicating that differential growth of sex-neutral jobs is not responsible for these changes.

TABLE 2.5
Indices of Dissimilarity (D), 1970–1986

Year	1970 occupational codes		1980 occupational codes
1970	70.7 (B&H)		67.6 (J2)
1971	69.5 (J1)	68.1 (B1)	
1972	66.9 (B&R)	67.4 (B1)	
1973		67.1 (B1)	
1974		66.4 (B1)	
1975		64.2 (B1)	
1976			
1977		64.7 (B2)	
1978			
1979			
1980			59.8 (J2)
1981	63.0 (J1)	61.7 (B2)	
1982	59.5 (B&R)		
1983			59.6 (J3)
1984			59.1 (J3)
1985			58.1 (J3)
1986			57.3 (J3)

SOURCES:
B1: Beller, 1984a; March CPS data.
B2: Beller, 1984a; CPS annual average data.
B&H: Blau and Hendricks, 1979; 1970 census data.
B&R: Bianchi and Rytina, 1986; CPS annual average data.
J1: Jacobs, 1986a; May 1971 and March 1981 CPS data.
J2: Jacobs, 1986a; 1970 and 1980 census data, 483 categories.
J3: New computations, CPS annual average data, 321 categories.

Table 2.6 displays trends since 1970 for the concentration and isolation measures introduced above. Women remained more concentrated in a limited number of occupations than men, but the gap narrowed from 15.1 points to 9.5 points between 1970 and 1986. The indices of intergroup contact shown in Table 2.6 indicate that the declines in the level of occupational sex segregation throughout the labor force were not experienced in the same way by men and women. Between 1970 and 1986, men's probability of sharing an occupation with women increased sharply, from .18 to .26. For women, the probability of contact with men increased slightly, from .29 to .32. The P^* statistics thus reveal the interesting asymmetry of change. Men may feel women have made great strides, since

TABLE 2.6

Indices of Unevenness, Concentration, and Isolation, Selected Years, 1970–1986

Year	Pct. women	Unevenness		Concentration			Probability of sharing an occupation			
		D	D (size-standardized)	C women	C men	RC	P^*WM	P^*WW	P^*MW	P^*MM
1970[a]	38.0%	67.7	67.8	68.4	53.3	15.1	.29	.71	.18	.82
1980[a]	42.4	59.8	59.8	65.9	54.7	11.3	.32	.68	.24	.76
1983[b]	43.7	59.2	60.3	64.1	54.0	10.1	.31	.69	.24	.76
1984[b]	43.7	58.5	58.8	63.3	53.7	9.6	.32	.68	.25	.75
1985[b]	44.1	58.1	62.2	63.2	53.5	9.7	.31	.69	.24	.76
1986[b]	44.4	57.3	57.9	63.0	53.5	9.5	.32	.68	.26	.74

[a] Calculated from census data, 483 categories (1980 census codes).
[b] Calculated from CPS data, 321 categories (1980 census codes).

women co-workers are significantly more evident to them. However, women have experienced much less change in the probability of sharing an occupation with men, which may reinforce a feeling that little has changed.

This pattern may also be relevant to understanding the discontent of groups struggling for social change. The process of change often involves changing proportions of different groups as well as changing opportunities. As proportions of different groups change, the perception of trends will systematically differ from the point of view of the minority and the majority. Evidence on trends in racial segregation in schools suggests a parallel development; black students, especially in the North, have experienced a smaller increase in contact with whites than whites have with blacks (Farley, 1984: 30).

Age Profile of Change in the 1970's

Table 2.7 presents data on trends in sex segregation by age between 1971 and 1981. This comparison employs CPS data with 1970 occupational codes. We can see a modest decline at each age level. The decline in segregation is as great among those in the 55–64 age group (−4.1) as it is among the 25–34 year olds (−3.9). When one considers the fact that occupational mobility rates decline sharply with age, this evidence becomes particularly striking. Census data from 1980 are also presented by age. These data imply somewhat larger changes for younger age cohorts, but it is striking that even for the 35–44 and 45–54 cohorts there is notable change compared to the earlier period.

Table 2.7 also allows us to follow cohorts over time. Here we find the largest change among those who were 25–34 years old in 1971 (−5.7), although the changes for each age category are notable. The rate of change was almost as large among the oldest cohort (−5.0). This evidence clearly contradicts the assumption that sex segregation declines exclusively among the youngest groups. In fact, each of the older cohorts has a faster rate of change than the 16–24-year-old group. The most strik-

TABLE 2.7

Index of Dissimilarity (D) by Age, 1971, 1980, and 1981

Age	1971	1981	Change by age group	Change by cohort	1980[a]
16–24	67.4	59.4	−8.0	−2.9	59.7
25–34	68.4	64.5	−3.9	−5.7	58.6
35–44	66.9	62.7	−4.2	−3.8	61.5
45–54	67.5	63.1	−1.1	3.1	63.9
55–64	68.2	64.1	−4.1	−5.0	64.4
65+	64.1	63.2	−0.9		66.3

SOURCE: Current Population Survey data, 1971 and 1981; census data, 1980.
[a]Figures for 1980 use 1980 occupational codes, and are therefore not strictly comparable to the preceding figures.

ing finding in Table 2.7 is the penetration of change across all age groups. As we will see, these changes have mostly been the result of women moving into more male-dominated occupations, rather than men moving into more female-dominated occupations.

Beller (1984a) presents evidence suggesting that individuals with more labor force experience have undergone smaller declines in sex segregation than more recent labor force entrants, but the differences she reports are small. She reports as much change by 1977 for those in the labor force in 1971 as across new cohorts of entrants between 1971 and 1977. And in her standardized analysis, the group with the most labor force experience changed more than new labor force entrants. Thus, at least through midcareer, sex segregation remained quite fluid in Beller's analysis.

A recognition of the age pattern of women's labor force participation suggests another way to reconcile these results with Beller's. Within each age cohort, there are women with relatively few years of labor force experience. If Beller is right that recent entrants (and reentrants) to the labor market are likely to be most affected by recent changes, then we would still expect this pattern to be represented in a wide age-spectrum of women. In short, the labor force interruptions of women extend the possibility of occupational change throughout much of their working lives, and make them more likely to be influenced by events in a particular period.

As we will see, the experience of change by individuals in different age groups is an important piece of evidence for our social control perspective on sex segregation. This pattern underscores one of the central arguments of this book, namely, that early socialization experiences are not sufficient to maintain the system of occupational segregation by sex. A series of social control mechanisms throughout the life cycle are needed to maintain this institution. When these mechanisms tend to weaken among the young, they also tend to weaken among those already in the labor force.

It should be noted that these are indicators of net change, not gross change. The question of the extent of gross mobility between male-dominated, sex-neutral, and female-dominated occupations will be addressed in Chapters 5 and 7.

Sex Segregation and Socioeconomic Measures of Inequality

Since studies of occupational mobility have long held a prominent place in sociological research, it is natural to compare our focus on mobility among male-dominated, sex-neutral, and female-dominated occupations with the more traditional focus on socioeconomic mobility. Until the 1970's, sociological studies of mobility were concerned primarily with the intergenerational transmission of advantage from fathers to sons. Research since 1970 has included women in the analysis and has compared the status attainment processes of men and women. These status attainment comparisons have revealed only relatively minor differences between men and women, leading many researchers to search for other approaches to understanding gender-based patterns of occupational inequality (England, 1979; Sewell, Hauser, and Wolf, 1980; Marini, 1980). The sex segregation of occupations is a dimension of occupational inequality that traditional socioeconomic and prestige measures are unable to detect.

The two most prominent measures of occupational standing are the Duncan Socioeconomic Index (SEI) and the NORC (National Opinion Research Center) occupational prestige scale.

Each obscures the sex segregation of occupations, but for different reasons. Duncan constructed his index by estimating the prestige accorded to male-dominated occupations on the basis of the income and education of men in these occupations (O. Duncan, 1961). He extrapolated his results to all occupations, including those in which men constitute a small minority. This means that the SEI score for nurses is based on the small fraction of nurses who are men. This procedure inflates the status accorded to women's occupations, since men in female-dominated occupations tend to be better paid than their female counterparts. A detailed examination of socioeconomic measures also reveals that the standard SEI metric accords inconsistent scale weights to the characteristics of men and women (Jacobs and Powell, 1987). Correcting for this bias and for intraoccupational inequality shows that working women are at a major socioeconomic disadvantage compared to men, and at a distinct disadvantage in the status attainment process.

The NORC occupational prestige scale also fails to capture gender-based inequality, but for a different reason. For the prestige measure, the subjective evaluations of individuals, not features of the construction of the scale itself, are at the heart of the matter. In several studies, we asked respondents to rate the prestige of occupations twice, once assuming female incumbents and once assuming male incumbents (Jacobs and Powell, 1984). We found striking differences in the prestige accorded to men and women in the same occupations. Men were rated higher in male-dominated occupations, while women were rated higher in female-dominated occupations. The male-vs.-female prestige gap correlated strongly with the sex composition of occupations. We interpreted these results as evidence that incumbency in sex-atypical occupational roles is associated with a "prestige penalty." These data can be viewed as suggesting that there is a cost to sex-role deviance. A number of other studies report patterns similar to ours (Olson, 1979; see Jacobs and Powell, 1984, for a review of these studies), but one study (Bose, 1985) failed to find these differences.

We concluded that respondents implicitly rate women's work by different standards, against a different mean, than men's work. When rating women's occupations, respondents use female-dominated occupations as the implicit point of comparison; when rating male-dominated occupations, they use male-dominated occupations as reference points. A single verticle measure of occupational inequality therefore obscures inequality associated with the sex segregation of occupations, whether measured by SEI or prestige measures. Chapter 3 argues that sex segregation is not only a dimension of inequality separate from socioeconomic inequality, but also that it is maintained by different mechanisms. While socioeconomic inequality is buttressed by the institutional support of educational inequality, sex segregation is maintained by a lifelong system of social control.

Summary

The particular occupations assigned to men or women vary across societies. A universal level of segregation by sex does not appear in all forms of societies. Segregation is usefully thought of as a multidimensional phenomenon, with unevenness, concentration, and isolation as distinct components. Each of these aspects of segregation yields a different picture of long-term historical trends.

Segregation has been stable in the U.S. labor force throughout most of this century, changes in census occupational categories notwithstanding. Nonfarm employment, however, has become less segregated by sex, especially since 1970. Women have also made progress from being concentrated in a few occupations at the turn of the century to a wider range of occupations in 1980, although they remain more concentrated than men. More dramatically, the structure of workplace contacts has changed substantially; men had a much greater chance of encountering women in the same occupations in 1980 than in 1900. We have also seen the way in which sex segregation is a dimension of occupational inequality not revealed by the traditional socioeconomic indicators of occupations.

We now turn our attention to theories of sex segregation. If sex segregation is broadly stable over time, how does this phenomenon maintain itself? If sex segregation has declined in recent years, how can we account for the fact that women in many age groups participated in this change? How is sex segregation reproduced in the careers of individuals? In the next chapter, we review a range of theories and propose our own theory of social control, which incorporates some of the insights of these different perspectives.

3

A Social Control

Approach

Sociological theories usually assume a congruence between social institutions, a complementarity of goals, processes, and outcomes. This is often as true of radical critiques of society as it is of functional analyses. Yet social institutions are often unsynchronized, and they may remain so for extended periods of time. The rapid rise of women's labor force participation has heightened the tensions between the socialization, educational, and occupational systems of our society. Individual women's careers become disjointed in the context of such macro-structural incongruities. The pattern of instability we describe will likely continue for some time, until a new pattern of social relations becomes institutionalized.

A principal telltale sign of discontinuity is in the relationship between education and gender inequality in the workplace. Socioeconomic inequality is mediated by differential access to education, while gender inequality is not. A variety of sociological studies have documented the centrality of education to socioeconomic inequality. Fathers are able to pass advantages along to their sons via the educational system. Education is undoubtedly the main mechanism for the intergenerational transmission of socioeconomic advantage in industrial and postindustrial society. To be sure, this process is mediated by a variety of institutional factors, such as the economic segmentation of the economy, the internal labor markets of large firms, and other structures, but by all accounts education is a central means of maintaining socioeconomic advantage. The differences between high-status men and low-status men are easy to maintain because a lack of educational credentials severely restricts low-status men from access to high-status occupations.

In contrast, gender differences at work are not principally rooted in differences in the level of educational attainment. The gender gap in educational attainment is small compared to differences among men at different socioeconomic levels. Indeed, the median educational attainment of women in the labor force has exceeded that of men for much of the century. Further, the sex segregation of occupations is not principally rooted in educational differences. At each educational level, sex segregation is nearly as high as it is in the labor force as a whole. Differences in educational levels account for only a small fraction of the massive and persistent sex segregation of the labor force. The role of education in explaining the occupational disadvantage of women is decidedly secondary. In Chapter 2 we showed that occupational status does not capture the dimension of inequality represented by occupational segregation by sex. Now we are suggesting that the process by which sexual inequality is maintained fundamentally differs from that which maintains socioeconomic status.

In this chapter we (1) bring together evidence to substantiate the above assertions; (2) offer an explanation for this fundamental difference, which rests on educational homogamy in marriages; (3) develop a theory for understanding why gender inequality in the workplace persists despite broad similarities in the educational levels attained by men and women; and (4) contrast our approach with the socialization, human capital, and labor market segmentation perspectives.

Education, Status, and Gender

Occupational status transmission rests on differential access to education. Status attainment research, beginning with Blau

and Duncan's pathbreaking book (1967), has amassed a wealth
of evidence highlighting the importance of education in the
process of reproducing socioeconomic inequality. In the United
States, the correlation between the status of fathers and the
years of education attained by sons has been substantial ($r =$
.45; Blau and Duncan, 1967: 169). Moreover, the preponderance
of the relationship between paternal status and filial status
is associated with the education fathers provide for their sons.
In the path diagrams Blau and Duncan (1967) and Jencks et
al. (1973) made familiar to social scientists, the arrows that
depict the educational connections are the most important
ones shown.

Educational credentials are the principal route to high-status
positions for men in our society. Access to high-status positions is severely restricted for those without extensive education. Whether one conceives of education as improving productivity, as the human capital school of economics has claimed,
or merely as performing a screening or credential-providing
role, as others have maintained, the importance of education
in attaining high-status occupations in industrial society is
widely recognized.

Educational differences have been equally important in perpetuating racial inequality, although of course discrimination
above and beyond educational differences has also played a
large role. Throughout the century, black males have received
far less education than their white counterparts. Lieberson
(1980) has highlighted this fact in his analysis of the divergent
paths of blacks and European immigrants in the American
economy.

Education at once offers an ideological justification for inequality and a set of institutional mechanisms for maintaining it. Our culture has championed education as a reason that
some are entitled to earn more than others. The vast apparatus
of educational certification, from standardized tests to vocational entrance exams and licensing, helps to enforce this
belief.

Table 3.1 presents 1980 census data comparing educational
levels for men and women employed in different occupational
strata. The importance of education in increasing access to

TABLE 3.1

Educational Attainment by Sex and Major Occupation, 1980

Occupational grouping	No. of years of schooling completed by men:		No. of years of schooling completed by women:		Index of segregation[a]
	< 12	16+	< 12	16+	
Entire labor force[b]	25.9%	20.6%	21.8%	15.8%	59.8%
Professional	2.8	73.7	3.5	63.5	54.8
Manager	8.7	57.9	9.2	50.6	15.7[b]
Sales	15.8	27.8	26.4	8.9	51.1
Clerical	16.5	17.0	10.2	7.4	55.8
Craft	30.4	5.4	34.9	5.4	59.8
Operative	38.7	2.7	48.9	1.7	40.5
Transport	41.4	2.8	32.3	2.7	51.1
Service	40.6	6.7	41.6	3.5	38.7
Farm	45.3	7.0	39.0	6.6	30.9
Laborer	47.8	2.6	46.8	1.6	55.1

SOURCE: U.S. Census of Population, 1980.
[a]Index of dissimilarity (D) calculated across 3-digit occupations, within each major occupational category.
[b]Aged 16 and over.
[c]The low level of segregation among managers is an artifact of the limited number of job classifications reported for managers.

white-collar, particularly professional, occupations is inescapable. As one proceeds from the high-status occupations at the top of the table to the low-status occupations at the bottom, one finds that the proportion of those who completed college steadily declines while the proportion of those who did not complete high school rises. The pattern is almost as consistent for women as it is for men.

In contrast, educational levels of men and women in the same occupational stratum have been quite similar. Women are underrepresented among college graduates and professional degree recipients, but they are more likely than men to finish high school. Thus women are underrepresented at the extremes but spend slightly more years in school on average than do men. In Table 3.1 the differences in educational attainment of men and women within the same occupational stratum are generally small compared to the differences across these occupations.

Educational differences simply are not responsible for the

bulk of occupational segregation by sex. One finds a high degree of occupational segregation by sex at all levels of education. The last column of Table 3.1 presents the degree of sex segregation in 1980 within each major occupation group. We see marked levels of sex segregation within major occupational groups despite the similar educational levels of men and women.

Table 3.2 presents a breakdown of occupational sex segregation by educational level for 1971 and 1981, using CPS data. Among men and women with the same level of educational attainment, a high degree of segregation is evident. In 1971 the degree of occupational segregation by sex was essentially uniform across educational levels. Since that time, the declines in sex segregation have been most evident in the professional occupations. Limited historical evidence also suggests the limited role of educational differentials in explaining occupational segregation by sex.[1]

Educational differences between men and women have been rather small over the long term, with differences typically favoring women. Table 3.3 presents historical data from the U.S. decennial censuses on the educational attainment of men and women. Censuses since 1940 have inquired about educational attainment; for decades prior to 1940, the age breakdown of the 1940 data was employed to obtain estimates of educational attainment (Folger and Nam, 1967). For the adult population, the median years of schooling completed by women ex-

TABLE 3.2
Index of Dissimilarity by Educational Attainment,
1971 and 1981

Years of schooling completed	1971 (D)	1981 (D)	Change
1–11	68.7	62.7	−6.0
12	65.6	62.9	−2.7
13–15	68.2	59.9	−8.3
16	64.9	49.7	−15.2
17+	61.5	42.0	−19.5

SOURCE: Current Population Survey data, 1971 and 1981.

42   *A Social Control Approach*

TABLE 3.3
Educational Attainment of the U.S. Population by Sex, 1910–1980

Year	<12	12	12+	13–15	16+	Median
			No. of years of schooling completed			
			WOMEN			
1980	34.2%	37.7%		15.3%	12.8%	12.4
1970	47.2	34.1		10.6	8.1	12.1
1960	57.4	27.8		9.0	5.8	10.7
1950	64.0	23.2		7.6	5.2	9.6
1940	73.7	16.4		6.1	3.8	8.7
1930	79.3		20.7%		3.1	8.5
1920	82.9		17.1		2.4	8.3
1910	85.4		14.6		1.9	8.2
			MEN			
1980	32.7%	31.1%		16.1%	20.1%	12.6
1970	48.1	27.7		10.7	13.5	12.1
1960	60.5	21.2		8.6	9.7	10.3
1950	67.5	18.2		7.0	7.3	9.0
1940	77.3	12.2		5.0	5.5	8.6
1930	82.5		17.5%		4.6	8.3
1920	85.5		14.5		3.9	8.2
1910	87.6		12.4		3.4	8.1

SOURCES: Data through 1960 are from Folger and Nam, 1967. Data for 1970 and 1980 are from the U.S. Census of Population, 1970 and 1980.
NOTE: The population analyzed in this table was aged 25 and older.

ceeded that of men in every year examined until 1980, when men edged ahead. When the focus is restricted to those in the labor force, women's educational advantage over men is even greater than the population figures indicate. Table 3.4 reports the educational attainment of men and women in the labor force from 1940 to 1980. We find that women in the labor force have historically been better educated than their male counterparts, despite their underrepresentation among college graduates.[2]

A variety of multivariate analyses have substantiated the conclusion that occupational segregation by sex is not primarily due to differences in the level of educational attainment of men and women. The educational attainment of women in male-dominated occupations does not significantly exceed that of women in female-dominated occupations. Much evidence suggests that the human capital theory by itself explains relatively little of the persistent pattern of occupational segregation by sex (England, 1982; Beller, 1982a; Corcoran, Duncan, and Ponza, 1984; England and Farkas, 1986). Measurable productivity-related characteristics of women in male-dominated occupations do not differ substantially from those of women in female-dominated occupations.

Given the similarity in educational attainment of men and women, restricting access to high-status occupations on the basis of educational credentials would fail as a strategy for defending men's privileged positions. Since there are women at all levels of educational attainment, the social control implicit in sex segregation must rely on other props. Men have not maintained an overall educational advantage over women the way whites have over blacks and the way the wealthy have over the poor.

TABLE 3.4

Educational Attainment of the U.S. Labor Force by Sex, 1940–1980

Year	<12	12	13–15	16+	Median
		No. of years of schooling completed			
		WOMEN			
1980	21.8%	41.9%	18.6%	17.7%	12.7
1970	38.0	39.3	11.4	11.3	12.3
1960	49.7	30.9	10.6	8.8	12.0
1950	55.0	26.5	9.8	8.7	11.2
1940	54.5	26.6	10.6	9.3	10.8
		MEN			
1980	25.1%	33.7%	18.4%	22.8%	12.7
1970	41.8	30.9	11.7	15.6	12.3
1960	55.9	23.8	9.4	10.9	11.1
1950	67.5	19.5	7.1	7.7	9.4
1940	71.5	15.4	6.3	6.8	8.3

SOURCES: Data through 1960 are from Folger and Nam, 1967. Data for 1970 and 1980 are from the U.S. Census of Population, 1970 and 1980.
NOTE: The population analyzed in this table was aged 25 and older.

*Education, Companionate Marriages, and Status
Transmission: A Speculation*

Why are women so well educated in our society? Why is
there so little gender inequality in the extent of education,
compared to the extreme inequality in jobs and other aspects of
social life? Why have men let women have access to education,
which for men is the route to status, power, and privilege? As
we have seen, women on the average spend as many years as
men in school. The human capital perspective has trouble explaining the extent of women's investment in education in
terms of women's expected lifetime economic payoff. Since
women will not spend as many years in the labor force as men,
their expected return on educational investments is lower than
that of men, and consequently women should not invest as
much in their educations.[3]

More to the point, however, is the historical role of education in the marriage system. Strict economic discussions of
motivations for education ignore the role of educational attainment in marriages. Education for women historically has played
a large part in attracting desirable husbands (Freeman, 1976).

Educational homogamy is well documented: on average,
highly educated men marry women who themselves are well
educated (Goode, 1982). While at times women risk becoming
too well educated (as women with bachelor's degrees were
sometimes considered at the turn of the century, and women
with Ph.D. degrees are sometimes considered today), in general, the more education a woman obtains, the more likely she
is to obtain a high-status husband. This pattern of educationally
homogamous marriages characterizes second marriages as well
as first marriages (Jacobs and Furstenberg, 1986). But this emphasis on the rationality of individual choices again begs the
question of the social context in which these choices are being
made. Why has education been available to women, and why
has it been viewed as acceptable?

We propose that the reason for the similarity in the education of boys and girls ultimately stems from the companionate marriage system deeply rooted in our culture. Education for women emerged because of a struggle by women for the right to education (Solomon, 1985), but the success of this struggle in part rested on the notion that husbands and wives should be friends and companions. The view of marriage as the coming together of consenting equals sharing not only responsibilities but also the opportunity for the realization of mutual fulfill-ment—by no means a universal view—provides an important justification for the extension of education to women.

The Protestant conception of the companionate marriage system dates back at least to the eighteenth century (Stone, 1977; Degler 1980). Such a marriage system emphasizes in-dividual choice rather than parental selection and evolves cultural forms that highlight romance and self-fulfillment as the means and ends, respectively, of marriages (Waller, 1938; Swidler, 1986). For our purposes, the most important conse-quence of this system is that it implies the desirability of roughly similar educational levels for husbands and wives. What better way to promote the ideal of companionship than to provide husbands and wives with the similar interests and refinements that education brings? Clearly, vast differences in the education of husbands and wives would interfere with the companionship held as our cultural ideal. The connection between the education of women and the ideal of companion-ate marriages has long been noted (Stone, 1977; Degler, 1980; Waller, 1938).

Education for women has historically been justified in terms of the benefits for marriage; indeed, the curricula of women's colleges often emphasized the role of education in improving a woman's performance as a homemaker. Kent and Durbin (1986) find that only part of the variation between states in college at-tendance by women at the turn of the century can be explained by career opportunities; they attribute much of the balance to the matrimonial function of women's colleges.

Our argument is not meant to suggest that this ideal of com-panionship is typically attained. Indeed, historians have suggested that married men and women have often lived in vastly different worlds, with same-sex friendships the accepted pattern (Smith-Rosenberg, 1985; Cott, 1977; Rubin, 1983). Nonetheless, the ideals we hold often do have force, and they may have had something to do with promoting the education of women.

In developing countries, as the ideal of companionship in marriage makes inroads into local cultures, the education of women also tends to become acceptable. Indeed, men increasingly seek out educated wives as the notion of companionship in marriage becomes prevalent. As education for women spreads, the age at marriage increases and the role of parents in arranging marriages tends to diminish (Caldwell, Reddy, and Caldwell, 1983, 1985).[4]

This social system, in which status is transmitted across generations by highly educated men marrying highly educated women who do not work for wages, no doubt has its internal logic, but it has proven to be unstable as highly educated women have become dissatisfied at home and have demanded a place in the work force. Thus the education of women, in part an element of the status maintenance system of families, and in part a concession to the demands of women, spurred the growth of the women's movement and greatly increased labor force participation by women (Klein, 1984). The emergence of education for women fit nicely with the emphasis on companionate marriages, but it produced a serious incongruity in social institutions as women entered the workplace in large numbers.

This is not the place to give a full account of these historical developments, but they are important in setting the context for the current state of affairs. These developments led to a situation in which women by and large are as educated as men, and in which women are increasingly active in the labor force. How then can an occupational system that is predicated on sorting by education manage to deprive highly educated women of the opportunities to obtain prestige, power, and an independent means of support? The answer, of course, is that the content of women's education has been oriented to only a few career options, and the sex segregation of work has left well-educated women with only a limited number of relatively poorly paying occupations to choose from. But how is sex segregation in education and in the workplace maintained?

One prominent possibility is the institution of marriage, and specifically the greater obligations of women for child care and other household tasks. There is undoubtedly much truth to this view, which is stressed both by conservative economists who defend the free market (Polachek, 1976, 1979) and by radical feminists who argue that inequality rooted in reproduction is the basis for patriarchy (Hartmann, 1976). But, as we have seen, the extent to which marriage and child rearing have kept women from working has varied historically and across societies. Further, the concentration of women with family responsibilities in female-dominated occupations explains little of the sex segregation of work (England, 1982). Interrupted participation in the labor force undoubtedly is responsible for a portion of women's economic disadvantage, as is evident in standard decompositions of the wage gap (U.S. Bureau of the Census, 1987), but the extent of this loss is as much culturally as economically determined. When a generation of men took several years off to fight in the Second World War, they did not suffer a wage penalty for the duration of their careers. But when women take time off for the socially essential task of child rearing, they are penalized for their lack of labor force "commitment."

Undoubtedly, family demands are central to the ideological justification for women's secondary status at work, in particular for the view that women's short tenures account for their lower earnings (but see Waite and Berryman, 1985). To the extent that marriage and family are responsible for the disadvantages of working women, one must ask how family values are reinforced over time. As we will see, questions about social channeling processes pertaining to marriage values are not entirely dissimilar to those regarding the employment issues on which we will focus.

Sex Segregation and Social Control

The thesis advanced here is that sex segregation is maintained by a lifelong system of social control. There is no central institutional structure like the educational system to prop it up. Sex segregation depends on the differential socialization of young men and women, sex-typed tracking in the educational system, and sex-linked social control at the workplace, at the hiring stage and beyond. Social control is operative at each stage of life. Indeed, the maintenance of sex segregation depends on a lifelong system of social control because of the marked lack of continuity in values and behavior from one life stage to the next. The similarity in educational levels between men and women allows for a degree of mobility between female-dominated and male-dominated occupations. Sex-role socialization helps to initiate occupational segregation by sex, but the values and beliefs learned by individuals at young ages are constantly reinforced. Without constraints on opportunity, socialization by itself would be insufficient to channel women into female-dominated occupations.

The social control perspective maintains that the pressure for women to pursue female-dominated positions does not end in early childhood. It is continually reinforced and recreated throughout young adulthood, and continues during the years in the labor market. Many women internalize these values, while others successfully challenge the constraints imposed on them. These two groups of women are not as distinct as many assume. Yet the cumulative effect of social control restricts the number of women working in male-dominated fields. Thus, occupational segregation by sex persists, even though the same women do not stay in female-dominated occupations.

Sex roles are a classic case of the enforcement of social definitions of deviance (Schur, 1984). "Unfeminine" behavior by women brings sharp signals of social disapproval. Similarly, disapproval accompanies "unmasculine" behavior by men; indeed, it is often thought that definitions of masculinity are more vigorously enforced than definitions of femininity

(Pleck, 1981). Vocational goals certainly have sex-role attachments, as do educational majors and occupational roles. Even young children are aware of the gender connotations of familiar occupations.

Definitions of deviance are enforced by a system of social control. Many stereotypes are applied to those who violate sex-role norms. For example, women managers are often stereotyped as pushy and aggressive, which is to say unfeminine. Research on sex differences in occupational prestige suggests that incumbents in sex-atypical occupations may suffer an evaluative penalty for sex-role deviance (Jacobs and Powell, 1984). Sex-appropriate behavior is enforced in ways ranging from subtle pressure to violent threats and harassment. Given a normative system that labels their employment in male-dominated occupations deviant, women continually face subtle and overt barriers to successful competition for employment in male-dominated settings, as well as barriers to effective performance once that employment is secured.

Kanter (1977) has discussed the ways in which social control of women is exerted in corporate settings. Particularly noteworthy is her discussion of the dilemmas of the token woman, who often finds herself in situations designed for failure. We should not be surprised to find a substantial attrition rate of such women. Yet as we will see, attrition begins before women are employed, in the period during which values are developing and educational choices are being made. Social control is not restricted to early-life socialization or to employment settings, but is a constant feature of social life that steadily reinforces occupational segregation by sex.

England and Farkas (1986) have noted that economists emphasize the choices of individuals, while sociologists focus on the constraints individuals face. Social control processes run the gamut from subtle control that appears as personal choice to harsher practices that appear as constraints; much of what economists would consider to be free choice is the result of socialization and other forms of the internalization of values. Yet as Wrong (1961) points out, we must not view socialization as a straitjacket on the individual's initiative. People make their own choices, but they do so in the context of prevailing norms and institutional constraints, and they may be treated as sex-role deviants when normative standards are violated. We view conformity as a contested process and the mobility documented here as evidence that these norms are contested.

We emphasize that sex typing relies on a more extended process and is less formally structured than socioeconomic tracking. But this is not to say sex discrimination is uninstitutionalized. As Roos and Reskin (1984) have shown, many organizational routines are set up in ways that disadvantage women. Thus, women confront a combination of institutional barriers and intentional discrimination (Feagin and Feagin, 1986). But without the supporting force of educational differences, these barriers are somewhat more permeable for a longer portion of life than is the case for socioeconomic or racial inequality.

Cumulative Disadvantage Versus Revolving Doors

Two competing versions of the lifelong social control perspective must be distinguished. The more familiar is what we label the "cumulative disadvantage" view, which we contrast with the "revolving door" perspective. The cumulative disadvantage model holds that occupational segregation by sex is the result of the accumulation of obstacles women face in their pursuit of careers. Thus, socialization is compounded by educational inequality and labor market discrimination, the cumulative force of which leaves women in a segregated set of occupations.

This view is clearly implicit in Berryman's discussion of women in science and engineering (1983). Women face obstacles beginning with ambivalent socialization about the importance of careers and the stereotype that science is an unfeminine pursuit. Women are underrepresented in science and engineering professions because of inadequate preparation in high school, attrition from science and engineering fields in college, and minority status and hostility on the job for those women who pursue such careers.

If the obstacles women confront in pursuing science and engineering careers are characteristic of male-dominated occupations, this model implies a number of specific predictions concerning sex segregation. The first is that segregation would increase over women's lifetimes as women continually leave male-dominated pursuits. One would expect to find more segregation as a cohort ages, as the disadvantages women face accumulate. Second, mobility observed between male-dominated and female-dominated occupations would take the form of attrition of women from male-dominated pursuits. Delayed entry into male-dominated occupations would be difficult; at the very least, delayed entries of women into male-dominated occupations should be less frequent than exits. Finally, if declines in sex segregation were to occur, this change would primarily take the form of changes between cohorts. The best one could expect for those already in the pipeline is to reduce the rate of attrition; real change must await a new cohort that is exposed to different socialization, broader opportunities in school, and less hostility on the job. One would not expect increased integration among those already in the labor force, since the cumulative effects of these social control processes are essentially irreversible.

While the cumulative disadvantage model is attractive because of its recognition of the pervasive nature of social control, three striking findings suggest that while social control is continuous, its effects do not increase over the life course. First, occupational segregation by sex does not increase as men and women grow older. Second, sex-type mobility involves substantial rates of midcareer entry into, as well as exit from, male-dominated occupations. Third, overall change in segregation is observed across different age groups, and is not simply the result of cohort replacement. In other words, where the cumulative disadvantage view holds that change must come about principally because a new cohort has different experiences, the evidence suggests that a general weakening of the system of controls broadens opportunities for those already in the labor force. As we will see, there is as much change in young women's aspirations over time as there is across new cohorts of women in the process of forming their aspirations. There is as much change for people already in college as there is among those entering college. In recent years, there has been a notable decline in segregation among those already in the labor market, as we saw in Chapter 2. The insight of the cumulative disadvantage view is that it recognizes the range of constraints imposed on women throughout their lives. Its limitation is that it assumes that the effects of barriers to women's opportunities are permanent and irreversible.

Thus we arrive at a lifelong social control perspective that is not characterized by cumulative disadvantage. In recognition of the dramatic levels of mobility we find, we refer to this view as the "revolving door" model of sex segregation. The revolving door perspective can account for extensive sex-type mobility because it recognizes a variety of stages in the career development process, and it recognizes a host of pressures women face. Most women will face one or more barriers to the pursuit of a career at some point; they are likely to overcome some of these and not others. Thus there are reasons to expect substantial flows of women into and out of male-dominated occupations, while overall the system changes only gradually.

This perspective also accounts for the patterns of change in sex segregation we are beginning to see. If social control is exercised throughout life, social change is likely to be experienced by women of different ages. Change should affect those already in the labor force as well as those entering it and those in the educational system. Theories that emphasize labor market entry as the decisive time for segregation cannot account for decreasing segregation among those already in the labor force. As we have seen in Chapter 2, the declines in labor market segregation by sex in the 1970's occurred throughout the age structure and were not simply restricted to labor market entrants.

There is a striking similarity in the dynamics of sex segregation in the development of aspirations, in the segregation of college majors, and in the sex segregation of the occupational structure. All three are characterized by change occurring among different age groups, and all three have striking levels of mobility between male-dominated, sex-neutral, and female-dominated fields. The similarities of these patterns in these diverse contexts and across different stages of life convince us of the utility of the social control / revolving door perspective.

Let us consider the various stages of life and the application of this perspective to the development and maintenance of occupational segregation by sex. A general theory of sex segregation will enable us to incorporate the insights of other approaches and to show more effectively their theoretical limitations. Our principal argument against each of the alternative views is that it telescopes the time frame during which the essential social control processes are occurring. Socialization theory holds that the crucial time during which sex segregation is reproduced is in the earliest stages of life. The human capital view emphasizes the period of educational decision making and the acquisition of on-the-job skills. And the labor market segmentation perspective holds that the period of participation in the labor force is the essential time during which effective gender tracking is enforced. The lifelong social control view, on the contrary, holds that the process is drawn out and needs more reinforcement than is implied by any of these approaches. While each properly recognizes an important component in the process of sex typing, a fully integrated social control perspective does more justice to the social processes involved. The following discussion of these prominent views on the maintenance of sex segregation shows the ways in which the social control / revolving door model builds on the insights of each of these perspectives.

Social Control and Sex-Role Socialization

Numerous studies show that sex-role socialization begins early in life. By elementary school, girls and boys can distinguish men's and women's roles (Miller and Garrison, 1982; Getty and Cann, 1981; Garrett, Ein, and Tremaine, 1977; McGee and Stockard, 1987). Pronounced sex differences in occupational aspirations are documented for adolescents and preadolescents (Marini and Brinton, 1984; Hesselbart, 1977). Girls and boys play different games, which affects their social skills and attitudes (Lever, 1978; Gilligan, 1982). Parents assign different tasks to their sons and daughters, intentionally or unintentionally preparing them for sex-segregated pursuits in the world of work (Duncan and Duncan, 1978; White and Brinkerhoff, 1981).

Recent evidence on the labor force experiences of teenagers further strengthens the case for socialization. Greenberger and Steinberg (1983) examine the work experiences of teenagers at four high schools in suburban California. Among teenage workers, they find a level of segregation by sex and a gender gap in wages similar to those in the adult labor force. These early work experiences are reinforced by sex-typed vocational training in high school and college (Kessler et al., 1985; Jacobs, 1985).

Marini and Brinton (1984) provide an excellent survey of theories and research linking sex-role socialization to occupational segregation by sex. They review the evidence on sex differences in career aspirations and work-related attributes. They explore a range of mechanisms through which socialization processes can influence boys and girls, including family behavior, parental role models, school influences, sex stereotyping in textbooks and other educational materials, guidance counseling, vocational tracking, and mathematics and science preparation. Marini and Brinton document numerous channels of information and sources of influence affecting values (see also Haber, 1980; Lifschitz, 1983).

Yet the connection between early socialization and vocational outcomes is less direct than this body of literature sometimes implies. In our industrial society, there are a number of factors that complicate the process of channeling women into female-dominated occupations. The process of matching people with jobs is a complex one requiring a great deal of social coordination.

One complicating factor is the elaborate division of labor in our industrial economies. Recent censuses report information on over 400 occupations, each representing an aggregation of often vastly different types of work. The *Dictionary of Occupational Titles* lists over 28,000 job titles, and even this detailed list is an understatement of the diversity of work in our economy (Cain and Treiman, 1981). One case study reported as many as 2,100 different job titles for 6,000 workers in a single firm (Edwards, 1979). This elaborate division of labor poses a problem for the socialization of youth. Children are aware of only a limited number of familiar occupations. As we shall see, even teenagers' occupational choices converge on a small number of popular jobs. The sex label of a given job must be analogized to familiar occupations, and such analogies are often ambiguous and contestable (Milkman, 1987).

Further, occupational roles are as volatile as they are diverse. The volatility of our economy requires adaptability; the choices the young must make must not be too deeply held, for they may well have to abandon them as circumstances dictate. The rise and fall of technologies do not match neatly with the desired trajectory of careers. An informed young person preparing for a career confronts a bewildering set of choices, a bewilderment compounded by the uncertainty of technological and economic trends. The limited life expectancy of particular vocational skills compounds the problem of vocational socialization.

The educational process further complicates the translation of childhood values into adult roles. Aspirations regarding adult roles are in most cases channeled through educational goals. The educational system allows for the development of tastes and interests that may correspond with neither the values obtained in early childhood nor the exigencies of adulthood. The ability of the educational system to meet the needs of the economy has been widely questioned by critics on the left and on the right. From the vantage point of students, schooling represents a time to question and change values.

The problem of matching people with occupations continues after they have entered the labor market. For most people, careers do not simply unfold as a series of promotions from one's first job. Americans' career histories are replete with unexpected twists and turns. Our economy allows for substantial occupational mobility. Careers are the final context in which gender roles may be redefined and renegotiated.

Therefore, while we should expect important values to be acquired during the process of early-life socialization, we should also expect substantial fluidity during subsequent life stages. As we will see, occupational aspirations are highly segregated by sex at an early age, but adult outcomes are far from determined at this stage of the social control system.

All industrial societies face these issues, yet the volatility of the matching system is greatest in countries, such as the United States, that depend on what Ralph Turner has called a "contest mobility" system (1960). Turner argues that the United States' stratification system is distinctive in its reliance on voluntary choices rather than institutional tracking. Turner maintains that in the United States, the predominant metaphor for mobility is that of entering a contest, where contestants win places in the status hierarchy. In other countries, mobility often takes on a more "sponsored" quality, representing the decision of elites to confer status on aspirants. In the United States, the contest is prolonged for as long as possible; our system is predicated on the belief that opportunities are available to those with effort and merit. Thus the process of matching people and occupations takes a longer time than it does in other countries. Where other countries rely on early examinations to channel students into further education and vocational preparation, American society generally relies on the widespread distribution of aspirations and subtle "cooling out" processes (Clark, 1960). Thus research on careers in Germany finds a tighter connection between sex-typed education and careers than we find in the United States, no doubt because the highly structured German vocational educational system requires early decision making on the part of teenagers and enforces a tighter link between education and career decisions than is generally the case in the United States (Blossfeld, 1987).

These considerations might seem to apply as much to socioeconomic inequality as they do to occupational segregation by sex. But socioeconomic inequality is reproduced via the educational system: without attaining a certain level of education, vertical mobility is difficult. Sex segregation, in contrast, is not primarily a function of educational level. There are opportunities for employment in male-dominated as well as female-dominated occupations at each educational level, as we have seen. Thus, the system of sex segregation must rely on less formal social constraints to a much greater extent than the class system does. And so vocational goals are more likely to change their sex type over time than their socioeconomic level.

These theoretical considerations provide the context for our examination of one of the key lacunae in research from the socialization perspective. Although, as we have seen, much research documents the development of gender-segregated vocational goals, to our knowledge virtually no research has examined the link between these goals and subsequent behavior. The above considerations suggest why these linkages are likely to be weaker than many expect. Consequently, socialization begins the lifelong system of social control. But socialization is too slender a reed on which to maintain the massive edifice of occupational segregation by sex. Our society reinforces the values imbued in early life in a series of later social control systems.

For women in recent years, socialization was probably less connected to careers than is usually the case. The 1950's, 1960's, and 1970's were characterized by dramatic developments that probably short-circuited the usual relationships between socialization and career outcomes. Dramatic declines in fertility and increases in divorce and labor force participation changed the rules of the game for women. A large number of women were in the labor force for much longer periods than they had expected to be as children. Furthermore, the women's movement presented a clear challenge to accepted traditional values. Thus, while there are good reasons to expect the effects of socialization to be weak in general, they are especially weak in terms of gender differentiation, and for recent cohorts of women in particular.

Social Control in Education

We have emphasized the similarity in the educational attainments of men and women, specifically the length of time young men and women spend in school. One of the ways that sex segregation is maintained is the differentiation in the type of education men and women obtain. Although men and women spend equal amounts of time in school, they are tracked in sex-appropriate lines of study. The differentiation in studies begins in high school, when specialization is first permitted. Women are less likely than men to pursue mathematics and science. In vocational tracks, men are given mechanical training while women are directed toward home economics and typing. In college, men and women tend to major in different fields.

Social control in educational institutions has ranged from the coercive to the subtle. For many years, school policies forced young women into home economics classes irrespective of their own interests. Women's colleges often had limited curricular options, and entry into many elite schools was prohibited to women. These coercive controls were most durable in postgraduate education, where until recently law school, medical school, and business school education were severely limited for women. Today, controls are likely to be more informal, with the pressure of guidance counselors (Walsh, 1977) and peers replacing the restrictive policies of the past.

The human capital perspective in economics has become the predominant form of analyzing labor force behavior. Economists suggest a parallel between investing in buildings and equipment and investing in people's skills: both forms of investment increase productivity and produce returns in the form of a stream of future income.

As we have seen, the human capital school has had difficulty in explaining occupational segregation by sex. The limited explanatory power of the number of years spent in school is in part due to differences in the content of education. Recent work from this perspective has highlighted the connection between particular majors pursued in college and occupational segregation by sex (Daymont and Andrisani, 1984; U.S. Bureau of the Census, 1987).

While we share with the human capital school the view that sex segregation during schooling plays a role in occupational segregation, our view differs from the human capital perspective in four fundamental ways. First, we differ on the educational decision-making process. Where human capitalists tend to emphasize the rationality of choices women pursue in college, we emphasize factors such as peer pressure (Weitzman, 1979) and the unreceptive environment women find in certain majors (Hearn and Olzak, 1981). More specifically, the remarkable mobility between majors in colleges raises serious difficulties for the lifetime earnings calculus assumed by the human capital viewpoint.

Human capitalists link educational decisions to family values, and to fertility behavior in particular. The most prominent human capital argument is that sex-typed educational decisions are rational in the framework of lifetime expected earnings. Women are held to maximize lifetime earnings by pursuing fields of study leading to jobs that do not penalize career interruptions (Polachek, 1978). But demographic research shows that fertility decisions are often short-term ones, that young men and women do not foresee their life trajectories very far in advance (Rindfuss, Morgan, and Swicegood, 1988). Thus, the rationality that economists often impute to young people assumes a much longer time horizon than these people actually employ. Given a shorter perspective, nonrational influences can have important effects on choices that may have enduring consequences.

Second, the connection between college majors and subsequent employment is often overstated. Many students change majors, and the connection between majors and subsequent work is often limited. In particular, extensive career mobility is likely to dissipate the initial effects observed in certain studies (Daymont and Andrisani, 1984).

Third, we differ with the human capital school on the question of discrimination in the labor market. Where the human capital economists emphasize the efficiency of markets, which tends to eliminate discrimination, we see organizational constraints—implicit in recent economic theories—that imply much greater rigidity. This view is developed at some length in Chapter 8. Finally, whereas economic arguments often are built on an assumption of stable differences in preferences between men and women, our evidence on sex-role socialization indicates that these preferences are often unstable and change in response to the emergence of new opportunities. Thus, to the extent that economic arguments rest on the assumption of sex differences in values, our critique of the socialization perspective is pertinent to economic perspective as well.

The social control / revolving door perspective is better suited to explaining the observed malleability of educational decisions and the extensive mobility between majors than the human capital perspective. Education is another necessary but insufficient link in the chain of social control.

Social Control in the Workplace

In contrast to the socialization and human capital perspectives, which emphasize the importance of sex differences that emerge prior to labor market entry, theories emphasizing discrimination and economic segmentation focus on events that follow entry into the labor market as the causes of women's disadvantaged position. In short, where socialization and human capital focus on factors that influence the supply of working women, discrimination and segmentation theories scrutinize the demand for women workers.

Economic segmentation theorists examine the way the structure of the economy mediates the attainment processes of individuals (Beck, Horan, and Tolbert, 1978; Berg, 1981). The economy is typically divided into a core and a periphery: the core has large, relatively stable firms with significant market shares and highly developed internal career ladders, while the periphery consists of small firms in competitive markets without a great deal of opportunity for career advancement. This perspective has been employed to highlight differences in the career processes of men and women in the different sectors of the economy (Kemp and Beck, 1981). The core-periphery distinction is not particularly powerful in informing our understanding of gender inequality at work. While women are slightly more concentrated in the periphery, there is nearly as much occupational segregation by sex within each sector as there is in the labor force as a whole, as we document in Chapter 7.

Another segmentation perspective is a view we term the "segregation as segmentation" thesis. This view holds that employers utilize arbitrary divisions between workers in a divide-and-conquer strategy. In this view, the segregation of work into male-dominated and female-dominated occupations is arranged by employers to reduce workers' ability to see their common interests and to organize in the workplace. Wharton (1986) has suggested that this underlies the high levels of sex segregation in blue-collar occupations. This perspective unfortunately is of relatively little help in our efforts to understand stability and change in women's careers. It says little about the mobility of individuals, and even less about the aggregate patterns of change in sex segregation.

Labor market discrimination, in contrast, can help to explain both the mobility of individuals and the aggregate patterns of change. Discrimination is the result of individual employers' actions, not of management working collectively, as in the "segregation as segmentation" view. Discrimination is likely to be consistent with a degree of mobility on the part of individual women, since a series of moves is likely to bring an employee into contact with some discriminatory employers and some nondiscriminatory employers. Nonetheless, this individual mobility is not likely to cumulate into structural change, because employers on average discriminate against women. Discrimination is also consistent with the evidence on aggregate change. Recent changes in the acceptability of discrimination against women have produced declines in discriminatory attitudes, or at least have caused them to be recognized as inappropriate even if they are still privately held. Consequently, there should be progress for women already in the labor force as discriminatory behavior declines. Thus we view labor market discrimination as the final component of our lifelong social control process.

Women are not only discriminated against at the point of hiring. Women are harassed at work by supervisors and co-workers after they manage to overcome discrimination at the hiring stage. They are not aided in informal training as men often are, they are often viewed with suspicion and not treated as part of the team, and they are not expected to seek advancement and are criticized when they seem too aggressive. Women complain that they must be twice as good as men to be recognized as competent, and that they risk being criticized for trying to "show up" the men. The experiences of women in male-dominated settings vary widely, and many do not experience these difficulties. But on average, women in male-dominated settings continue to face numerous impediments to effective on-the-job performance. Thus, in our view, discrimination is not solely the purview of management but extends to colleagues and co-workers as well. (A brief survey of evidence on women's experiences at work is presented in Chapter 7.) The attrition of women from male-dominated occupations is not a surprising consequence of work in such a context.

From a social control perspective, both human capital theory and socialization theories focus on an extremely limited period during which social control is exercised, namely, the pre–labor force years. They assume that once in the labor force, people's natural activities, reflecting either their economic interests or their acquired tastes, will perpetuate a system that is already in motion. Labor market segmentation and discrimination theories, on the other hand, focus on structural constraints in the labor market and minimize the importance of those processes that occur prior to entry into the labor force. The social control perspective proposed here insists that a lifelong system of social control is required to maintain a high level of occupational segregation by sex. The lifelong social control perspective thus serves as a metatheory that can incorporate insights from each of the perspectives discussed above. Further, this perspective alone takes mobility as a central finding, rather than as an inconvenient fact to be explained away.

While the notion of "adult socialization" captures a portion of the lifelong social control idea, our perspective is somewhat different and somewhat broader. Adult socialization typically refers to the continuing adjustments of personality to different stages in the life course (Rose, 1979; Elder, 1985). We focus on occupationally related sex-role values that are reinforced throughout life, rather than socialization associated with coping with midlife crises. Further, we include discrimination and harassment, behavior not generally discussed in terms of adult socialization, in our list of influences on women.

Summary

In this chapter we have seen the contrast between occupational segregation by sex and socioeconomic inequality among men. We have suggested that the high levels of education attained by women throughout the century were related to educational homogamy in marriages, which in the final analysis may be related to the companionate marriage system. Without the institutional support of educational inequality, sex segregation relies to a much greater extent on less formal social controls. These allow for substantial individual mobility while maintaining a high overall level of sex segregation. We have reviewed theories of sex segregation, noted their limited attention to the extent of change for individuals, and incorporated their insights into a lifelong social control perspective.

Unfortunately, most of the evidence we examine only tests our hypotheses indirectly. We do not have direct measures of the social influences that lead women to pursue female-dominated occupations or to enter male-dominated fields. What our national sample data do show is change. We try to infer the causes of change from the timing and direction of the mobility observed. We hope this research will stimulate efforts to pin down more precisely the causes of the patterns documented here.

4

Trends in Young Women's

Occupational Aspirations

In this chapter we track aggregate trends in young women's occupational goals. Research on women's career aspirations has focused on the concentration of women's choices in a limited set of fields and the predominance of female-dominated occupations among women's top choices. We consider how both of these phenomena have changed in recent years and examine variations in these trends by age, cohort, race, educational goals, and labor force experience. We also compare the trends for young women with those for young men. For both groups, we compare the aspirations of individuals in the labor force with the occupations they hold and trace changes in the level of segregation in aspirations.

Aspirations as Harbingers of Change?

A detailed examination of trends in aspirations raises many interesting questions regarding the connection between these trends and changes in employment patterns. It is often assumed or implied that aspirations are harbingers of things to come, that evidence of the increasing popularity of male-dominated occupations in the career choices of young women is a sure sign of a future world of work increasingly integrated by sex. This apparently reasonable position actually assumes a great many things that are not well documented and may not be true. It assumes (1) a degree of stability in the aspirations of individuals; (2) the ability of individual women to realize their aspirations; (3) that aspirations of new labor force entrants must change before occupational change can be expected; and (4) that employment patterns will change in accordance with changes in aspirations.

There are reasons to be skeptical about each of these assumptions. Aspirations may reflect current trends as much as they predict future ones. If so, we can expect to observe changes over time in the goals of individual young women, in addition to changes across cohorts of young women. The more changeable women's aspirations, the less we can rely on present aspirations to predict future occupational patterns. The instability of aspirations implies that projections may either understate or overstate present developments. If trends toward greater sexual integration reflect changes in social beliefs and mores, then future trends may depend on future changes in these beliefs, which could mean either faster or slower change in the future.

The ability of women to realize their aspirations is also clearly assumed by the "harbinger" position. The next chapter considers in detail the ability of individuals to achieve their goals. While individuals may not succeed, one may hold to a weaker assumption, namely, that aggregate trends in aspirations track general shifts in the occupational structure. Yet even this assumption is questionable. For particular occupations, we recognize that there may be a significant gap between pursuit and realization. For example, we do not predict future trends in employment in medicine, engineering, or business on the basis of the numbers of young people who aspire to these occupations. Yet for the pursuit of male-dominated occupations by young women, it is assumed that growing aspirations will result in the greater representation of women in a wide range of occupations.

This reasoning may reflect the assumption that young women's lack of interest is currently constraining the supply of women to male-dominated occupations. Yet if more women already aspire to male-dominated occupations than are employed in them, the assumption that greater interest will produce greater representation may be questioned. If there is a gap between aspirations and occupations, the "harbinger" view assumes that this gap is resolved by women increasingly achieving their goals. However, another possible resolution of this gap is that young women abandon their career goals when they realize the obstacles in their way. Alternatively, an aspiration-occupation gap may remain unresolved over time. Thus, trends in aspirations raise a great many possibilities for our consideration.

While many of the questions we have raised require an examination of trends in the aspirations of a cohort of individuals, most studies of trends in aspirations only examine the goals of successive cohorts. Consequently, these studies cannot provide answers to the questions we have posed. We examine both types of data in this chapter.

Two types of data constitute evidence of the adaptability of aspirations: (1) trends in aspirations that affect different age cohorts similarly, and (2) similarities between trends in occupations and trends in aspirations. If occupations and aspirations change in the same way during the same period, we may view aspirations as changing in step with the changes in opportunities. These changes will be distinguished from that associated with cohort replacement (new groups of young people with different goals) and from age effects (patterns associated with growing older).

As we argued in Chapter 3, the adaptability of aspirations constitutes evidence for the lifelong social control perspective: it indicates that the social constraints undergirding occupational segregation by sex are not fixed early in life but can change as the social context changes. If aspirations are changing to a similar extent for different cohorts, then the social control mechanisms operating across a wide age spectrum are weakening at the same time, and individuals are attentive to these changes and trying to take advantage of them. Mapping trends in aspirations will allow us to test certain implications of the socialization perspective, but it will be less powerful in distinguishing between sociological and economic viewpoints.

Data and Methods

Our principal source of data is the National Longitudinal Survey of Young Women (NLS), a survey of over 5,000 young women interviewed ten times between 1968 and 1980. In each survey year, the women were asked to name the occupation they aspired to be in at age 35. A percent-female score, based on the sex composition of each occupation in 1970, was assigned to the detailed (census three-digit) occupations to which respondents aspired.

The NLS Young Men's data set includes a question on the occupation respondents aspired to be in at age 30. We can thus compare the sex segregation of aspirations at different times and examine trends among cohorts. The men were not asked this question after 1976, and consequently our comparison of men and women does not cover all the years of the survey.

Data from the ACE-CIRP Freshmen Surveys were used for comparison. These large annual national surveys of college freshmen include a question about respondents' occupational goals. These data are extremely useful for the analysis of trends, since they focus on a specific age group over time. However, the occupational coding is far less detailed than that available in the NLS surveys, and these data do not permit us to follow the changes over time experienced by a group of individuals.

The concentration of women's aspirations in a limited range of occupations was measured with several indicators. We calculated the proportion concentrated in the top 10 and top 20 of these occupations as well as the relative concentration index (RC), which represents the degree to which women's goals are more concentrated than men's in a limited number of occupations.

The sex composition of occupations was coded in several

ways. Each detailed occupation was assigned a percent-female score, based on 1970 sex-composition data. The sex composition of individual occupations was treated as constant over time, a procedure that tends to understate the degree of change but that allows us to focus on the changing choices of occupations young women are making, rather than the degree to which a fixed set of choices has changed its sex composition.[1]

In summarizing trends, we first indicate the average percentage of women in the occupations desired by young men and women. We then divide the occupations into male-dominated, sex-neutral, and female-dominated categories. While these divisions are inevitably somewhat arbitrary, occupations that are 0–29.9 percent women are considered male-dominated; those 30–69.9 percent women are considered sex-neutral; and those with 70–100 percent women are considered female-dominated. The most important feature of this partition is the inclusion of a sex-neutral category, which allows for a more refined examination of the locus of change. (A statistical justification for these particular divisions is presented in Chapter 7.) Finally, we measure the degree of difference between distribution of men and women in both aspirations and occupations with our trusted index of dissimilarity, D.

Trends in the Career Goals of College Freshmen

The conventional view of trends in aspirations examines the extent of change in sex segregation with data on successive groups of people, such as high school seniors. Table 4.1 presents such an analysis, using the ACE-CIRP college freshmen data from 1967 to 1981. The index of segregation (D) between the occupational goals of freshmen women and men declined from 62.3 in 1967 to 37.4 in 1983. The trend toward increasing similarity of career choices for college freshmen and women is clearly evident from these data. The percentage of young women aspiring to be elementary or high school teachers declined from 36.4 in 1967 to 8.1 in 1983, while the proportion hoping to enter business rose from 3.3 to 12.8 percent. These changes represent an important shift in the career orientation of young women during this period. The concentration statistic extends this optimistic picture. While in 1967 women's aspirations were more concentrated in a handful of fields than were those of young men (C = 48.4 for women, 36.8 for men), by 1983 this pattern was reversed, with freshmen men's goals more concentrated than those of freshmen women (C = 43.0 for men, 36.3 for women). During this time, the proportion of men aspiring to be in business and engineering rose slightly, from a combined 32.5 percent in 1967 to a combined 33.6 percent in 1983, which constituted 57 percent of those aspiring to one of the occupations listed. The increased concentration of men, combined with the shift of women away from their historical focus on teaching, produced this historic reversal. The ACE-CIRP data thus depict a significant cohort shift in the occupational choices of young men and women.[2]

The greater concentration of men than women is not merely an artifact of the broad categories employed by the ACE-CIRP survey. In Table 4.1, we aggregated the ACE-CIRP statistics for the most recent years to preserve the comparability of results over time. Comparing the concentration of men and women across the 43 detailed occupations included in the 1983 ACE-CIRP survey shows that male college freshmen remain more concentrated in their choices (C = 51.7) than their female counterparts (C = 45.7).

We have no quarrel with the historical trends implied by these data, nor with the optimism with which many would view this development. Sex-role attitudes have changed substantially since the 1960's (Deaux, 1984; Scanzoni and Fox, 1980). However, extrapolating from this type of evidence requires rather strong assumptions about the process of change. The balance of this chapter examines evidence of change over time for a particular cohort of young women and men, rather than the comparison across cohorts found in Table 4.1. We follow the NLS Young Women and Young Men through the late 1960's and 1970's to examine whether the trends observed in

TABLE 4.I
Occupational Aspirations of College Freshmen by Sex, Selected Years, 1967–1983

Occupational goal	1967	1971	1975	1979[a]	1983[a]
			WOMEN		
Artist	8.1%	7.7%	6.5%	4.3%	3.7%
Businessman	3.3	4.4	10.0	10.9	12.8
Clergyman	.3	.2	.4	.1	.1
College teacher	.9	.6	.6	.2	.2
Elementary teacher	17.6	13.8	5.8	7.0	5.7
Engineer	.2	.2	1.1	2.3	3.3
Farmer	.1	.7	1.5	1.2	.5
High school teacher	18.8	11.0	4.5	3.4	2.4
Lawyer	.6	1.4	2.5	3.4	3.6
Medical doctor	1.5	2.0	3.3	2.9	3.4
Nurse	5.4	8.6	9.9	7.0	8.4
Health professional (other)	6.3	8.8	12.8	11.3	10.6
Scientist	1.6	1.5	1.5	1.3	1.2
Other	25.2	26.1	26.9	33.3	33.1
Undecided	9.9%	13.5%	12.6%	11.4%	11.3%
C	48.4	43.5	36.0	34.9	36.3
			MEN		
Artist	4.1%	4.9%	4.1%	3.8%	3.5%
Businessman	17.5	16.1	17.2	15.3	15.3
Clergyman	1.9	1.0	1.0	.7	.5
College teacher	1.4	.8	.6	.3	.3
Elementary teacher	.8	.9	.5	.5	.3
Engineer	15.0	9.7	10.2	16.8	18.3
Farmer	3.3	4.8	5.7	3.8	2.5
High school teacher	10.4	6.6	2.7	2.1	1.8
Lawyer	5.8	6.8	5.4	4.8	4.3
Medical doctor	6.4	6.4	6.6	4.0	4.5
Nurse	.1	.3	.3	.2	.3
Health professional (other)	2.6	3.8	5.2	4.8	4.3
Scientist	3.9	3.3	2.5	2.4	1.8
Other	16.7	21.7	24.5	28.8	32.6
Undecided	10.2%	12.9%	13.5%	9.4%	8.8%
C	36.8	31.1	35.0	39.3	43.0
D^b	62.3	56.5	44.8	40.7	37.4

SOURCE: ACE-CIRP data, 1967–83.
[a]Categories are collapsed together to maintain consistency. The number of respondents included in the "other" category is inflated, because more options are included.
[b]"Other" and "undecided" categories are excluded. Calculation assumes men and women reporting other occupations are as segregated as those reporting the listed occupations.

Table 4.1 parallel changes individuals experienced during this time. A richer view of the process by which recent changes have come about thus emerges.

The Adaptability of Aspirations: Evidence from Panel Data

Trends in the sex composition of occupations for NLS women and men are presented in Table 4.2. The table displays the average percentage of women in occupations chosen by women and by men. The table also shows the proportion of men and women in male-dominated, sex-neutral, and female-dominated occupations.[3] We see on Table 4.2 a slow and steady movement of this group of young women toward more male-dominated occupational goals. The average percentage of women in occupations chosen by women dropped from 68.8 in 1968 to 58.9 in 1980. The decline in the average percentage of women is due to an increase in the proportion of young women choosing male-dominated occupations and a decrease in the proportion choosing female-dominated occupations. The proportion of young women choosing male-dominated occupations doubled in this period (from 12.1 percent in 1968 to 25.9 percent in 1980), while the proportion of young women choosing female-dominated occupations showed a corresponding decline (from 52.8 to 42.2 percent). The proportion in sex-neutral occupations fell only slightly.

These data indicate that there was roughly as much change in aspirations for this cohort of women as there was across cohorts of college freshmen women, as Table 4.1 showed. In other words, the aspirations of young women remain adaptable well into their twenties and early thirties. Even after young women have entered the labor market, they remain as sensitive to trends in opportunities as new cohorts of women about to enter the labor force.

Young men's occupational choices, in contrast, moved only slightly toward more female-dominated occupations; the average percentage of women in occupations chosen by men in-

TABLE 4.2

Sex Composition of Occupational Aspirations of NLS Young Women and Young Men, 1968–1980 and 1966–1976

Year	Avg. pct. female	Std. dev.	Pct. in male-dominated occupations	Pct. in sex-neutral occupations	Pct. in female-dominated occupations	n
		NLS YOUNG WOMEN				
1968	68.8%	27.7%	12.1%	35.0%	52.8%	2,397
1969	70.1	26.7	10.9	33.5	55.5	2,101
1970	68.3	27.3	13.3	34.7	52.0	2,103
1971	67.0	27.3	14.6	39.1	46.3	2,133
1972	67.5	26.9	13.1	41.2	45.7	2,174
1973	66.0	28.6	15.7	38.5	45.8	2,144
1975	65.4	30.0	18.4	31.1	50.5	2,285
1977	63.4	30.4	20.9	32.0	47.1	2,354
1978	60.2	30.9	24.4	32.8	42.8	2,241
1980	58.9	31.6	25.9	31.9	42.2	1,908
		NLS YOUNG MEN				
1966	17.6%	20.9%	77.0%	20.6%	2.4%	4,198
1967	18.0	18.9	78.2	18.4	2.4	3,889
1968	18.1	20.3	78.2	18.4	3.4	3,767
1969	18.9	20.2	77.4	19.8	2.8	3,459
1970	19.3	20.5	77.6	18.8	3.6	3,326
1971	18.7	20.0	77.9	19.7	2.5	3,364
1973	18.5	19.9	77.3	20.3	2.4	2,676
1975	18.7	20.3	77.7	19.1	3.2	2,348
1976	18.7	20.3	77.7	19.1	3.2	1,966[a]

[a]Projected from 1975.

creased from 17.6 to 18.7. Thus women, but not men, experienced a significant change in the sex-composition of their occupational choices in this period. The index of segregation between the occupational goals of young women and young men fell from 71.5 in 1970 to 63.8 in 1975. Although this change may appear small relative to the changes across cohorts of college freshmen, the rate of change is actually quite similar. This NLS comparison of men and women covers only a five-year period, while the ACE-CIRP data covers fifteen years, and the NLS data include young men and women not bound for college.

The average percentage of women in young women's occupational choices declines consistently as they get older, from 73.1 percent at age 14 to 59.4 percent at age 34 (data not shown in table). Thus, this period was one of significant reconsideration of the acceptability of choices for young women. Dividing the sample into two age cohorts reveals only a small difference across cohorts: the average percentage of women in the choices of the younger group is roughly two points lower than for the older group, a rather small difference compared to the major changes experienced by each group.

Racial and educational differences in the sex type of aspirations are evident, but the patterns of change are roughly parallel across races and educational groups. Black and Hispanic women start out choosing more female-dominated occupations than whites, but the gap shrinks throughout the 1970's (the difference in the average percentage of women in chosen occupations drops from 4–5 percent in the late 1960's to 1–2 percent by the late 1970's). Educational differences are larger and remain constant. Young women who plan to receive a college degree are found in occupations with about 5 percent more men than occupations chosen by women who do not plan to complete college.[4]

Table 4.3 compares trends in the sex composition of aspirations with trends in the sex composition of occupations actually held by young women and men in the labor force. This comparison is restricted to employed women. We see a movement toward more male-dominated pursuits for both women's aspirations and their occupations in this period. The extent of change was slightly greater for aspirations than occupations, but this difference was not large (a decline in the percentage of women of 10.6 percent for aspirations and 8.7 percent for occupations). These parallel developments are strong evidence of the sensitivity of aspirations to changes in opportunity: change in the sex composition of women's aspirations did not wait for a new generation of women with different aspirations, but changed along with the changes in women's actual career options. As more women were employed in male-dominated occupations, more women aspired to these occupations.

TABLE 4.3

Sex Composition of Occupations Aspired to and Held
by NLS Young Women and Young Men,
1968–1980 and 1966–1976

Year	Avg. pct. women in occupations aspired to	Avg. pct. women in occupations held	n
NLS YOUNG WOMEN			
1968	68.6%	71.3%	689
1969	70.8	70.8	1,107
1970	68.2	72.0	1,234
1971	67.2	69.8	1,320
1972	66.7	70.6	1,389
1973	65.8	69.4	1,413
1975	64.2	67.5	1,654
1977	59.0	63.8	1,605
1978	58.5	63.5	1,674
1980	58.0	62.6	1,511
NLS YOUNG MEN			
1966	17.5%	23.6%	2,866
1967	18.0	23.6	3,390
1968	18.2	22.9	2,946
1969	18.8	22.7	2,875
1970	19.2	22.2	2,871
1971	18.6	21.0	3,061
1973	18.4	20.5	2,402
1975	18.7	20.3	2,152
1976	18.7	20.3	2,340[a]

[a]Projected from n for 1975.

An interesting and important statistic is the consistent difference between the percentages of women in the occupations
young women aspire to and in the occupations they hold. This
difference might be termed a realization gap, an index of the
degree to which goals outstrip opportunities. Table 4.3 documents a small but consistent tendency for women to aspire to
more male-dominated occupations than they hold. The difference in the sex composition of the occupations women aspire
to and the occupations they hold hovered between 3 and 5 percentage points throughout the 1970's. Pressure for more change

was consistently evident, since women were more likely to aspire to male-dominated occupations than they were to be employed in them. Part of this gap may be due to the fact that the aspiration question is asked with respect to age 35, while the current occupation is being reported by women under 35. Yet the aspiration/occupation gap does not decline with age. A 3–5 point aspiration/occupation gap is consistent throughout. This pattern also does not mask experience effects. The aspiration/occupation gap remains about the same size as the number of years of labor force participation increases. Women consistently aspire to more male-dominated pursuits than those in which they are employed. The small but consistent aspiration/occupation gap is evident whether the data are displayed by age or by labor force experience. It should be noted that this is the *average* difference between aspirations and occupations in terms of their percentage of women; the disparities of individual men and women, discussed below, are much greater.

In the data for men's aspirations and occupations presented in Table 4.3, an interesting pattern of convergence is found. Men moved slowly to choose more female-dominated occupations, while the jobs in which they were employed became slightly more male-dominated. Initially, young men's occupations were about 6 percent more female-dominated than the occupations they aspired to, and this gap diminished to about 2 points by 1975. Thus both men and women chose more male-dominated occupations than they were able to obtain. The difference between the sexes is that women on average aspire to occupations with 60 percent women, while men aspire to occupations with an average of about 20 percent women.

One summary measure of change is a comparison of the index of segregation for 1970 and 1975. Occupational segregation declined from 70.3 to 65.5 during this period, a drop of 4.8 compared with the 7.7 point drop in the segregation of aspirations. Thus, there was slightly more convergence in the aspirations of young men and women than there was in the actual jobs in which they were found.

Turning now to the issue of concentration, the NLS panel data also indicate a clear pattern of increasing dispersion of as-

TABLE 4.4

Concentration (C) of Occupational Aspirations
of NLS Young Women and Young Men, 1968–1980 and 1966–1976

Year	Pct. aspiring to top 10 occupations	Pct. aspiring to top 20 occupations	C	n of occupations	n of cases
		NLS YOUNG WOMEN			
1968	65.5%	81.1%	79.6	109	2,397
1969	62.1	78.8	79.0	105	2,101
1970	60.4	77.4	77.5	108	2,103
1971	59.8	77.2	77.7	116	2,133
1972	61.5	77.4	77.8	116	2,174
1973	57.8	75.2	75.9	126	2,144
1975	54.3	71.6	72.8	143	2,285
1977	52.8	70.0	71.8	151	2,354
1978	52.5	70.7	72.8	151	2,241
1980	52.5	70.7	72.8	143	1,945
		NLS YOUNG MEN			
1966	39.3%	57.1%	67.8	194	4,198
1967	41.7	57.6	67.5	192	3,889
1968	41.4	57.4	65.8	204	3,767
1969	41.4	57.1	64.9	212	3,459
1970	42.9	58.4	64.5	204	3,326
1971	45.7	60.8	64.4	211	3,364
1973	43.8	58.8	64.1	198	2,676
1975	43.8	59.3	64.3	200	2,348
1976	43.0	59.8	64.5	202	1,966

pirations for women. Table 4.4 presents trends in the level of concentration in the aspirations of young women and young men. These data reveal the limited range of occupations to which this cohort of young women initially aspired. In 1968, 65.5 percent chose among only ten occupations, and 81.1 percent chose among twenty occupations. In all, only 109 of the 301 census-detailed occupational categories were represented in women's choices. The index of concentration (C) was 79.6 in 1968, indicating a high level of concentration in a limited number of occupations. Throughout the 1970's, the concentration in aspirations for this group of women declined. The proportion of women in the ten most popular occupations dropped from 65.5 to 52.9 percent, while the proportion aspiring to the top twenty occupations dropped from 81.1 to 70.2 percent. The number of occupations chosen grew from 109 in 1968 to 151 in 1978. The index of concentration dropped from 79.6 to 71.3. While one may choose to view some of the increased dispersion of choices as reflecting the increased familiarity with a diverse array of options that young women acquire as they enter the labor force, we view the change predominantly as a reflection of contemporaneous influences and not as an age effect, because men did not experience a similar dispersion.

The trends for men are distinctly different from those for women. The proportion in the top ten and top twenty grew slightly for men, but the concentration measure, calculated across the entire distribution, declined slightly.[5] The proportion of men in the top twenty choices grew to 59.8 from 57.1 percent, where women's choices consistently became less concentrated.[6]

While the NLS young women remained concentrated in a smaller set of occupations than the young men, this group was clearly moving in the same direction as the cohorts of college freshmen described in Table 4.1. A clear pattern of change for women characterizes the concentration of aspirations as well as the segregation of these choices.

The trends for the young women are not simply a reflection of the entry of younger women with less traditional aspirations into the picture, but rather are the result of movement within each age group. The changes are particularly pronounced during the teenage years, as young women became familiar with a broader range of possible choices. However, aspirations should not be considered stable even for women in their twenties who have largely completed their education. The declines when the young women were in their twenties were significant for each of these cohorts.

We turn now from a statistical summary to a discussion of the popularity of particular choices. Tables 4.5, 4.6, and 4.7 list the top 20 aspirations and occupations for women for 1970, 1975, and 1980. Tables 4.8 and 4.9 list the corresponding figures for men for 1970 and 1975.

Among the top choices of young women are secretarial work,

TABLE 4.5

Comparison of Leading Aspirations and Occupations
of NLS Young Women, 1970

Title	Aspirations		Occupations		Ratio of aspirations to occupations
	Rank	Pct.	Rank	Pct.	
Secretaries	1	10.3%	2	7.1%	1.45
Teachers, elementary school	2	9.5	10	3.0	3.17
Nurses, professional	3	8.3	13	2.2	3.77
Clerical workers, nec	4	5.6	1	8.6	.65
Teachers, nec	5	5.4	–	–	–
Hairdressers and cosmetologists	6	4.5	18	1.7	2.65
Teachers, high school	7	4.3	14	2.1	2.05
Managers, officials, and proprietors, nec	8	3.9	–	–	–
Professional, technical, and kindred workers, nec	9	3.2	–	–	–
Social and welfare workers	10	3.1	–	–	–
Office machine operators	11	2.7	11	2.2	1.22
Artists and art teachers	12	2.5	–	–	–
Technicians, medical and dental	13	1.8	–	–	–
Therapists and healers, nec	14	1.8	–	–	–
Bookkeepers	15	1.7	8	3.4	.50
Nurses, practical	16	1.6	–	–	–
Attendants, hospital, and in other institutions	17	1.6	9	3.2	.50
Typists	18	1.6	5	4.5	.36
Operatives and kindred workers, nec	19	1.3	17	1.7	.76
Sewers and stitchers, mfg.	20	1.3	12	2.2	.59

NOTES: Dashes denote occupations not among the top 20. "Nec" means "not elsewhere classified."

TABLE 4.6

Comparison of Leading Aspirations and Occupations
of NLS Young Women, 1975

Title	Aspirations		Occupations		Ratio of aspirations to occupations
	Rank	Pct.	Rank	Pct.	
Nurses, professional	1	8.7%	4	5.3%	1.64
Teachers, elementary school	2	8.2	3	8.6	.95
Secretaries	3	7.9	1	10.2	.77
Managers, officials, and proprietors, nec	4	6.6	7	3.4	1.94
Clerical workers, nec	5	5.7	2	7.6	.75
Teachers, high school	6	4.6	6	3.9	1.18
Bookkeepers	7	3.3	5	4.0	.83
Social and welfare workers	8	2.9	19	1.5	1.93
Nurses, practical	9	2.6	16	1.8	1.44
Professional, technical, and kindred workers, nec	10	2.1	17	1.7	1.23
Operatives and kindred workers, nec	11	2.1	8	3.4	.62
Attendants, hospital, and in other institutions	12	1.9	10	3.0	.63
Hairdressers and cosmetologists	13	1.8	18	1.7	1.06
Typists	14	1.8	11	3.0	.60
Salesmen and sales clerks, nec	15	1.8	9	3.3	.55
Technicians, medical and dental	16	1.7	–	–	–
Teachers, nec	17	1.5	–	–	–
Sewers and stitchers, mfg.	18	1.3	14	1.8	.72
Office machine operators	19	1.3	15	1.8	.72
Artists and art teachers	20	1.3	–	–	–

NOTES: Dashes denote occupations not among the top 20. "Nec" means "not elsewhere classified."

TABLE 4.7

Comparison of Leading Aspirations and Occupations
of NLS Young Women, 1980

Title	Aspirations		Occupations		Ratio of aspirations to occupations
	Rank	Pct.	Rank	Pct.	
Managers, officials, and proprietors, nec	1	11.7%	3	5.7%	2.05
Clerical workers, nec	2	7.5	1	11.1	.68
Secretaries	3	7.9	2	8.5	.93
Nurses, professional	4	6.3	4	5.1	1.24
Teachers, elementary school	5	4.9	5	4.6	1.07
Bookkeepers	6	4.2	6	4.1	1.02
Professional, technical, and kindred workers, nec	7	3.0	17	1.2	2.50
Salesmen and sales clerks, nec	8	3.0	8	2.9	1.03
Teachers, nec	9	2.6	–	–	–
Operatives and kindred workers, nec	10	2.3	7	3.2	.72
Hairdressers and cosmetologists	11	2.2	12	1.9	1.16
Social and welfare workers	12	2.1	–	–	–
Accountants and auditors	13	2.0	19	1.1	1.82
Attendants, hospital, and in other institutions	14	1.9	10	2.7	.70
Teachers, high school	15	1.7	9	2.7	.63
Nurses, practical	16	1.7	–	–	–
Office machine operators	17	1.7	11	2.3	.74
Technicians, medical and dental	18	1.7	13	1.5	1.13
Therapists and healers, nec	19	1.2	–	–	–
Artists and art teachers	20	1.1	–	–	–

NOTES: Dashes denote occupations not among the top 20. "Nec" means "not elsewhere classified."

TABLE 4.8

Comparison of Leading Aspirations and Occupations
of NLS Young Men, 1970

Title	Aspirations		Occupations		Ratio of aspirations to occupations
	Rank	Pct.	Rank	Pct.	
Managers, officials, and proprietors, nec	1	20.2%	2	7.8%	2.56
Operatives and kindred workers, nec	2	3.4	1	8.8	.39
Foremen, nec	3	3.2	10	2.0	1.60
Mechanics and repairmen, automobile	4	3.2	7	2.6	1.23
Farmers (owners and tenants)	5	2.8	16	1.6	1.75
Truck and tractor drivers	6	2.7	6	3.3	.82
Professional, technical, and kindred workers, nec	7	2.5	9	2.1	1.19
Accountants and auditors	8	2.3	19	1.4	1.64
Policemen and detectives	9	2.3	20	1.1	2.09
Salesmen and sales clerks, nec	10	2.2	4	5.1	.43
Lawyers and judges	11	2.1	–	–	–
Teachers, high school	12	1.9	8	2.2	.86
Mechanics and repairmen, nec	13	1.6	11	1.9	.84
Teachers, nec	14	1.5	–	–	–
Engineers, electrical	15	1.4	–	–	–
Electricians	16	1.4	–	–	–
Clerical and kindred workers, nec	17	1.4	5	3.3	.42
Artists and art teachers	18	1.4	–	–	–
Excavating, grading, and machinery operators	19	1.4	–	–	–
Teachers, elementary school	20	1.3	–	–	–

NOTES: Dashes denote occupations not among the top 20. "Nec" means "not elsewhere classified."

82

TABLE 4.9

Comparison of Leading Aspirations and Occupations
of NLS Young Men, 1975

Title	Aspirations		Occupations		Ratio of aspirations to occupations
	Rank	Pct.	Rank	Pct.	
Managers, officials, and proprietors, nec	1	20.1%	1	10.8%	1.86
Salesmen and sales clerks, nec	2	3.9	3	5.0	.78
Farmers (owners and tenants)	3	3.6	12	1.9	1.89
Truck and tractor drivers	4	3.5	6	2.9	1.21
Operatives and kindred workers, nec	5	3.0	2	5.7	.53
Mechanics and repairmen, automobile	6	2.8	7	2.8	1.00
Professional, technical, and kindred workers, nec	7	2.3	13	1.7	1.35
Mechanics and repairmen, nec	8	2.2	5	3.4	.65
Policemen and detectives	9	2.2	14	1.5	1.47
Foremen, nec	10	2.2	10	2.2	1.00
Laborers, nec	11	2.1	4	4.8	.44
Teachers, high school	12	2.0	11	2.0	1.00
Electricians	13	1.7	17	1.4	1.21
Carpenters	14	1.6	9	3.3	.48
Accountants and auditors	15	1.5	19	1.3	1.15
Lawyers and judges	16	1.4	–	–	–
Teachers, elementary school	17	1.3	–	–	–
Clerical and kindred workers, nec	18	1.3	8	2.4	.54
Excavating, grading, and machinery operators	19	1.0	–	–	–
Linemen and servicemen, telegraph, telephone, and power	20	1.0	15	1.4	.71

NOTES: Dashes denote occupations not among the top 20. "Nec" means "not elsewhere classified."

teaching, nursing, managing, social work, and bookkeeping. The aspirations included in the top 20 choices of women stay reasonably consistent: 18 of the top 20 choices in 1970 remained in the top 20 in 1980. However, the relative popularity of these occupations changed more significantly. For the 18 occupations included in both 1970 and 1980, the correlation of the proportion choosing these occupations in the two years was only .54.

Some of the leading choices in 1970 declined in popularity over the decade. The young women lost interest in being secretaries, teachers, professional nurses, hairdressers, and social workers. The big gainers in popularity were managers and proprietors, which shot up from 4 to nearly 12 percent, and bookkeepers, which moved from 1.7 to 4.2 percent (from fifteenth to sixth position). Some occupations are more popular than the distribution of employed women indicates. In Tables 4.5–4.9 an indicator of the ratio of aspirations to employment is presented. For example, in 1980 twice as many women aspired to be managers and proprietors as were so employed. Among the most popular choices, this disparity was also evident for nurses, social workers, and accountants and auditors. Examples of occupations employing more women than the aspirations of young women would predict in 1980 were clerical workers, hairdressers, hospital attendants, and waitresses.

The agreement between aspirations and occupations was thus far from perfect, but it improved over the decade. The index of dissimilarity between aspirations and occupations for women was 50.5 in 1970, declining to 22.8 in 1975 and 20.2 in 1980. Thus, the distribution of aspirations at first diverges substantially from the occupations women find themselves in, and over time this disparity declines. The figures just cited are aggregate statistics: they indicate the difference between the proportion aspiring to occupations and the proportion in those occupations. An even more dramatic indicator of the lack of correspondence between aspirations and occupations is the proportion of individuals whose aspirations do not correspond with their occupations. This figure was a whopping 73 percent in 1970, declining to 38.6 percent in 1975 and 38.7 percent in 1980. The resolution of this divergence was due in about equal measure to changes in aspirations and to changes in employment. The degree of change in aspirations between 1970 and 1980, as indicated by the index of dissimilarity, was 30.7, compared with 32.4 in the occupations women held. Thus, the increasing overall agreement between the distribution of aspirations and occupations is roughly the equal result of changes in aspirations and changes in occupations.

Young men's leading goal is far and away to enter managerial and proprietary positions. Over 20 percent cited this choice in both 1970 and 1975; no other choice represented more than 4 percent of the responses. The proportion of men actually employed as managers and proprietors grew from 7.8 to 10.8 percent in this period. This contributed to the decline in dissimilarity between aspirations and occuptions, which dropped from 38.3 to 24.3 between 1970 and 1975. The proportion of employed men who chose occupations other than those in which they were employed declined from 62.2 to 38.5 percent over this five-year period. For men as for women, the aspiration/occupation gap was resolved roughly equally by changes in occupations and in aspirations (the index of dissimilarity between 1970 and 1975 is 17.5 for aspirations, 20.3 for occupations).

Thus, young women's occupational goals dispersed and moved into more male-dominated occupations, while young men experienced fewer net changes. For both sexes, there was increasing convergence between goals and employment, with changes in each contributing in about equal measure.

Another interpretation of these concentration data presents itself. The sex segregation of occupations can be directly attributed to sex-typed aspirations only for that limited set of occupations to which young men and women actually aspire. Other occupations must be given sex-type labels by analogy. Yet the process of analogizing may leave room for ambiguity. There can be disagreement as to whether the work content of a particular job is more like women's work or men's work. For example, the appropriate sex label for new jobs in automobile and electrical manufacturing studied by Milkman (1987) was often the subject of extended discussion and debate. Thus one could argue that sex-typed aspirations are of limited predictive power in explaining the sex segregation of the labor force because young men and women aspire to only a small subset of the wide range of occupations they will enter. The elaboration of analogies from the paradigmatic sex-typed jobs to other jobs requires sex-role tracking later in life, including the sex-typing of fields of study in college and the steering of men and women into different career paths on the job.

Discussion

In the areas in which they overlap, these results match closely with other recent studies of trends in aspirations. Herzog (1982) reports a decline in the sex segregation of aspirations of high school seniors from 49.8 in 1976 to 36.3 in 1980, based on choices of 15 occupations. Lueptow (1981) also indicates declining sex typing in occupational choices of high school seniors between 1964 and 1975.[7] These studies compare successive cohorts of individuals, rather than following a group over time. Harmon (1981) follows 391 young women six years after they entered college. She indicates that respondents remain clustered in typically female-dominated occupations, but she does not report measures of change in concentration or sex-atypicality. She does, however, indicate that on average her respondents considered nine alternative occupations in the six years following high school graduation. These findings are also consistent with the early trends documented by Brito and Jusenius (1978), which is encouraging, since they examine the same NLS data we have employed in our analysis.[8]

The trends examined here indicate the significance of change in recent years. Successive cohorts of young women are increasingly dispersed in their occupational goals and increasingly likely to pursue careers in occupations that have traditionally been male-dominated. The changes over time in the sex composition of the occupations to which young women aspire appear to reflect the influences young women in the labor force experienced. The forces of change affect those in their twenties as well as those in the early stages of formulating their goals. Perhaps the clearest evidence of the adaptability of aspirations is the fact that aspirations have been changing in much the same way as occupations. If current trends continue, we may see further changes in both aspirations and occupations. Yet if the climate of opinion changes, both occupations and aspirations may slow down or even reverse present trends.

The evidence suggests that sex-role socialization is not sufficient to fix occupational goals for young women. Other pieces of evidence that are inconsistent with the "harbinger" view are the findings that aspirations are as likely to change to accommodate the realities of the workplace as they are to reflect changes in young people's goals; that the aspirations of women in the labor force diverge substantially from the occupations they hold; and that young women's aspirations are consistently more male-dominated than the occupations they hold.

The similarity in trends of aspirations and occupations is due to the fact that the same forces are working on both. We should not simply assume that if girls think positively they will be able to succeed. Future trends in occupational patterns will reflect in part the political environment in which the country finds itself. Political choices affecting affirmative action, comparable worth, child care, efforts to combat harassment at work and other policy matters will affect the ability of young women to realize their aspirations. Our examination of these data suggest the need to revise a simple "harbinger" perspective. The adaptability of aspirations should make us reluctant to predict future occupational developments on the basis of trends in aspirations.

These results are consistent with a lifelong social control perspective. The direction of women into female-dominated occupations begins with the formation of aspirations. Yet aspirations are adaptable; in the period studied here, aspirations changed in step with changes in the occupational structure. The social control perspective makes this pattern understandable by stressing the enduring social control needed to maintain occupational segregation by sex. The results suggest that as social controls in the labor force are relaxed, young women's aspirations change. One does not need to wait for a new generation to be socialized to a new value structure to observe changes in goals. Thus, we suggest that the simultaneous change in aspirations and occupations is due to the simultaneous relaxing of controls in the occupational sphere and in the ideological sphere, and indicates the responsiveness of individuals to these changes.

One might argue that these results are not necessarily inconsistent with an economic perspective. If young women during this period increased their expected number of years in the labor force, their aspirations and occupational choices might both have changed accordingly. Thus an economist might maintain that the trends documented above are rational responses to changing expectations about women's economic future. But if part of the increase in women's expected labor force participation is due to noneconomic motives, then the cultural and social influences emphasized by the social control perspective need to be taken into consideration. Econometric analyses suggest that only part of the increase in women's labor force participation can be explained by purely economic motives; perhaps one-third is accounted for by a secular trend toward increasing participation (Goldin, 1983). Thus, if part of the increase in women's labor force participation represents the declining force of cultural inhibitions, then the social control factors we have emphasized are necessary elements in this explanation. While an exclusively economic interpretation of these trends seems unpersuasive, we are unable to distinguish with these aggregate data the economic from the sociological components of these developments.

5

The Instability of

Vocational Aspirations

In this chapter we continue our examination of the contribu-
tion of sex-typed vocational socialization to sex-segregated careers. Whereas Chapter 4 focused on trends in aspirations and
the link between occupational aspirations and employment
trends, this chapter focuses on the strength of this link for
individuals.

Sex-Role Socialization Theory

Socialization is often accorded an important if not decisive
role in shaping the labor force experiences of women. This perspective can be analytically separated into two parts. First,
boys and girls acquire different values and attitudes about work.
Second, socialization experiences lead some girls into female-
dominated occupations and others into male-dominated occupations. The former proposition is the focus of the preponderance of the research in the area, but the latter is a necessary
corollary.

Various theories of socialization stress different psychological mechanisms and different influences on the young. Among
the common threads in this literature is the thesis that so-

cialization instills in girls a sensitivity to family obligations and a feminine value orientation. Women are taught from a young age that their primary role will be the maternal one, which reduces their commitment to lifelong employment. They choose jobs with flexible schedules and opportunities to express feminine values such as nurturance. As a result, women pursue a limited set of occupations, such as clerical work, teaching, social work, and nursing, that allow them to realize these values. Boys are taught to be competitive, to strive to achieve, and to expect no tension between work and family commitments. They consequently seek out a wider range of careers than girls and devote themselves more completely to the pursuit of success. As we saw in Chapter 3, a great body of research has documented various aspects of the acquisition of sex-typed vocational goals.

In this chapter, we present evidence indicating that these early aspirations are necessary but not sufficient to produce sex-segregated careers. Evidence of the temporal instability of the sex type of aspirations and occupations raises questions about the proposition that early beliefs and experiences lead directly to occupational choices and pursuits.

As noted above, an important component of the socialization thesis is that socialization leads some young women to prefer employment in male-dominated occupations. If traditional aspirations channel women into female-dominated occupations, women who break out of this traditional mold should be found in male-dominated occupations. The identification of factors associated with increased preference for employment in male-dominated occupations is thus an important line of inquiry for the socialization perspective. If women's preferences are crucial in channeling them into male-dominated occupations, then finding those factors that influence these preferences is important to understanding the maintenance of occupational segregation by sex (Brito and Jusenius, 1978; Daymont and Statham, 1981; Waite and Berryman, 1985). Socialization not only must account for sex differences, but also must differentiate those women who pursue male-dominated occupations from the majority who do not.

Empirical support for the socialization perspective requires documenting the following five propositions, which connect individuals' early values with their later behavior: (1) specific features of early family life are responsible for people's sex-role orientation; (2) sex-role orientation is directly connected with occupational aspirations; (3) the sex type of individuals' occupational aspirations remains constant over time; (4) the sex type of occupational aspirations predicts the sex type of initial occupational choices; and (5) the sex type of the first job corresponds with the sex type of the occupations held over the course of a career. This chapter focuses on the last three propositions, which underscore the connection between socialization and career outcomes. Evidence from the National Longitudinal Survey of Young Women indicates that none of these three propositions has strong empirical support.

The stability of young women's aspirations (with respect to the sex type of their occupational choices) has not been examined, and the link between aspirations and subsequent employment remains unexplored. The evidence presented by Marini and Brinton on the connection between socialization and labor force outcomes is instructive. They indicate that there is a close correspondence between the level of sex segregation in aspirations and the level of sex segregation in the labor force. Marini and Brinton report an index of segregation of 61.0 between the occupational aspirations of young men and women, compared with 66.1 for the labor force as a whole (1984: 202). The correspondence cited here, however, does not indicate a direct causal relationship. The missing link is evidence of a connection between the sex type of people's aspirations and the sex type of their subsequent jobs.

Marini and Brinton do not examine the stability of aspirations over time. They report studies that indicate young children hold sex-typed values and attitudes. However, they present no studies that show whether the same girls who aspired to female-dominated occupations as youngsters persist in such desires as teenagers. Nor do they report studies that examine the serial correlation (the correlation of the same variable at two points in time) in sex-typed aspirations for women in their teens and early twenties. The data have long been available, but no studies have examined the serial correlation in the sex type of occupational aspirations.

In addition to being stable, aspirations must also be effective in generating occupational outcomes. Marini and Brinton recognize the importance of a correlation between attitudes and behavior. They cite studies indicating that after ten years only 15 to 25 percent of the respondents are employed in the same occupation to which they aspired in high school (1984: 202). These data suggest that the link between socialization and later occupational behavior is not simply a matter of aspiring to a particular occupation and subsequently pursuing that choice. Less than 25 percent of sex segregation could be explained by this connection alone, since after ten years fewer than 25 percent of young adults pursue their preferred occupations. Rather, the socialization thesis rests on the proposition that women end up in jobs similar to those to which they aspired. Specifically, if sex segregation is a result of the sex-typical aspirations of young women, then women must end up in occupations with the same sex type as the occupation to which they aspired. The continuity of the underlying dimension, in this case sex type, rather than the continuity of commitment to a particular occupation, is the crucial proposition for the socialization perspective.

Marini and Brinton present just this kind of evidence to support the proposition that socioeconomic aspirations predict the socioeconomic status of occupations. Although young people frequently change jobs, the socioeconomic level of their jobs is closely related to the socioeconomic level of their aspirations. Sewell, Hauser, and Wolf (1980) have shown a substantial but far from perfect correlation between the socioeconomic level of high school students' aspirations and the socioeconomic level of their first jobs ($r = .461$ for females and $.541$ for males). We address the same question with respect to the sex type of occupations that Sewell, Hauser, and Wolf ask with respect to socioeconomic status.

The final issue is the stability of the sex type of occupations young women hold. Students of career mobility recognize that individuals often change occupations. Even if socialization were a powerful predictor of the sex type of women's first jobs, substantial career mobility between male-dominated and female-dominated occupations would vitiate the impact of socialization. In order for socialization to account for the sex type of the occupations women hold during the middle of their careers, not only must socialization predict the sex type of women's initial occupations, but the sex type of occupations women pursue over the course of their careers must be relatively stable.

Data and Methods

Data are obtained from the NLS Young Women and the NLS Young Men samples. The serial correlation is used as a measure of the consistency of occupational aspirations. The analysis focuses on employed women in the labor force, so that the results will not reflect high school students' unrealistic and changing aspirations. The results thus constitute a conservative test of the consistency of aspirations. The analysis also examines the degree to which the sex type of occupational aspirations predicts the sex type of occupations in which the women were actually employed. Finally, the continuity in occupations over time is examined. Just as we can measure the serial correlation in the sex type of aspirations, so we can measure the serial correlation in the sex type of occupations held by the women.

Stayers and Movers

Researchers who study occupational mobility have found it fruitful to distinguish between "stayers" and "movers." The distinction between stayers and movers has a long history in the study of career mobility (Blumen and McCarthy, 1955; Jacobs, 1983b). Stayers are people who remain in the same detailed occupation over the period under examination; movers are those who change their detailed occupations. Distinguishing stayers from movers is important in understanding mobility processes. No matter what attribute of occupations is examined, the serial correlation in this attribute will be stable for the group remaining in the same occupation over time. However, the attributes of movers' occupations may remain the same or change as the movers change occupations. It is important to distinguish between those attributes of work that remain with people even as they change jobs, and those that last only as long as they continue in the same job.

For example, if we assign a random code number to each detailed (census three-digit) occupation, we will find a significant serial correlation for this random code for all employed women but not for movers. If we calculate the serial correlation between 1970 and 1980 for randomly generated occupational codes, we obtain a modest but statistically significant relationship for all women employed in both years ($r = .17$, $p < .001$, $n = 1,252$). However, for all women changing occupations, the serial correlation is essentially zero ($r = .01$, $n = 982$). This feature of employment is stable only to the extent that people stay in the same occupations; among movers the relationship vanishes.

Movers are not a small, aberrant, and uninteresting group. Nearly 35 percent of the experienced civilian labor force changed detailed occupations between 1965 and 1970, a rate reasonably consistent with other data on rates of occupational mobility (Somers and Eck, 1977; Rosenfeld, 1979). A recent reanalysis of the 1970 census revealed substantial numbers of occupation changers even among such professions as law, medicine, and engineering (Evans and Laumann, 1983).

Young women are most likely to change occupations. Of the NLS Young Women employed in both 1970 and 1980, nearly 80 percent changed occupations in the interim, and over 80 percent changed the occupations to which they aspired. Komarovsky (1985) reports that over 80 percent of the college women she surveyed changed their occupational goals at least once during the college years. Angrist and Almquist (1975) report that only 4 of 87 college women they followed until graduation maintained the same occupational goal throughout college. The separation of stayers and movers is less restrictive than the quasi-independence model often employed in mobility analyses (Hout, 1983), since a mover can change detailed occupations but still remain in the same sex-typed category.

We will apply the distinction between stayers and movers in our investigation of the relationship between the sex type of aspirations and the sex type of occupations. We will examine the strength of this relationship over time and the extent to which it is more than simply a reflection of persistence in the same occupations.

Another methodological question is the appropriate categorization of the sex type of occupations. We begin by treating the sex type of occupations in a continuous manner: each detailed occupation is assigned a percent-female score from 0 to 100. We subsequently group occupations into male-dominated, sex-neutral, and female-dominated categories, in order to analyze the cumulative patterns of aspirations and employment.

The Volatility of Aspirations

Table 5.1 presents the serial correlation of the sex type of occupational aspirations for the NLS Young Women. The sex type of aspirations for each year between 1968 and 1978 is compared with the sex type of aspirations in 1980. In this section, the sex type of aspirations is treated as a continuous variable, with each occupation coded from 0 to 100 percent female. The first column includes all women employed at both times; the second column includes women who changed their detailed occupational aspirations in the intervening period.

The results indicate a high degree of instability in the sex type of occupational aspirations. The serial correlation between 1970 and 1980 for all employed women who answered the question both times is weak ($r = .25$). Thus, just over 6 percent of the variance in the sex type of aspirations can be explained by the same measure obtained ten years earlier. This relationship is only slightly stronger than the relationship for the random occupation codes discussed above over the same time period. Furthermore, as noted above, this analysis over-

TABLE 5.1

Serial Correlation of Sex Composition of Occupation
Desired for Age 35 by NLS Young Women, 1968–1980

	1980			
	All women		Women changing desired occupation	
Year	r	n	r	n
1968	.17**	668	.06	552
1969	.22**	936	.08*	769
1970	.25**	944	.08*	754
1971	.29**	991	.11**	776
1972	.29**	1,047	.08**	810
1973	.35**	1,072	.15**	821
1975	.43**	1,161	.16**	806
1977	.43**	1,290	.12**	820
1978	.55**	1,412	.24**	842

NOTE: The women analyzed in this table were employed during both
years in which they were surveyed.
*$p < .05$ **$p < .01$

states stability, because it holds the sex type of occupations
constant.

Even more dramatic is the weakness of the relationship for
those who changed their occupational aspirations. As indicated earlier in the discussion of methods, we can distinguish
between two groups: those who changed their aspirations and
those who remained loyal to their earlier preferences. Among
the loyalists, we know in advance the serial correlation is perfect: there can be no change in the sex type of occupation if there
is no change in the occupation. The crucial question, then, is
the correlation for those who changed their aspirations.

The analysis of the large group that changed aspirations
between 1970 and 1980 (over 80 percent of the women) indicates an extremely weak serial correlation in occupational sex
type. Between 1970 and 1980, the correlation for women who
changed aspirations is barely statistically significant ($r = .08$,
$p < .05$). Thus, less than 1 percent of the variance in sex type
of aspiration for movers is explained by the same measure ten
years earlier.

TABLE 5.2

Correlation of Sex Composition of Occupation Desired for Age 35 with Sex Composition of Occupation Held in 1980 by NLS Young Women, 1968–1980

	1980			
	All women		Women whose occupation differed from desired one	
Year	r	n	r	n
1968	.21**	1,077	.06*	860
1969	.15**	1,390	.04	1,187
1970	.18**	1,407	.03	1,171
1971	.24**	1,463	.09**	1,211
1972	.23**	1,536	.03	1,229
1973	.28**	1,534	.07**	1,203
1975	.36**	1,703	.08**	1,152
1977	.37**	1,829	.06*	1,168
1978	.34**	1,835	.04	1,196
1980	.54**	1,674	.06*	718

NOTE: The women analyzed in this table were employed during both years in which they were surveyed.
*p < .05   **p < .01

The relationship weakens as time elapses. Aspirations measured two years apart seem reasonably strongly related (between 1978 and 1980, r = .55 for all women, .24 for movers). The relationship gradually diminishes over the course of the decade. This indicates that there is short-term consistency in the values and preferences of young women. This consistency, however, does not constitute support for the socialization thesis, which requires that early values predict later values. Socialization presupposes a strong relationship over the long run. The evidence demonstrates that early aspirations are only weakly related to later ones.

The evidence points to the instability of aspirations. The relationship between aspirations and subsequent behavior is likely to be even weaker. The effectiveness of aspirations in predicting the occupations pursued by young women is examined in Table 5.2. Again, the interval from 1970 to 1980 indicates only a modest positive relationship. For all women employed in 1980, the sex type of aspiration in 1970 is weakly related to the sex type of occupation in 1980 (r = .18), explaining less than 4 percent of the variance in 1980. For those who did not pursue the occupation to which they aspired, there is no predictive power for the sex type of occupational aspirations (r = .03, p > .1).

Again, over the short term, aspirations do correlate with subsequent occupational pursuits. For example, the correlation between the sex type of aspiration in 1978 and the sex type of occupation in 1980 is .34 for all women (r = .04 for movers). Thus, the women's preferences and behavior are related in a sensible way. But early values predict behavior as much as ten years later only for women who persist in the same occupations. For those changing occupations in the ten-year interval, there is no long-term relationship between aspirations and behavior.

The effects of occupational mobility on sex type of occupation are indicated in Table 5.3. The sex-type correlation is weak for all women employed in 1970 and 1980 (r = .21) and absent for those who changed occupations during the decade (r = .04, p > .1). Thus, even if socialization perfectly explained

TABLE 5.3

Serial Correlation of Sex Composition of Occupation
of NLS Young Women, 1968–1980

| | 1980 | | | |
| | All women | | Occupation changers | |
Year	r	n	r	n
1968	.14**	1,024	.02	855
1969	.18**	1,137	.05*	916
1970	.21**	1,252	.04	982
1971	.21**	1,317	.01	985
1972	.27**	1,428	.07**	1,048
1973	.32**	1,569	.07*	1,078
1975	.40**	1,654	.08**	997
1977	.47**	1,798	.13**	955
1978	.54**	1,894	.15**	888

NOTE: The women analyzed in this table were employed during both years in which they were surveyed.
*p < .05   **p < .01

the sex type of women's initial occupations, career mobility that crosses sex-type lines completely vitiates this relationship for the majority of women. The mobility across sex-type categories is striking.

The mobility of women is not random: in socioeconomic terms, aspirations are reasonably stable, aspirations predict subsequent employment, and later occupations are moderately strongly related to earlier ones. The serial correlation for the socioeconomic status of aspirations between 1970 and 1980 for occupation changers is .40 ($r = .51$ for all women employed in 1980); the relationship between the status of aspirations in 1970 and the status of employment in 1980 for occupation changers is .42 ($r = .51$ for all women employed in 1980); and the serial correlation of status for occupation changers is .30 ($r = .45$ for all women employed both times). Thus, movement is not random, nor is the sex-type mobility presented above an artifact of the methods employed. The socioeconomic status of occupations is linked to aspirations, while the sex type of occupations is not.

The occupational mobility of young women is dramatic. The NLS data have a high rate of occupational change, which suggests that they may overstate the degree of mobility. This may result from the use of the error-prone occupational codes of the 1960 census, and from the tendency of different interviewers to code the same job in different ways. Because retrospective data avoid these problems, we examined a one-year retrospective question on occupations in the Current Population Survey for comparison. The March 1981 CPS data provide a comparison of occupations held in 1980 with occupations held in March 1981. The data are described in a U.S. Bureau of Labor Statistics publication (1976). The serial correlation in the sex composition of occupations for women aged 16–24 who changed occupations between 1980 and 1981 was .09 ($n = 1,770$); for women aged 25–34 the serial correlation was .14 ($n = 1,142$). Thus, for an extremely large national sample, the serial correlation in the sex composition of occupations is quite weak. The structure of these mobility patterns is examined in greater detail in Chapter 7.

The Instability of Vocational Aspirations   99

TABLE 5.4
Serial Correlation of Sex Composition of Aspirations
and Occupations of NLS Young Men, 1966–1975

	1975 aspirations		1975 occupations	
	r	n	r	n
All men				
1966 aspiration	.20**	1,076	.23**	2,131
1966 occupation			.21**	2,506
Occupation changers				
1966 aspiration	.14**	940	.14**	1,798
1966 occupation			.11**	2,141
All men				
1970 aspiration	.33**	1,237	.34**	2,380
1970 occupation			.37**	2,784
Occupation changers				
1970 aspiration	.12**	902	.14**	1,749
1970 occupation			.12*	1,870

NOTE: The men analyzed in this table were employed during both years in which they were surveyed.
$*p < .05$ $**p < .01$

Table 5.4 presents comparative figures for the NLS Young Men. The first panel examines the 1966–75 transition. During this period, there was a weak relationship between the sex type of initial aspiration and destination aspiration ($r = .20$), between initial aspiration and destination occupation ($r = .23$), and between initial occupation and destination occupation ($r = .21$). Each of these relationships diminishes when the focus is restricted to occupation changers ($r = .14$ for initial vs. destination aspirations, $r = .14$ for initial aspiration and destination occupation, and $r = .11$ for initial vs. destination occupations).

These figures may overstate mobility because the young men were quite young in 1966. Therefore, we also considered the 1970–75 transition. The sex-type correlations are stronger for this later stage in the young men's development toward career maturity, but among occupation changers the relationships remain weak. For young men changing occupations, the sex-type correlations between 1970 and 1975 are .12 for initial vs. destination aspirations, .14 for initial aspiration and destination occupation, and .12 for initial vs. destination occupations. While these relationships are quite weak, they are stronger than those observed for women. The extent of mobility for men is further reduced because men are more concentrated in male-dominated occupations than women are in female-dominated occupations.

These mobility data suggest that men who aspire to or pursue female-dominated occupations are likely to return eventually to male-dominated occupations. Men are unlikely to pursue female-dominated occupations, but even among those who aspire to them, the likelihood of pursuing a female-dominated occupation is only slightly less than if the outcome were based solely on chance. Thus, sex-role social control is a lifelong process for men just as it is for women. Sex-typed attitudes and related occupational behavior are not fixed early in life but are constantly reproduced or reinforced throughout a person's lifetime.

Cumulative Aspiration Patterns

The extensive mobility between male-dominated, sex-neutral, and female-dominated occupations suggests that individuals will stand a good chance of aspiring to more than one of these categories. In this section, we examine the cumulative probability of aspiring to each sex-type category and compare these probabilities with the probability of employment in each occupational group. We present results for the conventional definition of male-dominated (0–39 percent female) and female-dominated (40–100 percent female) occupations as well as for the tripartite partition introduced in Chapter 4.

This analysis begins in a straightforward manner. We simply count the proportion of women who ever aspired to each of the sex-typed occupational categories over the ten survey periods. However, we must adjust these results for sample attrition, and for the fact that not everyone answered the aspiration question in each survey. As a result, simply adding up all those who ever aspired to a male-dominated occupation understates the actual number, since not everyone had the opportunity to respond ten times.

We address this truncation problem in two ways. First, we display the results by the number of times the respondent answered the aspirations question, and then we present averages adjusted for the average labor force participation rate. The rationale behind this adjustment is that the distribution of aspirations and employment ought not to reflect the thoughts of women who were never employed, but should focus on those who are actually employed. This strategy also facilitates comparing the cumulative distribution of aspirations and occupations.

Table 5.5 presents data on the cumulative probability of aspiring to a female-dominated occupation for the NLS Young Women. The probability of aspiring is listed in terms of the number of aspirations reported. The results are dramatic. After ten surveys, virtually all women had aspired to a female-dominated occupation at least once (98 percent), while about three-fifths had aspired to a male-dominated occupation (63 percent). The sex-neutral occupations were also likely to be chosen by 60 percent of young women when aspirations are grouped into three categories. Table 5.6 presents data on the cumulative probability of employment in each sex-type category. The cumulative employment patterns are quite similar to the aspiration patterns. After ten years in the labor force, virtually all women can expect to have been employed in a female-dominated occupation at least once, and nearly 60 percent can expect to have been employed in a male-dominated occupation.

Table 5.7 compares the cumulative aspirations data with the cumulative employment patterns. The first column shows aspirations results adjusted by the average number of responses volunteered; the second shows the results adjusted for the typical number of years in the labor market. Whereas Tables 5.5 and 5.6 indicate the probabilities by the number of opportunities to respond, Table 5.7 reports the average probability of aspiring to and being employed in each occupational group. In short, Table 5.7 adjusts the results to reflect the average years of employment experienced by this sample.

The clear picture from these results is that a very sizable minority of women are employed in male-dominated occupations at some point in their early years in the labor force (44 per-

TABLE 5.5
Cumulative Probability of NLS Young Women's Aspiring to Sex-Typed
Occupational Categories by Number of Aspirations Reported, 1968–1980

Occupational category	No. of aspirations reported									
	1	2	3	4	5	6	7	8	9	10
Male-dominated (0–39% female)	.24	.35	.37	.47	.49	.56	.56	.53	.55	.63
Female-dominated (40–100% female)	.76	.90	.94	.94	.98	.95	.95	.99	.98	.98
Male-dominated (0–29% female)	.16	.27	.29	.38	.41	.46	.48	.47	.39	.60
Sex-neutral (30–69% female)	.39	.50	.60	.64	.70	.68	.76	.82	.77	.77
Female-dominated (70–100% female)	.45	.65	.73	.72	.79	.80	.82	.85	.86	.74

NOTE: Ten surveys were conducted over the twelve-year span.

TABLE 5.6
Cumulative Probability of NLS Young Women's Employment in
Sex-Typed Occupational Categories by Years in the Labor Force, 1968–1980

Occupational category	No. of years in labor force									
	1	2	3	4	5	6	7	8	9	10
Male-dominated (0–39% female)	.14	.22	.36	.40	.47	.51	.48	.55	.54	.57
Female-dominated (40–100% female)	.79	.91	.96	.98	.99	.99	.99	.98	.97	.99
Male-dominated (0–29% female)	.08	.14	.26	.29	.35	.38	.38	.44	.46	.47
Sex-neutral (30–69% female)	.31	.47	.54	.66	.66	.72	.72	.75	.75	.75
Female-dominated (70–100% female)	.54	.73	.83	.82	.87	.89	.92	.90	.89	.86

TABLE 5.7

Cumulative Probability of NLS Young Women's
Aspiring to and Being Employed in Sex-Typed
Occupational Categories, 1968–1980

Occupational category	Aspirations		Employment
	Adjusted for sample attrition	Adjusted for years in labor force	Adjusted for years in labor force
Male-dominated (0–39% female)	.45	.49	.44
Female-dominated (40–100% female)	.90	.92	.93
Male-dominated (0–29% female)	.37	.42	.34
Sex-neutral (30–69% female)	.64	.62	.65
Female-dominated (70–100% female)	.72	.74	.82

cent); and an even larger proportion aspire to work in a male-dominated occupation at one time or another (49 percent). Women's cumulative chances of employment in male-dominated occupations are slightly lower than their chances of aspiring to men's jobs. At the other end of the spectrum, female-dominated occupations at some point are desired by or employ the overwhelming majority of women (92 percent and 93 percent, respectively).

One reading of these results is that they speak to the power of sex-role socialization. They indicate that few women are able to escape its spell at some point. Nearly all women at one point or another aspire to a female-dominated occupation. Thus socialization is important in this early stage of life: the evidence demonstrates the prevalence of social influences.

However, the continuity between life stages is weaker than many suspect. These results indicate that the serial correlation in the sex-type of occupations is quite weak, not only for occupation changers, but for the sample as a whole; most women are likely to have expressed interest in sex-neutral or male-dominated occupations at some point. Indeed, many women have had some employment experience in sex-neutral and male-dominated occupations. If all of the women who ever aspired to or were employed in male-dominated occupations remained in them, sex segregation would be far less severe than it is. Thus, sex-role socialization, while a powerful force in influencing attitudes and behavior, needs continuing reinforcement and support to be effective in channeling young women into female-dominated occupations.

How does all the mobility documented here support the thesis of social control? The instability of sex-typed occupational choices indicates that early-life social control is inadequate by itself to maintain high levels of sex segregation. Thus, we observe that most young women aspire to both male-dominated and female-dominated occupations at one point or another. If social control were to end in adolescence, the sex segregation of occupations could not be maintained. Sex segregation persists into adulthood because sex-appropriate attitudes and behavior are reinforced in the educational and occupational settings. Thus, social control is not so tight as to preclude mobility, nor does its effectiveness increase over the life course. Rather, it is an enduring and imperfect set of influences that allow a notable degree of mobility in both directions while maintaining the overall system of segregation.

Discussion

Theories of socialization rest on a mountain of data and a highly plausible (and in many ways appealing) view of the connection between childhood experiences and adult behavior. Yet the temporal connection, which is central to this perspective, is not as strong as many assume. The data indicate that over a ten-year period the connection between occupational aspirations and subsequent achievements is extremely weak. The relationship is mostly due to that small minority of young women who pursue the same occupations they initially desired.

Angrist and Almquist (1975) report high rates of change in the sex type of career goals for their sample of college women.

They found that 21 percent of women "converted" from their original sex-atypical goals to sex-typical occupational choices, while 17 percent converted from female-dominated to male-dominated fields; another 26 percent fluctuated back and forth. Our findings follow a larger national sample for a longer period of time, and they confirm the qualitative finding that there is substantial instability in the sex type of career goals.

The women examined here were in their late teens, twenties, and early thirties. We would suspect much greater instability in aspirations among girls in their early teens and under ten. Thus, the evidence that young girls and boys can distinguish "men's work" from "women's work," while interesting and informative, says little about which boys and which girls will end up in any particular job. Some little boys want to become firemen, and some little girls want to become nurses, but children may revise these inclinations countless times before they enter the world of work.

The results discussed above provide a basis for understanding several important studies of women's careers. First, they indicate why it has proved so hard to predict which women will aspire to and choose male-dominated occupations (England, 1982). Brito and Jusenius (1978) examine what they refer to as the sex atypicality of occupational aspirations for the NLS Young Women. They are able to explain only 7 percent of the variance in aspirations. This is due to the instability in aspirations. Clearly, background factors can be of limited influence if there is a constant flux in the dependent variable. A longitudinal analysis might explain even less variance, since the serial correlation in aspirations is so low. Waite and Berryman (1985) find stronger relationships for the sex type of occupational choices for a national sample of women aged 14–21 in 1979 ($r^2 = .18$), reflecting a lengthy list of independent variables employed. However, these relationships are likely to weaken over time as young men and women change their aspirations, and as women move from female-dominated occupations to male-dominated occupations.

Daymont and Statham (1981) examine the sex atypicality of occupations held by the NLS Mature Women. Their equations explain 3 percent of the variance in occupational atypicality for whites and 1 percent for blacks. Again, the present findings shed light on the limited effectiveness of social scientists in explaining the occupational behavior of women. On the one hand, the failure of sustained inquiries by highly professional researchers is due to the temporal instability in the sex type of occupational preferences of women and to the rate at which women cross sex-type boundaries. On the other hand, if one were to try to explain variation among women in ever aspiring to female-dominated occupations, one would find little or no variation to explain. The data suggest the near-ubiquity of aspiring to female-dominated occupations at some point in the lives of young women.

This chapter has documented the remarkable instability of aspirations and the weakness of the connection between the sex type of aspirations and occupations. This evidence raises further serious doubts for the early-life socialization perspective; the young respondents seem to have difficulty in holding on to their goals and in realizing the aspirations they settle on. The data demonstrate that, for individuals, the connection between intentions and outcomes is relatively weak with respect to the sex-typing of occupations, especially compared to the stability of the tie between socioeconomic intentions and outcomes.

The patterns of mobility documented here raise serious questions for an economic model of occupational sex segregation. Economists assume stable preferences; these data, however, clearly indicate that preferences are not stable. Economists assume that stable differences in values lead men into male-dominated occupations and women into female-dominated occupations. But the data suggest otherwise. Individuals report frequent changes in intentions, and thus a central premise of the economic perspective is undermined. Moreover, the career mobility into and out of male-dominated occupations is particularly problematic from the standpoint of the human capital approach. If there were a steep human-capital gradient such that male-dominated occupations required higher levels of investment than female-dominated occupations, individuals would find it difficult to move into male-dominated jobs, and they would find little reason to move out of such jobs. The extensive mobility documented in both directions suggests that a human-capital differential is not the principal force responsible for the sex segregation of occupations (Corcoran, Duncan, and Ponza, 1984).

The evidence is consistent with a lifelong social control perspective, which emphasizes the continuous if imperfect social control mechanisms that operate to maintain the sex segregation of occupations. Socialization tracks young men and women into different career paths, but these differences are unstable without continuing social controls. Individuals can and do change direction, but the cumulative force of sex-role reinforcement reproduces sex segregation during the early labor force years. The system as a whole remains segregated even while individuals change their goals and plans. The cumulative disadvantage model is not supported, since movement is observed in both directions, and over time a cohort of young women has moved into more male-dominated occupations. The revolving door model is a more appropriate characterization of these patterns.

6

Sex Segregation During
the College Years

As we have seen in Chapter 3, gender-based inequality in education is not primarily a matter of the level of educational attainment. Women have led men, on average, in school attendance, although they have been underrepresented among high school dropouts as well as recipients of college and graduate degrees. Thus, gender inequality in education is more a matter of the differentiation of specialties than of inequality in the number of years spent in school. Segregation by field of study is the educational analogue to occupational segregation by sex. Informal social pressures direct women to pursue different fields from their male counterparts.

The sex segregation of higher education is interesting for several reasons. First, the educational connection is central to the traditional views of sex segregation we have been criticizing. If early socialization is held to be responsible for occupational outcomes, the sex-typed values should persist long enough to result in stable choices of college majors, which subsequently lead to occupational outcomes. The more mobility in the college context, the less we can hold early socialization accountable for later life outcomes.

The segregation of college majors is also a prominent feature of the human capital perspective. To the extent that career differences are attributed to differences in skills acquired, differences in the type of education acquired by men and women should be an important part of the story. The human capital perspective has characterized the sex-typed choices of college majors as a rational response to the expectation of career interruptions for women (Polachek, 1978). The instability of the choice of college major suggests that factors other than the desire to maximize lifetime income emphasized by economists influence the selection of majors. College students are often too uncertain about their interests and preferences to conduct the lifetime calculus economists predict, and they are thus susceptible to social influences. If the choice of major in part reflects barriers to women in the college setting, then a portion of the sex difference in earnings attributed to differences in education ought to be attributed to pre–labor market discrimination. Net change may partly reflect changing expectations regarding future labor force participation for young women, as we noted in our discussion of changes in aspirations, yet a strictly economic explanation of such changes is too narrow. An expanding sense of opportunities and the increasing social acceptability of women's labor force participation reflect a weakening of the social controls we have emphasized. Further, as we will see, it is more difficult to link the attrition of women from male-dominated fields to changing expectations about labor force attachment on the part of women.

We expect sex segregation in higher education to be another context in which informal social control dynamics are at work. Here we have sex segregation without the direct application of the profit motive, without segmented labor markets at work, without formal institutional support. How does it work? How does it persist? How much individual change is evident?

The sex segregation of majors ought to display the same social control processes that influence aspirations and the choice of jobs. We have argued that the process of sex typing is a dynamic one; there should be substantial individual mobility, and any change that occurs should be experienced by people of different ages. If we can demonstrate the same social control dynamics at work in college that are found in the diffuse context of the aspirations process and later in life on the job, we will have mustered dramatic evidence for the social control view we are proposing.

We do not mean to ignore those who do not pursue higher education. There may be similar questions to be addressed with regard to the choice of courses in high school, but the degree of specialization in high schools is more limited and panel data on issues such as the choice of courses are not available.

In this chapter we document trends in sex segregation among bachelor's degree recipients, track the net changes in the distribution of students across majors during the college years, and examine stability and change in the choices of individuals between the freshman and senior years. (See Jacobs, 1985, for a comparison of trends in sex segregation among associate, bachelor's, master's, and Ph.D. degree recipients.)

Significance of the Field of Study

Higher education in the United States has undergone striking changes since the Second World War. Overall enrollment, the proportion of degrees granted in junior colleges, and the proportion of students enrolled in coeducational settings all have soared, transforming the college and university system.

The 1964 Civil Rights Act, the burgeoning women's movement, and the 1972 Title IX Amendments to the Higher Education Act all pointed to increased opportunities for women in higher education. By one measure of opportunity—enrollment—women have made dramatic strides in recent years. Women now receive more than half of all associate degrees (two-year degrees typically granted by community colleges), half of all bachelor's degrees, one-third of all doctoral degrees, and one-quarter of all professional degrees. In 1950, women received only one-third of all bachelor's degrees and less than one-tenth of all doctoral and professional degrees. Female enrollments have grown at all levels of higher education.

The central indicator of opportunities for our purposes is the fields of study women pursue. Men and women have always been concentrated in separate majors (Beller, 1984b; Lyson, 1981; Thomas, 1980; Lloyd and Niemi, 1979; Polachek, 1978; Jacobs, 1985). Fields such as business, engineering, chemistry, and physics have traditionally been male bastions, while foreign languages, fine arts, literature, nursing, and psychology have enrolled disproportionately high numbers of women. Nearly one-half of women bachelor's degree recipients in 1960 received their degrees in one specialty: teaching. By 1984 this proportion had dropped to 14 percent. While all specialties are formally open to men and women, informal social processes work to channel men and women into separate specializations (Weitzman, 1979).

The field of study chosen by students represents an important part of the college experience. The organization of courses of study into majors or fields of concentration has been termed "the dominant feature of undergraduate education today" (Levine, 1978: 28). The vast majority of colleges and universities require students to select a primary field of study. The requirements for majors vary but are generally substantial: 30–40 percent of the total course load is typical of bachelor of arts programs and 40–50 percent is typical of bachelor of science programs (Levine, 1978: 32–33).

The field of study constitutes a social as well as an intellectual environment for the student. College majors facilitate frequent contact between students having similar interests, shaping patterns of acquaintance and friendship (Feldman and Newcomb, 1969). Some evidence suggests important differences between majors in the social dimensions of instruction (Hearn and Olzak, 1981). Other studies indicate that within colleges there is substantial variation between majors in the effort devoted to instruction (Trow, 1977; Stark and Morstain, 1978) and in the quality of instruction provided (Hartnett and Centra, 1979). Political attitudes and grades also vary systematically across college majors (Astin, 1977).

Finally, and perhaps most importantly, college majors influence later occupations and earnings. Bielby (1978) and Daymont and Andrisani (1984) have linked the field of study chosen by women in college to subsequent employment in female-dominated occupations. Census Bureau reports indicate that the salaries of humanities graduates average 60 percent of those earned by engineering graduates (National Center for Educational Statistics, 1982: 187; see also Angle and Wissman, 1981; Astin, 1977). A recent Census Bureau report (1987) finds that 12 percent of the sex gap in wages of college graduates is due to the sex segregation of college majors.

However, one should not overstate the connection between choice of major and subsequent career. There is a great degree of instability in the choice of major; the connection between the field of study and the subsequent job is often indirect for many specialties; and the first job after schooling by no means determines one's entire career. Overall, only 55 percent of a national sample reported a direct connection between the major they pursued in college and the subsequent employment they obtained (National Center for Educational Statistics, 1982: 186). Nonetheless, a notable relationship between field of study and subsequent career options is indisputable, especially in certain fields. Thus, the educational choices of young women are arguably a better harbinger of future trends than are the occupational goals they hold. In short, both the college experience and subsequent opportunities are demonstrably related to the field of study.

The choice of majors by undergraduates has been extensively studied. Prominent among the findings in this literature is the important effect of gender on the choice of major (Astin and Panos, 1969; Davis, 1965; Peng and Jaffe, 1979; Polachek, 1978; Strange and Rea, 1983). Gender directly affects the choice of major and also mediates the influence of other determinants of major choice (Astin and Panos, 1969; Davis, 1965). The educational arena is a particularly interesting setting in which to study patterns of segregation by sex, because of the substantial role of informal social controls in maintaining a highly stable structure of segregation.

Trends in Segregation

How have the changes in higher education since the 1950's affected the fields men and women pursue? Were changes in higher education faster than those observed in occupational segregation by sex, which declined relatively slowly during this period? The present investigation utilizes the complementary indicators of segregation we have discussed and places the analysis in the context of a social control perspective on sex segregation.

The analysis here draws on the National Center for Educational Statistics (NCES) data on degree recipients described in Chapter 1. We follow the trends through 1984. The data are based on complete or virtually complete reports from all colleges and universities throughout the United States. We employ measures of three dimensions of segregation, as in previous chapters: the index of dissimilarity (D, as well as a size-standardized D), indices of concentration (C, RC), and measures of group contact and isolation (P*).

It should be noted that the P* statistics presented here refer to contact between men and women in classes, not in other settings. More specifically, the figures measure the likelihood of sharing the same major for men and women. One must also note that these figures represent national averages. The sex composition in a given school may differ substantially from these national averages, with single-sex colleges being the extreme case. In that instance, the statistic refers to the likelihood that a random individual specializing in one's field of study is a man or a woman, not the direct probability of contact with a male or female classmate at one's college or university.

Table 6.1 presents data collected by the National Center for Educational Statistics on the size and sex composition of fields of study for bachelor's degree recipients in 1952, 1968, and 1984. Women constituted just over half of the degree recipients in 1984. Female-dominated fields of study included home economics (93.8 percent women), library science (87.1 percent women),

TABLE 6.1

Bachelor's Degrees Received by Sex and Field of Study, 1952, 1968, and 1984

Field of study	1952 Total	1952 Pct. received by women	1968 Total	1968 Pct. received by women	1984 Total	1984 Pct. received by women
Agriculture	9,595	1.5%	8,308	3.2	19,317	31.6%
Architecture	2,210	5.1	2,955	4.3	13,938	45.0
Area studies					2,879	58.9
Biology	11,196	26.1	31,826	27.8	38,640	46.8
Business	46,683	12.0	79,528	8.7	230,031	43.5
Communications	2,772	29.3	4,363	40.7	40,165	58.6
Computer science					32,172	37.1
Education	62,951	60.9	134,905	75.9	92,382	76.0
Engineering	30,549	.2	37,368	.6	94,444	12.8
Fine arts	15,981	56.6	25,521	59.3	39,833	62.1
Foreign languages	4,418	61.4	19,254	72.7	9,479	73.2
Health professions[a]	14,544	38.5	17,429	77.8	64,338	84.3
Home economics	7,716	99.2	7,350	97.3	16,316	93.8
Letters[c]	16,508	52.0	53,728	62.0	40,174	60.7
Library science	629	86.5	814	90.3	255	87.1
Mathematics	4,721	28.2	23,513	37.1	13,211	44.2
Military science	201	0	2,029	.5	195	8.2
Physical sciences	12,145	11.0	19,380	13.6	23,671	27.6
Pre-law[b]			477	5.9	1,272	58.1
Psychology	6,622	42.9	23,819	42.1	39,872	67.9
Public affairs					27,050	54.2
Social sciences	38,819	29.9	123,291	36.1	93,212	44.1
Theology	7,139	15.7	4,575	32.3	5,914	26.2
Interdisciplinary[d]	14,731	24.6	11,856	23.1%	35,549	52.3
TOTAL	310,130	33.5%	632,289	43.4%	974,309	50.5%

SOURCE: Data are from the National Center for Educational Statistics (unpublished tabulations for 1984). [a] D.D.S. and M.D. degrees removed in 1952. [b] Excluded in 1952 because J.D. and B.A. were not differentiated. [c] Includes philosophy. [d] Includes trade subjects in 1968; liberal studies in 1984.

education (76 percent women), and psychology (67.9 percent women). These fields were disproportionately female in 1952 as well, when only one-third of graduates were women. There has been more change in the sex composition of fields dominated by men in the earlier period. Fields with a substantial increase in the representation of women over this period included architecture (45 percent women in 1984), biology (46.8 percent women), business (43.5 percent women), and mathematics (44.2 percent women). Fields remaining dominated by men in 1984 included military science (8.2 percent women), engineering (12.8 percent women), and physical sciences (27.6 percent women).

The 24 fields of study displayed in Table 6.1 were employed as the units of analysis in order to maintain comparability over time. Careful analysis of the properties of these categories is reassuring (Jacobs, 1985). First, these major categories capture a large proportion of the segregation revealed by the most detailed categories. The major categories consistently capture between 80 and 90 percent of the index of dissimilarity revealed by the detailed categories. Second, the major categories appear as robust in 1980 as in 1952. There is no apparent secular decline in the proportion of segregation captured by the major categories. In spite of increasing specialization, the major categories employed here are reliable indicators both of the level and of the trend in specialization of educational majors.

Table 6.2 presents data on bachelor's degree recipients from 1952 to 1984. The year, the percentage of women, the index of segregation (D), measures of concentration (C and RC) and the probabilities of sharing a major (P*) are presented. Indices were calculated for each year; every fourth year is presented in the tables.

For bachelor's degree recipients, the index of segregation rose during the 1950's, then declined slowly and steadily from the early 1960's through 1984. The 1984 index of segregation was 31.0, indicating that 31 percent of women would have had to change majors to be distributed in the same manner as men. To give an indication of how this figure compares to others, the index of occupational segregation by sex in 1986 in the U.S. la-

TABLE 6.2

Indices of Unevenness, Concentration, and Isolation for Bachelor's Degree Recipients, Selected Years, 1952–1984

Year	Pct. women	Unevenness		Concentration			Probability of sharing a major			
		D	D (size-standardized)	C women	C men	RC	P^*WM	P^*WW	P^*MW	P^*MM
1952	33.5	46.2	45.9	.54	.46	−.08	.49	.51	.25	.75
1956	36.8	49.4	45.9	.57	.48	−.09	.44	.56	.26	.74
1960	36.1	49.6	46.1	.58	.48	−.10	.45	.55	.25	.75
1964	42.9	51.4	51.6	.57	.52	−.05	.39	.61	.28	.72
1968	43.4	47.5	50.8	.56	.50	−.06	.40	.60	.31	.69
1972	43.5	45.7	52.6	.54	.49	−.05	.41	.59	.32	.68
1976	45.4	39.7	46.3	.46	.43	−.03	.43	.57	.36	.64
1980	49.0	35.2	39.0	.42	.43	+.01	.42	.58	.40	.60
1984	50.5	31.0	35.0	.41	.43	+.02	.42	.58	.43	.57

SOURCE: Data are from the National Center for Educational Statistics.

bor force was over 57; the index of occupational segregation between white and black men in 1981 was just over 35. Thus the
degree of segregation between men and women in bachelor's
degree programs was similar to the degree of racial segregation
of occupations but much lower than that of the sex segregation
of occupations.

The size-standardized measure of dissimilarity shows a similar picture over this period, which suggests that almost all of
the change is attributable to the changing sex-composition of
fields, and not to changes in the size of fields. One exception to
this pattern was evident in the period between 1964 and 1972,
when the declines in segregation were due to the shrinking of
highly segregated fields such as teaching, which fell from 25 percent of graduates in 1964 to 20 percent in 1972.

The concentration measures indicate a notable reversal over
this period. In 1952, women were more concentrated in a limited set of fields than men. This gap grew until 1960, when it
began to close. By 1980, however, the difference in concentration favored women by a small amount. Thus, women are now
more evenly distributed across majors than are men.

The probability of women's sharing a major with men (P^*WM)
has *declined* from .49 in 1952 to .42 in 1984. This figure indicates that women bachelor's degree recipients on the whole
have not found themselves an isolated minority. As we saw in
Chapter 2, women's representation as well as the level of segregation contribute to changes in women's contact with men. For
women, these two changes work in opposite directions. From a
woman's point of view, the increased representation of women
increases her chances of sharing a major with another woman,
while declines in the level of segregation increase her chances
of sharing a major with a man. Since the Second World War, the
representation effect has outweighed the decline in segregation: on the whole, women are less likely to share a major with
a man today than 30 years ago.

Men, on the other hand, have historically been much less
likely to share majors with women. The probability of men's
contact with women (P^*MW) has grown from .25 in 1952 to .43
in 1984. This asymmetry reflects the fact that men have until

recently exceeded women in enrollment and have been segregated from women in the majors they pursue. The declines in segregation and increases in women's enrollments combine to increase the chances that women will share a major with men. The probability figures in Table 6.2 exemplify the asymmetric nature of change: women, a sizable and growing minority group in this case, have had declining chances of sharing a major with men, while men have had increasing chances of sharing a major with women.

The data suggest that our nation's colleges and universities have experienced a much greater decline in sex segregation than the American occupational structure. While occupational segregation by sex has declined slowly since the 1960's, higher education has experienced substantial change. Higher education appears far more susceptible than private employers to the influence of government decree and organized pressure groups. Yet the formal equality of higher education continues to coexist with substantial segregation in the studies men and women pursue.

The declines in sex segregation described here began during the 1960's, as the women's movement started to emerge as a significant force in American life. The call for greater opportunities for women in higher education was among the leading issues of the women's movement from the earliest days of the current revival of feminism. Betty Friedan's *Feminine Mystique* (1963), often cited as marking the beginning of the new wave of feminist activism, emphasized the exclusion of women from professional education. Friedan wrote critically of "feminine" higher education, which defines sociology, anthropology, and psychology as acceptable for women but excludes "pure science (since abstract theory and quantitative thinking are unfeminine)" (1963: 152). The higher education of women has consistently been a focal concern of the women's movement.

The women's movement also directly affected the sex segregation of American higher education by pressuring institutions of higher education to change their recruitment and admissions procedures. The increased attendance of women in professional schools, and the resultant increased integration of professional and master's degree recipients, was in no small measure the result of pressure to eliminate enrollment quotas and other practices restricting admission for women (Rossi and Calderwood, 1973; Westervelt, 1975). This pressure culminated in the 1972 Title IX Amendments to the Higher Education Act, which proscribed sex discrimination in higher education. Subsequent programs developed at all levels of higher education, including the associate degree level, have been introduced to attempt to reduce inequities related to sex. The declines over time are due in part to the influence of the women's movement, and not simply to changes in women's labor force participation. During the 1950's, women's labor force participation increased, but so too did the segregation of college majors.

Stability and Change During College

Now we will turn to the dynamic aspects of sex segregation in college. As in the case of aspirations, we will look for both net changes and individual mobility. We argued in our discussion of aspirations in Chapter 4 that the malleability of aspirations constituted evidence for the social control perspective. If aspirations change over time for a cohort, then the forces affecting those aspirations must persist after the early years crucial to the socialization perspective. Our thesis regarding educational change is identical: if there is as much change for those in college as for successive waves of new college entrants, then the forces affecting educational decision making remain at work during the college years.

Our second argument is that extensive individual mobility characterizes a revolving door, as opposed to a cumulative disadvantage, model of social control. As we suggested in Chapter 3, the cumulative disadvantage model posits extensive attrition of women from male-dominated pursuits, in this case fields of study such as math and science in college. The revolving door thesis predicts extensive mobility in both directions, entrance of women into as well as attrition from male-dominated fields. Thus we view with particular interest two types of data: the pattern of net changes, and the extent of individual change, during the college years.

In this section we will examine the influence of college on the choice of major. About one-half of students will change their field of study at some point in their undergraduate years (Astin, 1977; Davis, 1965; Levine, 1978; Komarovsky, 1985). This mobility allows for substantial effects of the college environment on the distribution of students into specialized areas of study. College has the potential to dramatically increase or dramatically decrease the degree to which men and women specialize in different areas of study. (The terms "college" and "college experience" are used here to refer to all four-year institutions of higher education.)

One view of the effect of college on students sees college as introducing a variety of new ideas to young men and women. College exposes students to other students with different backgrounds, assumptions, and values. College also exposes students to courses of instruction and fields of study they are unfamiliar with. The consequence of these broadening social and intellectual experiences may be a growing tolerance for diversity of attitudes and behavior. Several studies have concluded that the college experience has a liberalizing effect on a range of student attitudes and behaviors (Bressler and Wendell, 1980; Trow, 1977). Astin finds that college has generally liberalizing effects but that sex roles are a notable exception (Astin, 1977).[1] One consequently might expect the college years to break down the stereotypes and prejudices about sex-appropriate roles freshman women and men may bring to college with them. If this tendency were dominant, the net effect of college would be to reduce the degree of sex segregation of college majors.

An alternative possibility is that the college experience reinforces sex-role differences among undergraduates, an expectation consistent with the cumulative disadvantage perspective. A number of studies have specifically examined the issue of attrition of women from math, science, and other male-dominated fields (Baruch and Nagy, 1977; Ott, 1978; Jacobs, 1985; Fiorentine, 1987; Adams, 1987). The difficulties women have in pursuing male-dominated fields include lack of family and peer support, lack of institutional support, and harassment (Hearn and Olzak, 1981; Komarovsky, 1985; de Cani et al., 1985; Weitzman, 1979). The scarcity of women in certain majors itself constitutes an obstacle and is associated with a number of behavioral consequences impeding women's performance and persistence in these settings (Alexander and Thoits, 1985). The implication of this perspective is that there will be net flows of women from male-dominated fields to sex-neutral or female-dominated fields. If men also tend to leave female-dominated specialties, the overall tendency will be toward increased sex segregation over time. Upon graduation, women college students would be more segregated by specialty from their male peers than they were in their freshman years.

A final possibility is that the changes experienced during the college years may be the result of influences outside the identifiable college environment. Both the liberalization and reinforcement views outlined above assume the salience of factors within the college. Yet students may be as readily susceptible to outside influences as to those in the immediate environment. In addition, colleges themselves are influenced by the trends in society. As a result, the college experience itself and the changes experienced during the college years may vary substantially over time. If the net change during the college years varies significantly in extent or direction over time, this may indicate that external influences may determine the extent of the changes in the college years. As we found in the discussion of trends in aspirations in Chapter 4, evidence regarding parallels between changes in college and changes occurring outside college are indicative of social forces during this period that affect choices and attitudes in the community as a whole.

The effect of college will be examined with data spanning the 1970's and with a large-scale study of the class of 1961. The availability of this series of data allows a test of the hypothesis that the effect of the college experience was constant over the past 10 to 20 years. If the effect of college changed significantly in size or direction over this period, and if these changes paralleled other trends outside the academy, then we will conclude that external influences directly or indirectly affect the direction and extent of the effects of the college experience. As we noted in our discussion of aspirations, contemporary influence on choices is one piece of evidence in support of our social control model.

First we consider the net effect of college on the sex segregation of majors. Do men and women undergraduates become more or less segregated over the course of their years in school? And do these changes in college reflect trends in the external environment? We subsequently consider the stability of choices for individuals.

Net Change in Segregation During College

Students enter college with plans to major in certain fields. We will characterize the degree of divergence in the plans of young men and women entering college by measuring the degree of segregation evident at the conclusion of the college years. We will determine whether the level of segregation increased or declined by comparing the levels of segregation evident at the beginning and at the end of the college years. Our trusted standby, the index of dissimilarity (D), will be employed to measure the level of segregation for initial and final choice of majors. Thus, a comparison of entry and exit levels of segregation by sex in the choice of college majors will provide an indication of the effect of college on the pattern of sex-segregated choice of majors.

One might object to the examination of freshmen's intended major on the grounds that these intentions may well be little more than wild guesses. The evidence on mobility between majors, cited above, indicates that there is a great deal of switching before students settle on a major. Yet if this switching were simply random changes, there would be no net change in the proportion enrolled in different majors, a finding that would contradict the hypotheses outlined above. The hypotheses under consideration can be tested even if there is a degree of random movement reflecting randomness in freshman responses.

Data on freshmen's intended majors have been gathered yearly by the American Council on Education–sponsored Cooperative Institutional Research Program (ACE-CIRP), as discussed in Chapters 1 and 4. These extremely large annual surveys (including 250,000 students in over 500 colleges and universities) provide a highly reliable description of the characteristics of the freshman class.

The ACE-CIRP data are the source of the entry or origin data. Two different terminal or destination groups can be argued to provide the most appropriate comparison: (1) all degree recipients, and (2) the same students four or more years later. This chapter will examine both types of data.

We analyze the degree recipient data published by NCES. These data are available for every year, and they consequently allow us to consider trends over time. The problem with comparing freshman intentions with degrees received is that some freshmen do not complete college, others do not do so in four years, and some who receive degrees in a given year began college much earlier or transferred from two-year colleges. In short, the population receiving degrees is not the same as the group of freshman who started four years earlier. Thus, some of the differences between entry and exit data may be due to differences in attrition and different characteristics of students transferring to colleges. These disadvantages are at least partly outweighed by the comprehensiveness of the data, since these data provide us with a virtually complete account of graduates. Nonetheless, the present investigation will supplement the degree data with four longitudinal studies of students. By following up the same students four years after college entry, these data avoid the potential problems of divergent populations that the degree data present. Longitudinal data will help to measure the extent of the biases in the degree-recipient data.

The first major national longitudinal study of college students was conducted by Davis on the class of 1961, for the National Opinion Research Center (Davis, 1965). These data include retrospective information on intended majors. CIRP researchers have followed samples of students four years after college entry in certain years. The data on the 1967–1971 cohort and the 1978–1982 cohort will be examined here (Bayer, Royer, and Webb, 1973; Green et al., 1983). Finally, the National Longitudinal Survey of the High School Class of 1972 included a four-year follow-up in 1976 (National Center for Educational Statistics, 1976). These four studies are all large national samples of students with high response rates for follow-up interviews. The college class of 1961 and the high school class of 1972 data were examined for the individual level analyses.[2] In each case, freshman year data (plans of high school seniors in the case of the NLS data) will be compared with the students' actual majors four years later. Each type of data will serve as a check on the reliability of the other.

ACE-CIRP data are divided into college and university data. These data were combined to produce overall figures for four-year institutions. College and university data were weighted to reflect the relative size of enrollments in these institutional categories, as reported in national enrollment figures (National Center for Educational Statistics, 1971–82). Data for freshman classes of 1966–76 were analyzed and compared with the graduating classes of 1970–80.

The data for degrees conferred were collapsed into the same broad categories presented in the CIRP publications. Collapsing these detailed majors into broad categories results in some loss of precision, but, as discussed above, the major field of study categories available for the CIRP data capture over 80 percent of the segregation between men and women.

It should be noted that the consequence of the aggregated measurement is the attenuation of the effects revealed. By hiding a portion of the true level of segregation, the measures reduce the degree to which the college experience can be said to influence sex segregation. Rather than undermining the validity of the findings, the aggregation of the data on field of study produces relatively conservative estimates of the effect of college. But since the degree of imprecision introduced is quite modest, the results represent only a relatively minor attenuation of the effects considered.

TABLE 6.3

Comparisons of Sex Segregation by Field for College Freshmen
and Degree Recipients, 1970–1980

| Class | Segregation of freshmen | | Segregation of degree recipients (D) | Net change | Net adjusted change | Freshman cohort comparison[b] |
	Unadjusted D	Adjusted[a] D				
1966–70	48.7	46.8	44.1	−4.6	−2.7	
1967–71	48.3	47.2	44.8	−3.5	−2.4	
1968–72	48.1	46.9	43.2	−4.9	−3.7	
1969–73	48.9	47.2	40.1	−8.8	−7.1	
1970–74	47.5	46.0	39.7	−7.8	−6.3	−1.2
1971–75	46.1	44.2	38.5	−7.6	−5.7	−2.2
1972–76	45.3	45.1	36.3	−9.0	−8.8	−2.8
1973–77	43.4		37.8	−5.6		−5.5
1974–78	37.4		34.1	−3.3		−10.1
1975–79	35.2		34.3	−0.9		−10.9
1976–80	34.5		34.0	−0.5		−10.8

SOURCE: Freshman data are from ACE-CIRP annual surveys. Data on degrees received are from the National Center for Educational Statistics.
[a] Adjusted by removal of the preprofessional category, which is not employed in series after 1973.
[b] Compares freshmen with those entering four years earlier. For example, 1970 freshmen segregation was 47.5; 1966 freshman segregation was 48.7. Thus there was a decline of 1.2 points in this period for incoming freshmen.

Table 6.3 compares the indices of segregation for freshmen and degree recipients for graduating classes 1970 through 1980. It presents changes in the indices of segregation between freshman and senior years, and also presents adjusted scores that remove the preprofessional category from the analysis.[3] The comparisons reveal a striking uniformity. In all years, degree recipients were less segregated by sex in the distribution of majors than were freshman students four years earlier. This conclusion is consistent across the 11 years studied for both the adjusted and unadjusted segregation scores.

Table 6.3 also reveals notable variation in the extent of change. The effect of college is quite modest for the graduating classes from 1970 to 1972. The decline in sex segregation during the college years is greatest for the classes between 1973 and 1977; the three following classes exhibit a sharp diminution of this effect. This pattern suggests that in the mid-1970's college had a heightened influence on students. The liberal atmosphere of many college campuses and the societywide reevaluation of sex-role attitudes may have created a particularly adaptable cohort during this period. As Astin has pointed out, the effects of college in part reflect the college environment and in part reflect change occurring in society at the time (Astin, 1977). The external influences hypothesis thus finds support in these results.

One way to shed light on the question of external effects is to compare the changes experienced by students after four years in college with the changes experienced by incoming freshmen during the same four years. If the same declines in sex segregation are experienced by these two groups, the changes may not be the result of the college experience per se but rather the result of societywide reevaluation of sex roles.

The last column of Table 6.3 compares levels of sex segregation for four cohorts of freshmen at four-year intervals. The change revealed by comparing freshmen at four-year intervals indicates the rate of change due to changes in social trends, not changes due to the college environment. Changes in college students appear to be quite similar to changes between cohorts of freshmen. For both groups, the rate of change accelerates from the early 1970's through 1976. The declines in sex segregation were greater for college students from 1970 to 1973, while the changes were larger for incoming freshmen for 1974 to 1976.

The rate of change for college students varies over time, broadly in step with changes among incoming freshmen. These data can be viewed as evidence that changes in social attitudes regarding sex roles affected college-bound high school students and college students to similar degrees during this period. The extent of change in the college years varies over this period, and the variation appears to follow the same pattern for those outside the college environments.

Table 6.4 reports comparisons of freshman data and four-year follow-up data for NORC, CIRP, and NLS longitudinal data. As noted earlier, these data allow for a comparison of origin and destination distribution effects for the same individuals, avoiding the potential problem resulting from comparing different

TABLE 6.4

Indices of Sex Segregation for College Freshmen
and Follow-up Sample Four Years Later

Study	Years	N of cases	Sample persistence rate	N of categories	Freshman segregation (D)	Follow-up segregation (D)	Change in D
NORC	1957–61	33,982	100%[a]	8	50.4	48.5	−1.9
CIRP	1967–71	34,346	59	16	48.3	42.8	−5.5
NLS	1972–76	5,503	89[b]	21	40.0	36.3	−3.7
CIRP	1978–82	2,500	?	10	31.7	32.4	+0.7

[a] Freshman data were gathered retrospectively.
[b] The sample size refers to the population attending college; the persistence rate was obtained for the whole sample.

populations. The NORC data on the class of 1961, the CIRP data on the class of 1971, and the NLS data on the class of 1976 all show a slight decline in the degree of sex segregation over the period of college enrollment. These data parallel the pattern found in the CIRP freshman intentions and NCES degree recipient data. These two sets of analyses together provide compelling evidence that the effect of college throughout the 1960's and most of the 1970's was to increase the level of integration in the specialties pursued by men and women undergraduates. Sharp changes in the extent of change suggest that it is external trends in sex-role attitudes rather than college per se that are responsible for these changes.

The 1982 CIRP follow-up of the freshman class of 1978 indicates a slight increase in the level of segregation. This may be due in part to the very high degree of aggregation of these data. The 1982 data were available for ten major subject areas, whereas other data analyzed were grouped into 16 or 20 categories. This small positive effect, on closer inspection, actually differs only slightly from the small negative effects obtained with the degree recipient data for the late 1970's. It is reasonably consistent with the CIRP-NCES comparisons presented in Table 6.3 which indicate that the net effect of college has moderated in recent years.

Early-life sex-role socialization is not able to explain the ex-

TABLE 6.5

Fields of Study of the Class of 1980 by Sex and College Year

Field of study	Freshmen (1976) Men	Women	Degree recipients (1980) Men	Women	Change in pct. men	Change in pct. women	Change in D
Agriculture	4.0%	1.3%	3.4%	1.5%	−0.6%	+0.2%	−0.4
Biology	9.3	7.7	5.7	4.3	−3.6	−3.4	−0.1
Business	22.2	12.4	26.2	13.8	+4.0	+1.4	+1.3
Education	5.4	16.9	6.5	19.1	+1.1	+2.2	+0.6
Engineering	15.6	2.2	13.2	1.4	−2.4	−0.8	−0.8
English	.8	2.0	1.8	3.7	+1.0	+1.7	+0.4
Fine arts	6.2	7.6	4.6	6.2	−1.6	−1.4	+0.1
Health	1.7	13.7	2.4	11.5	+0.7	−2.2	−1.5
History	5.6	3.7	6.2	3.8	+0.6	+0.1	+0.3
Humanities	1.8	3.1	3.2	3.8	+1.4	+0.7	−0.4
Mathematics	1.8	1.3	1.4	1.1	−0.4	−0.2	−0.1
Physical sciences	5.5	1.8	3.8	1.2	−1.7	−0.6	−0.5
Social sciences	4.3	9.8	13.2	16.8	+8.9	+7.0	−1.0
Other—technical	6.2	5.3	2.2	1.0	−4.0	−4.3	+0.1
Other—nontechnical	9.6	11.2	6.2	10.8	−3.4	−0.4	+1.5
	D = 34.5		*D* = 34.0			Change in *D* = −0.5	

SOURCE: Freshman data are from ACE-CIRP annual surveys. Data on degrees received are from the National Center for Educational Statistics.

tent or direction of change during the college years. The data indicate the importance of continuing socialization and reinforcement of sex-role attitudes during college years. The evidence demonstrates that college students continue to be susceptible to changes in opportunities; indeed, they are as susceptible to change as precollege students in the same period. This pattern of change constitutes support for the social control model. The direction of change does not correspond with the predictions of the cumulative disadvantage perspective. Sex segregation declines during college, whereas the cumulative disadvantage view predicts an increase in segregation. There is some attrition of women from male-dominated fields, as we will see, but net change during college results in increased integration. The revolving door model of social control is consistent with the observed changes. This model emphasizes continuing susceptibility to change but does not predict increasing segregation throughout life.

Table 6.5 presents net changes in fields of study for the class of 1980. Several male-dominated fields lost female students at higher rates (but in lower numbers) than male students. These include biology, engineering, and physical sciences. Agriculture, business, and mathematics fit this pattern in 1970 but did not lose women at a higher rate in 1980. The disproportionate rates of attrition of women from these fields cannot be accounted for by lower grades or inadequate preparation (Adams, 1987; Fiorentine, 1987). These changes suggest the continuing importance of sex-role conformity pressures during the college years.

Other fields, however, moved in the opposite direction. Some relatively integrated fields, such as history, the humanities, and the social sciences, gained both men and women during this period. Other highly segregated fields, such as the female-dominated health sciences, declined in size during the college years. Thus, the overall changes during college reflect continuing social control pressures, but the net effect is a slight decline in segregation. The pattern of change conforms to a revolving door pattern rather than to the cumulative disadvantage model. Segregation declines, reflecting the weakening barriers to opportunities for women, and this change is reflected by cohorts of entering freshmen as well as by students already in college. Individual patterns of mobility, to which we now turn, constitute more direct evidence for the revolving door thesis.

Individuals Changing Fields of Study

Until now, we have considered aggregate changes during college. Let us now consider the serial correlation between the sex type of college plans and the sex type of the field in which the degree is received. Data are examined from the college class of 1961 and the National Longitudinal Survey of the high school class of 1972. These data provide us with more college graduates and more detailed data on majors over time than do the NLS Young Women data.

Let us first consider the data on the high school class of 1972. We assigned a percent-female score to each major on the basis of national data on degrees received in 1976 (National Center for Educational Statistics, 1976). Two sets of correlations were considered. The first relates freshman plans in 1972 to degrees received in 1976. The second relates freshman plans in 1972 to expected areas of degrees for those who had not received their degrees by 1976. As in the discussion of the mobility between male-dominated and female-dominated career goals, we are careful to distinguish between stayers and movers. In this case, stayers are those who remain in the major that they planned to enter as freshmen; movers are those who changed majors before graduation.

For young women in the high school class of 1972 who received their degrees in 1976, the correlation between the sex type of their intended major as freshmen and the sex type of the field of their degree was .44 ($n = 823$). The correlation between the intended major as freshmen and the intended field of degree for women who had not completed college by 1976 was .28 ($n = 729$). For both groups, there is a moderately strong positive correlation between the sex type of plans and the sex type of degrees received for all women. However, for women who changed their majors, this relationship disappears. The sex-type correlation for the women (approximately half of the total) who changed majors in the interim is negative. The sex-type correlation for degree recipients who changed their majors during college was $-.10$ ($n = 410$); for those still in school, the relationship was $-.09$ ($n = 461$). This weak negative relationship in part reflects a problem of "lumpiness": the definitions of fields for the class of 1972 data remain relatively broad, and consequently a student who changes his or her major is relatively unlikely to find another major with a similar sex composition. For the occupational data, each occupation is relatively small compared to the sex-type categories we constructed. Here, majors are relatively large with respect to the sex-type categories. Thus, we expect that finer measures would produce a sex-type correlation closer to zero.

As in the case of young women's aspirations, we find that there is a remarkably weak connection between intentions and outcomes. Further, this relationship is confined strictly to stayers; for the one-half of all students who change majors at one point or another, no positive connection between intentions and outcomes is evident.

Our analysis of the college class of 1961 data reveals strikingly similar results. The 1961 freshman intentions data are retrospective, collected from seniors about their previous inclinations. These data consequently are likely to understate change. As for the high school Class of 1972, we assigned each major a percent-female score on the basis of the national averages obtained for 1961 (National Center for Educational Statistics, 1961). The correlation of the sex type of the intended major and the sex type of the field in which the degree was received was .14 for women who changed fields and .26 for men who changed fields. While these results show a slightly stronger relationship than was evident in the class of 1972 data, both groups exhibit a great deal of movement between male-dominated, sex-neutral, and female-dominated majors. The slightly stronger relationship in the 1961 data may be due to the inflation of retrospective reports about previous majors and to the greater detail in the classification of fields of study.[4]

Discussion

There have been significant declines in the sex segregation of college majors since the 1950's. The informal tracking system in college has not been effective in blocking women's progress. Yet there is continued evidence of social control at work. Women leave some male-dominated majors in higher percentages (but smaller numbers) than men during the college years. More research is needed to explain the disproportionate attrition of women from male-dominated fields of study.

The rate at which net change occurs during the college years appears to reflect the rate of change in sex-role attitudes in the society at large, rather than the distinctive influences of the college environment. This evidence indicates the power of social trends to influence the attitudes and behavior of young people. Psychological and sociological investigations that assume constant effects of socialization and psychological orientation are unable to explain the changes evident in the college years. Further, the connection between individual intentions and subsequent outcomes is quite modest and restricted to students who persisted in their initial choices. The sex segregation in majors is thus reproduced during the college years.

While some of the patterns of change observed in college are consistent with a human capital view, others raise questions that the view cannot answer. The increasing integration of majors could be explained as a reflection of women's expectations of increasing labor force participation. Yet the extent of change during the college years suggests that students are often uncertain about their future plans, and that in the face of limited information they are susceptible to social influences and peer pressure. Further, the attrition of women from male-dominated fields of study suggests that barriers still exist to women's pursuit of male-dominated fields. The social control perspective explains the declines in segregation as evidence of the weakening barriers to opportunity for women and their expectation of greater opportunities at work. Both the varying rates of net change during the college years and the high rates of sex-type mobility found for individual students indicate the continued susceptibility of college students to sex-typed social control influences. Social control in college is not a case of cumulative disadvantage, as the level of sex segregation generally declines during the college years. The movement of men and women across majors represented a revolving door pattern, with extensive movement in both directions found among the large group of students who change majors. The social control forces evident during the college years continue as students enter the working world.

7

Sex-Type Mobility in

Women's Careers

The primary goal of this chapter is to document the extent of mobility among male-dominated, sex-neutral, and female-dominated occupations. In Chapter 5 we saw that the sex composition of young women's occupations were not stable over time. Now we explore this matter further with log-linear models of occupational mobility. We examine whether the labor market segmentation perspective can be employed to understand occupational segregation by sex. We assemble evidence from various case studies that is consistent with the mobility patterns we described. Finally, we briefly explore medicine and law as two unlikely instances of support for our social control framework.

Labor Market Segmentation and Occupational Sex Segregation

A variety of structural approaches to inequality have been proposed in recent years. They share the view that individual attainment processes are mediated by the contexts in which they take place. The conceptualization of the relevant contexts varies from economic dualism to class location to local labor market conditions (Berg, 1981; Wright, 1979; Parcel and Mueller, 1983). The sex segregation of occupations is similarly viewed as mediating between individual attributes and labor market outcomes (Kemp and Beck, 1981). In the terms of the social control perspective we have developed, these theories emphasize social control exerted during the labor market experience rather than before labor market entry. To what extent do these theories offer an explanation for occupational segregation by sex, and what are the implications they hold for women's career patterns?

Among the most prominent of the structuralist theories is the economic segmentation model, which divides the economy into a core of large, stable firms with market power, and a periphery of small firms in competitive industries (Beck, Horan, and Tolbert, 1978). This dualistic treatment of labor markets has been the subject of a great deal of research (Berg, 1981). Some have heralded this model as reintroducing social structure into the discussion of individual attainment processes, while critics have faulted the coarseness of the dualistic model (Baron and Bielby, 1980; Jacobs and Breiger, 1988).

The dual economy model directly explains little of the sex segregation of occupations. There is nearly as much occupational segregation by sex within each of these sectors as there is in the labor force as a whole. In 1981, the degree of occupational segregation by sex was 65.3 for men and women working in core industries and 59.5 in peripheral industries.[1] Wharton (1985) indicates that among blue-collar workers, sex segregation is higher in the periphery than in the core, but the difference is not great. The core-periphery division constitutes less of a barrier to mobility for women than for men (Jacobs, 1983b; Rosenfeld, 1983). Further, women are only modestly concentrated in the peripheral sector. In 1981, 41 percent of women were located in peripheral industries, compared to 39 percent of men. Thus the economic dualism perspective is only of limited value in explaining occupational segregation by sex.

Yet the core-periphery distinction may help to define the context for two more useful structuralist approaches. The first, which we may call the "internal labor market" thesis, is set in the large organizations that are predominantly located in the core and public sectors of the economy. Internal labor markets and career ladders have been the focus of a good deal of interest in stratification research since Baron and Bielby (1980) called for more attention to the role of firms in the allocation of rewards (Baron, 1984).

There is growing evidence for the gender effects of internal labor markets. It is clear that women in clerical jobs have limited promotion opportunities within firms (Glenn and Feldberg, 1979), and evidence is accumulating regarding the deleterious effects of promotion ladders on women's careers (Rosenbaum, 1984; DiPrete, 1987). Coverman argues that female-dominated occupations "operate under a set of often implicit rules and procedures which can be distinguished from those to which men are subjected" (1986: 143). Coverman maintains that women's work is not integrated into bureaucratic lines of authority and, implicitly, into male-dominated career ladders. This perspective cannot account for segregation between firms (Talbert and Bose, 1977; Blau, 1977) or between industries (Bridges, 1982), but the prevalence of firms with internal career ladders underscores the importance of this view.

A second line of structuralist reasoning, which we may term "the segregation as segmentation" thesis, suggests that the sex segregation of occupations itself constitutes a form of segmentation (Bridges, 1982). Burris and Wharton (1982) have claimed that segregating workers by sex is a way of stratifying the work force to effect employers' strategy of divide and conquer. They argue that rather than employ lower-paid women in all possible areas in order to minimize their wage bills, employers draw on existing cultural definitions about the appropriate sexual division of labor to drive a wedge between workers and obscure their common interests. They explain the persistence of occupational segregation by sex despite the neoclassical economic prediction of its demise by referring to the desire of employers to fragment the organization of work and the characteristics of workers. This reasoning may be particularly applicable in the periphery of the economy, where the technical division of labor is less elaborate and where there are fewer detailed job ladders to divide workers.

Thus two separate strands of structuralist logic offer explanations for the persistence of occupational segregation by sex. One important implication of both views is that there is little mobility between female-dominated and male-dominated occupations. The internal labor market thesis implies that women and men are segregated because their careers are segregated. The structure of opportunities built into job ladders promotes and reinforces occupational segregation. Thus, a large degree of movement between female-dominated and male-dominated occupations would be contrary to the internal labor market thesis. For the segregation as segmentation thesis, the rationale for segmenting work also implies a motivation to differentiate the career lines of men and women. Specifically, one would predict little movement from female-dominated occupations to male-dominated occupations, for this movement would undermine the division of workers that constitutes employers' motive for segregation.

The present analysis seeks to examine these suggestions empirically. Can sex segregation itself be considered a type or dimension of labor market segmentation? To answer this question, data on three specific issues will be examined: (1) How much mobility do women experience between male-dominated, sex-neutral, and female-dominated occupations? (2) What are the boundaries of the sex composition–based segments? (3) How does this segmentation intersect with other structural and demographic variables?

Both Rosenfeld (1983) and Corcoran, Duncan, and Ponza (1984) present evidence indicating a significant amount of mobility between male-dominated and female-dominated occupations. This work raises the distinct possibility that the assumption of immobility at the core of labor market segmentation theory is not supported empirically. It strongly suggests that there is more mobility than people recognize, mobility that is consistent with the social control perspective we have advanced throughout this book.

However, research to date on these mobility patterns has been limited. Corcoran, Duncan, and Ponza rely on relatively crude two-digit occupation and industry data, which mask a good deal of occupational segregation by sex. Rosenfeld considers mobility across a discrete male-dominated/female-dominated boundary over a one-year period and focuses on the explanation of these mobility patterns rather than on the overall extent of mobility. We will consider a range of possible boundaries between the male-dominated and female-dominated occupational spheres, employing data over longer time periods, and employing as much detail as is possible with survey data.

The broad significance of this question for theories of labor market segmentation should be apparent. A finding of little or no mobility between male-dominated and female-dominated occupations would be consistent with the labor market segmentation perspective. Substantial mobility would cast doubt on a primary assumption of the segmentation approach; it would, however, be consistent with our social control model.

The social control model stresses the fact that sex segregation is not the result of stable attributes brought by individuals to the labor market. We have seen the instability of aspirations and the mobility between college majors. We have also documented the fact that sex segregation has declined across a wide spectrum of age groups, and not simply among new entrants into the labor market. Continuing mobility across sex-typed occupational lines constitutes the final evidence in support of this perspective. During the labor market years, sex segregation is not simply the product of institutional barriers women face but rather is the result of a dynamic process. Women have difficulty getting hired in male-dominated occupations, getting the assistance they need to learn the ropes, and getting the recognition they deserve for the work they do. Kanter (1977), for example, has argued that minority status per se creates a host of problems for women, including systematic misperception by the majority, a lack of political allies, and difficulties in winning acceptance from peers and subordinates. Thus, the barriers to success for women in male-dominated occupations do not disappear once they have succeeded in being hired.

Data and Methods

Even if there are barriers to mobility, consistent with the predictions of a segmentation perspective, the barriers observed must conform to the predictions of a segmentation model. Two necessary specifications of a labor market segmentation model are that mobility should be (1) infrequent between segments and (2) frequent within segments. Segments must be discrete, homogeneous categories. The boundaries of the segments must constitute barriers to mobility. If there were no such barriers, it would be difficult to make a case for the existence of segments. If the segments are not internally homogeneous, then segments cannot be distinguished from strata or from a continuous model of sex segregation. Thus, in the case of sex-based segments, one must show not only that mobility from female-dominated to male-dominated occupations is difficult, but also that mobility within each of these divisions is easy.

This reasoning places the number of categories and their boundaries at the center of the analysis. Studies of sex segregation are not in accord regarding how to define male-dominated and female-dominated occupations. Researchers generally pick an approach for the purpose at hand without considering possible statistical justification for their choice. Some of those who advocate a two-category approach focus primarily on entry into male-dominated occupations. For them, everything over 20 or 30 percent female is grouped together in a single category (see, for example, Beller, 1982b). Others are interested in the concentration of women in female-dominated occupations (for example, Oppenheimer, 1970). They chose 70 or 80 percent female as the dividing line, collapsing all other occupations into a "not-female-dominated" residual category. Typically, only two categories, male-dominated and female-dominated, are employed, despite the large number of women employed in sex-neutral occupations and despite theoretical reasons to question the grouping of such occupations with the extremes (Kanter, 1977). While it is often noted that relatively few occupations are sex-neutral, a substantial proportion of people work in these occupations. Over one-third of women in 1970 (34.2 percent) worked in occupations that were between 30 and 69.9 percent women.

Breiger (1981) has argued that the choice of appropriate categories should be the focus of analysis, rather than a decision made prior to the beginning of analysis. This is particularly true for hypotheses regarding segmentation, since the existence and boundaries of the segments are themselves the objects of analysis. We will employ the Breiger (1981) and Goodman (1981) models for partitioning mobility tables for testing labor market segmentation hypotheses. The analysis will determine whether the sex-typed mobility table can be collapsed into a small number of discrete categories or segments. These models will be employed to test for the existence of sex composition–based segments and to aid in determining the boundaries of the segments.

A final set of issues for analysis is the possibility of interactions of sex segregation with other labor market structures and with demographic variables. We will examine whether the patterns of mobility observed interact across economic segments and for different types of workers. This analysis will indicate the generality of the patterns observed.

The NLS Mature Women sample will be examined, and the 1980–81 CPS data will be used for comparison. As before, we will compare the sex type of current occupation with the sex type of previous occupation. The presentation of statistical results is divided into three sections. The first section presents evidence on the extent of sex-typed mobility. The second section examines the partitioning models of the sex-type mobility table. The third section presents log-linear models of the generality of the mobility patterns for several labor market situations and for a range of demographic groups.

Sex-Type Mobility Patterns

In this section, we examine the patterns of movement for NLS women between 1967 and 1977, viewing this period as a single occupational transition. Panel A of Table 7.1 presents the

TABLE 7.1

Three-by-Three Sex-Type Mobility Table for NLS Mature Women,
1967—1977

A. All Employed Women

		1977			
	count row %	0–29.9% female	30–69.9% female	70–100% female	row total
1967	0–29.9% female	183 46.9	96 24.6	111 28.5	390 10.4
	30–69.9% female	173 12.9	827 61.4	346 25.7	1,346 35.8
	70–100% female	214 10.6	386 19.1	1,426 70.4	2,026 53.9
	column total	570 15.2	1,309 34.8	1,883 50.1	3,762 100%

chi-squared = 1086.3   4 df   r = .38 (p < .001)

B. Female Occupation Changers

		1977			
	count row %	0–29.9% female	30–69.9% female	70–100% female	row total
1967	0–29.9% female	50 19.5	96 37.4	111 43.2	257 11.9
	30–69.9% female	173 21.1	299 36.6	346 42.3	818 37.7
	70–100% female	214 19.6	386 35.3	492 45.1	1,092 50.4
	column total	437 20.2	781 36.0	949 43.8	2,167 100%

chi-squared = 1.8   4 df   r = .02

C. Ratio of Observed to Expected Occupation Changers

		1977		
	count row %	0–29.9% female	30–69.9% female	70–100% female
1967	0–29.9% female	.97	1.04	.99
	30–69.9% female	1.05	1.02	.97
	70–100% female	.97	.98	1.03

cross-tabulation of the sex type of a woman's detailed occupation in 1977 by the sex type of a woman's detailed occupation in 1967, based on three categories: male-dominated (0–29.9 percent female); sex neutral (30–69.9 percent female); and female-dominated (70–100 percent female). Panel A compares the sex type of (last or current) occupation for women in 1967 with their (last or current) occupation in 1977.[2] The correlation between percentage of women in 1967 and percentage of women in 1977 is only moderately strong (Pearson's $r = .38$).

Included in Panel A is a large number of women who did not change occupations. This group is found entirely on the main diagonal, which has the effect of inflating the observed relationship. Panel B is restricted to women who changed their detailed occupational category between 1967 and 1977. It reveals no correlation between the sex type of occupation in 1967 and the sex type of occupation in 1977 for women who changed occupations in the interim. For occupation changers, a great degree of movement is indicated. Panel C presents the ratio of observed values to expected values for women occupation changers. The values are all close to 1.0. The striking result is that, for occupation changers, the sex type of destination occupation is independent of the sex type of origin occupation.

In 1967, 390 women were employed in male-dominated occupations. Of these, only 183, or 46.9 percent, remained in these occupations in 1977. Of the 257 women who changed occupations in the interim, only 50 (19.5 percent) remained in male-dominated occupations. Also notable is the fact that the rate of occupation change is higher for women in male-dominated occupations (65.9 percent) than in sex-neutral (60.8 percent) or female-dominated (53.8 percent) occupations. Thus, exit from male-dominated occupations is high for women occupation changers, and the probability of being an occupation changer is disproportionately high for women in male-dominated occupations. Yet in absolute numbers, more women entered male-dominated occupations than left. More women were employed in male-dominated occupations in 1977 (15.2 percent) than in 1967 (10.4 percent), confirming the net entry of mid-career women into male-dominated occupations documented

TABLE 7.2

Three-by-Three Sex-Type Mobility Table for CPS
Occupation Changers, 1980–1981

A. Female Occupation Changers

		1981			
	count row %	0–29.9% female	30–69.9% female	70–100% female	row total
	0–29.9% female	243 28.6	240 28.2	367 43.2	850 21.2
1980	30–69.9% female	274 24.4	270 24.0	579 51.6	1,123 27.9
	70–100% female	388 19.0	543 26.6	1,114 54.5	2,045 50.9
	column total	905 22.5	1,053 26.2	2,060 51.3	4,018 100%

chi-squared = 45.5   4 df   r = .10 (p < .001)

B. Male Occupation Changers

		1981			
	count row %	0–29.9% female	30–69.9% female	70–100% female	row total
	0–29.9% female	2,701 76.6	637 18.1	187 5.3	3,525 76.9
1980	30–69.9% female	559 69.3	182 22.6	66 8.2	807 17.6
	70–100% female	157 62.5	58 23.1	36 14.3	251 5.5
	column total	3,417 74.6	877 19.1	289 6.3	4,583 100%

chi-squared = 54.8   4 df   r = .11 (p < .001)

in Chapter 2. Thus, the net effect of this revolving door pattern is a modest decline in occupational segregation by sex.

Supplemental data from the March 1981 CPS sample corroborate these findings. Panel A of Table 7.2 presents the three-by-three sex-type mobility table for all CPS sample women occupation changers employed in both years. The correlation for women occupation changers is quite low (r = .10). The year-to-year sex-type correlation is only slightly positive. The correlation for the 35–44 age group, which is the same age range as the NLS sample, is .06, compared to .02 for the NLS sample. Neither correlation is statistically significant. Panel B of Table 7.2 presents the sex-type mobility table for all employed men in the CPS sample. The sex-type correlation for male occupation changers is also quite low ($r = .11$). The evidence indicates a very substantial amount of sex-type mobility for men as well as women.

One should be cautious in comparing the NLS and CPS results. The NLS data cover a ten-year period; the CPS data, a one-year period. Thus, the NLS women may be changing occupations more than once, which may have the effect of reducing the correlation. On the other hand, there is almost certainly more coding error in the NLS data, which has the consequence of increasing the correlation for occupation changers.[3] Taken together, the two sets of data provide strong support for the conclusion that the sex-type correlation for women occupation changers is no more than slightly positive. It seems clear that, while occupational segregation changes only slowly at the aggregate level, it is much more fluid at the micro or individual level. While the structure of occupations is highly segregated, individuals do have some degree of flexibility in changing the sex type of their occupations during their careers.

In addition to the 1967–77 transition, the transition from the first job ever held to the job held in 1967 was examined for the NLS data. For the 46 percent of the sample of women who changed occupations between their first job and their job in 1967, there is no correlation between the sex type of initial occupation and the sex type of 1967 occupation ($r = -.02$, $p < .20$, $n = 2,342$). Because most of the NLS mature women started their first job in the late 1940's or early 1950's, this result indicates that the sex-type mobility patterns presented in Table 7.2 are not a recent development but have been characteristic of the career patterns of women since the Second World War. For this transition, sex-type mobility reproduced the overall level of sex segregation, while in more recent years the mobility patterns are slowly bringing more women into male-dominated occupations. This evidence clearly indicates that for extremely large, representative national samples, the serial correlation of the sex composition of occupations for women who change occupations is extremely weak.

Partitioning the Sex-Type Mobility Table

In the previous section, a three-by-three sex-type mobility table was presented. In this section, a more detailed examination of the structure of the sex-type mobility table is presented. Initially, we can determine whether the weak relationship documented above is the result of excessive collapsing of the sex-type mobility table. Table 7.3 presents a set of correlations from the 1981 CPS data. The figures on Table 7.3 clearly indicate that whether the variables are measured in a continuous or discrete manner, the sex-type correlations remain low.

Bielby and Baron (1984) have documented extremely high levels of sex segregation using data on job titles within firms. Their data raise the possibility that the mobility documented here is more apparent than real, an artifact of overly broad occupational classifications. Bielby and Baron's data are three lev-

TABLE 7.3

Sex-Type Correlations by Measurement Detail for CPS Female and Male Occupation Changers, 1980–1981

Degree of detail in sex-type measurement	Women ($n = 4,018$) r	Men ($n = 4,583$) r
3 categories[a]	.10	.11
5 quintile categories	.11	.11
10 decile categories	.11	.14
Continuous measurement	.11	.15
Continuous measurement, detailed occupation by detailed industries	.14	.17

[a] 0–29.9 percent female; 30–69.9 percent female; 70+ percent female.

els more detailed than those employed here: they can distinguish industries, firms, and job titles within firms. We can assess the significance of the first of these with the data at hand.

The final row on Table 7.3 presents the sex-type correlation for sex composition measured continuously for detailed occupation by industry categories. A sex composition score was calculated for each occupation by industry category if it differed from the occupational average by 10 percentage points or more. This procedure produced 63 new occupational categories, increasing the number of categories from 426 to 489, or 15 percent. The sex-type correlation using this more detailed measure of sex composition is slightly higher than that found using the 426 detailed occupational categories ($r = .14$ for women; $r = .17$ for men). Thus while the effect of more detailed measurement is to increase the correlation, as expected, the change is not large. Increasing the detail of the units employed here to the maximum possible only slightly increases the sex-type correlation.

A more direct test of the appropriateness of the proposed partition of the sex-type mobility table can be approached via loglinear analysis of the sex-type mobility table. Table 7.4 presents tests of the three-category model for both the Breiger and Goodman models. The starting point is a ten-by-ten sex-type mobility table, the rows and columns of which are the percent-female deciles noted above. The analyses test whether the three categories presented throughout the chapter are homogeneous. For the three-category model proposed, tests of Breiger's model involve tests of homogeneity within nine subtables; Goodman's model involves tests of homogeneity within three broad subtables. Results are shown for the model, which excludes the diagonal, the approach most often reported in the literature.

The three-category model fits the CPS data for both the Breiger and Goodman models. The CPS data fit both models even with the diagonal included. The Breiger model fits the NLS data for the first-job-to-1967-job transition; the Goodman does not fit this table. Both the Breiger and Goodman tests are rejected for the NLS data for the 1967-to-1977 transition. A

TABLE 7.4

Tests of Partitions of Sex-Type Mobility Tables for Breiger
and Goodman Models

	Breiger Model (df = 39)		Goodman Model (df = 67)	
Data	Partition 1[a] L^{2c}	Partition 2[b] L^{2c}	Partition 1[a] L^{2c}	Partition 2[b] L^{2c}
CPS 1980–1981	29.59	29.32	66.08	58.14
(n = 4,018)	$p < .90$	$p < .90$	$p < .60$	$p < .80$
NLS first job–1967	44.06	52.45	96.79	95.22
(n = 2,342)	$p < .30$	$p < .10$	$p < .01$	$p < .05$
NLS 1967–1977	72.14	49.36	130.42	134.63
(n = 2,167)	$p < .001$	$p = .20$	$p < .001$	$p < .001$

[a]Partition 1 is the three-category partition discussed throughout the chapter. The male-dominated occupations are those 0–29.9 percent women; the sex-neutral occupations are those 30–69.9 percent women; and the female-dominated occupations are those 70–100 percent women.
[b]Partition 2 follows Partition 1 except that the male-dominated category is broader, ranging from 0–39.9 percent women.
[c]L^2 designates the likelihood ratio of goodness of fit.

slightly modified partition, including 0–39.9 percent female occupations in a single male-dominated category, produces an acceptable fit for the Breiger model for all three mobility tables, although the alternative partition produces higher chi-squared statistics for the first NLS table than does the initial partition. No three-category partition produces a fit of the Goodman model for the NLS 1967–77 table.

All contiguous two-category partitions of these tables were tested. There is no such partition that produces an acceptable fit in all three tables for either the Goodman or Breiger model. These tests indicate that a three-category partition of the sex-type mobility table fits the data, but the precise boundary between the male-dominated and sex-neutral category is not entirely consistent across all three tables examined. These results also underscore the utility of the Breiger model in fitting partitions of large mobility tables.

These results indicate the presence of three distinct segments comprising male-dominated, sex-neutral, and female-dominated occupations. Yet the boundaries between these segments are weak, as indicated by the pervasive mobility discussed above. The extent of mobility limits the analytic force of the segmentation model.

Variation in Mobility Patterns

Table 7.5 presents tests of the uniformity of the sex-type mobility table across several dimensions of the occupational structure and for a variety of demographic groups. This analysis is designed to indicate whether the patterns found here apply to a broad range of labor market settings and to individuals with a variety of demographic characteristics.

Log-linear tests of the proposition that sex-type mobility is consistent across these independent variables presented in Table 7.5 models include all two-way relationships but exclude

TABLE 7.5
*Three-Way Log-Linear Models of Sex-Type Mobility
for CPS and NLS Mature Women*

Variable	CPS 1980–1981 ($n = 4,018$)			NLS 1967–1977 ($n = 2,167$)	
	df	L^2	$p <$	L^2	$p <$
Occupation and industry					
Blue-collar vs. white-collar	6.04	4	.20	18.04	.01
Four occupational cate-					
gories[a]	18.57	12	.10	14.84	.30
Economic Sector—Tolbert-					
Beck-Horan Model	3.72	4	.50		
Economic Sector—Bibb-					
Form Model	6.12	4	.20		
Demographic					
Race	5.04	4	.50	6.73	.20
Age	13.64	12	.40	7.45	.20
Education	33.81	16	.01	28.48	.01
Marital and family status	15.35	12	.22	8.22	.80

NOTE: Models fit all two-way relationships, and test whether these relationships vary for the independent variables.
[a]Professional, other white-collar, service, and other blue-collar.

the three-way interaction, namely, the dependence of the sex-type correlation on the independent variable.

The labor market variables examined are the collar-color of occupation; a four-category occupational scheme that contrasts professional and managerial with other white-collar occupations and service with other blue-collar jobs; and the economic sector, as measured both by the Tolbert-Beck-Horan model and the Bibb-Form models (Tolbert, 1982).

The demographic variables examined are race (white vs. nonwhite); age (14–24; 25–34; 35–44; 45+); education completed (1–11 years; 12 years; 13–15 years; 16 years; 17+ years); and marital and family status (ever married with children; never married with children; ever married without children; never married without children).

With the exception of education, each of the tests fits the CPS data, indicating that the pattern of sex-type mobility does not vary with race, age, collar-color, economic sector, or marital and family status. Education interacts with the mobility relationship for both the CPS and the NLS data, but the relationships do not take the same form for these two data sets. The strongest relationship for the CPS data is found for the group with 13–15 years of education; in the NLS data, the group with 1–11 years of schooling has the least mobility. Collar-color does not fit for the NLS data, but it does fit when the diagonal is excluded ($L^2 = 7.8$, $df = 8$), and the more detailed four-category occupational model also fits the data. Similar analysis conducted on the NLS Young Women sample indicated a similar weakness of independent variables in explaining sex-typed mobility patterns.

The effect of a number of other independent variables on the pattern of circulation described here has been examined. A detailed discussion of these results is found elsewhere (Jacobs, 1983a). Other occupational characteristics, such as socioeconomic status and self-employment, were considered. Factors potentially affecting work commitment, including number and ages of children, weeks employed, and hours worked per week, were examined, and other background factors, such as region and urbanism, were studied. None of these variables dramatically altered the pattern of circulation described here. The sex-type correlations for the CPS 1980–81 transition cluster in the range of .05 to .2 for women and men for all subgroups of the above variables. A high degree of sex-type mobility is evident among a broad spectrum of workers at all age levels and in a wide variety of employment settings.

These results indicate the generality of the patterns observed across different occupational settings and for working women with different attributes. For example, the results indicate that it is not simply women's conflict between work and family that is responsible for the mobility patterns observed. The principal self-selection mechanisms emphasized by economists do not account for the sex-type mobility we observe. The sex-type mobility patterns we document are a prevalent, though little recognized, aspect of women's work experiences.

Our analysis has relied on data obtained from large national surveys. Does the same picture emerge from in-depth studies of women in male-dominated occupations? Interviews with women employed in male-dominated jobs reveal a history of previous employment in female-dominated occupations. Typically, women in male-dominated blue-collar jobs have previously held female-dominated clerical or service jobs (Meyer and Lee, 1978; Walshok, 1981; Schroedel, 1985). For white women, clerical jobs are a more common background; for black women, service and low-level factory jobs are more typical precedents (Walshok, 1981). Movement from the more traditionally female, lower-paying jobs to the higher-paying blue-collar jobs is often a matter of opportunity and on-the-job experience. At least 20 of the 25 women in male-dominated blue-collar jobs that Schroedel (1985) interviewed had previous experience in female-dominated jobs. Most had been waitresses, dental assistants, clerical workers, or factory workers, although there were also nurses and teachers who had moved into craft jobs in order to obtain better pay.

Such qualitative studies also suggest that atypical sex-role socialization is not a precondition for entry into male-dominated occupations. Walshok reports that "more than half of the women interviewed indicated no particular prior interest in nontraditional work, and they describe their movement into nontraditional fields as directly related to the appearance of better opportunities" (1981: 138). Thus, while these studies have a very different focus from ours, they report data consistent with the picture portrayed by the large-scale survey data. Many women in male-dominated occupations previously were employed in female-dominated occupations.

Harassment

To what extent may sexual harassment be responsible for the patterns we have observed? Sexual harassment has been shown to cause psychological and emotional problems (Loy and Stewart, 1984; Crull, 1982), loss of motivation (Jensen and Gutek, 1982), lowered job satisfaction (O'Farrell and Harlan, 1982), negative attitudes toward co-workers and supervisors (Gruber and Bjorn, 1982), high absenteeism and turnover (Gutek and Namamura, 1980; U.S. Merit Systems Protection Board, 1981), and a lower sense of job competence (Benson and Thompson, 1982). (For general discussions of harassment, see also MacKinnon, 1979; Tangri, Burt, and Johnson, 1982; and Mc-Caghy, 1985.) Our concern is whether harassment of women on the job is connected to sex segregation. When harassment has the intent or effect of inhibiting women from entering male-dominated occupations or inducing them to leave, then harassment becomes a mechanism of social control that promotes sex segregation in the workplace. Along the internalized-coercive continuum, harassment falls at the coercive extreme. If some women leave male-dominated occupations as a result of harassment, this movement constitutes self-selection, or, more specifically, differential persistence, but hardly the internalization of female norms.

Women in male-dominated occupations report more harassment than women in sex-neutral or female-dominated occupations. Gutek and Morasch (1982) report that 42.7 percent of women in male-dominated jobs had suffered one or more negative consequences of sexual harassment, compared to 30.3 percent of the entire sample. O'Farrell and Harlan (1982) found that 30 percent of women in male-dominated blue-collar jobs said male co-workers gave them a hard time on the job. A third survey reported that as many blue-collar women (20 percent) said that men's attitudes toward them were "definitely accepting" as said that men were "strongly resentful" (Meyer and Lee, 1978). Both co-workers and supervisors are responsible for the harassment of women on the job (Carothers and Crull, 1984; Gutek and Morasch, 1982).

Sexual harassment on the job appears to be experienced by a minority of women (although the figures may well be understated, since they do not include the significant group of women who left such jobs, perhaps at least in part because of harassment). Yet even this minority experience may play a major role in perpetuating the sex segregation of occupations. O'Farrell and Harlan (1982) report that half of the women in white-collar female-dominated occupations who considered moving into blue-collar male-dominated positions expected that they would be subject to harassment. Thus, the fear of harassment may constitute as large a barrier as harassment itself in constraining choices women make regarding their careers.

Different types of harassment are associated with male-dominated and female-dominated positions. Harassment of women in female-dominated occupations often involves unwanted sexual advances and pressure for dates; rejection may result in retaliation that includes the threat of firing. Harassment of women in male-dominated occupations more frequently involves a sexually demeaning work environment, including pinups on walls, sexual jokes, slurs, and unwanted physical contact; it may also involve the sabotage of women's work (Carothers and Crull, 1984). Thus, the harassment of women in male-dominated occupations is more overtly hostile even at the outset than in female-dominated occupations (Carothers and Crull, 1984). Harassment of women in male-dominated occupations also involves the isolation of women and their exclusion from critical informal on-the-job training (O'Farrell and Harlan, 1982; Deaux and Ullman, 1983). If men succeed in undermining women's ability to do their jobs, they achieve the double victory of excluding women and maintaining the view that men's jobs are an extension of their masculinity. Thus, the withholding of informal on-the-job training may be an especially important mechanism for inhibiting women's persistence in male-dominated occupations. Harassment in male-dominated occupations is more a matter of hostility than sexual advances. It is exclusionary.

The direct evidence linking harassment to attrition is thin, but for good reasons. Surveys of women in male-dominated occupations are limited to those who remain; since those who have left are unrepresented, we generally don't know if they left because of harassment. Further, the large longitudinal studies have not probed the area of harassment; if they did, problems of attribution might arise. Nonetheless, Gutek and Morash (1982) report that 9 percent of their total sample quit a job at some point because of sexual harassment, but over 20 percent of women in male-dominated jobs had done so. An additional 9 percent of women in male-dominated occupations had lost a job at some point because of harassment. Many of these women may return to female-dominated domains after experiencing rejection in male-dominated fields. Harassment is a factor before women enter the labor force as well. There is evidence of extensive harassment of women on college campuses (de Cani et al., 1985), which may be connected to the sex segregation of college majors, although this connection has yet to be explored.

Why do men resist the entry of women into male-dominated positions? Both sex-role and economic motives are involved. The sex-role perspective has been developed by Gutek (1985), following the earlier work of Kanter (1977). For Gutek, the workplace is a sexual place, as workers are unable to completely separate the work role from their sex role. Sex roles "spill over" into the workplace, and sex-atypical occupational choices are treated as deviant behavior because they are inconsistent with the constellation of behaviors associated with the male or female sex role. Thus, she argues that the prevalence of sexual harassment in male-dominated occupations is simply a by-product of the sex composition of the job. Because men are predominant, women stand out, and their sex becomes especially salient. Because men in such jobs are used to seeing women in other roles, they are inclined to treat them as mothers, pets, or sex objects. Gutek further argues that women's jobs become sexualized; by their very predominance in such jobs, feminine attributes such as nurturance and flirtation become institutionalized as part of the jobs.

Compatible with Gutek's perspective, but left out of her discussion, is the sexuality that becomes built into male-dominated positions. There are two distinct components to the masculinization of male-dominated jobs. The first is the importance of male camaraderie. The sociological literature on working men has long emphasized the role of camaraderie in coping with the subordination and alienation of the workplace (Gutman, 1977). This companionship is based on competitive banter regarding such masculine topics as sports, cars, and the pursuit of women. Men often feel that they need to alter their behavior in the presence of women. Women are often made to feel outsiders in the effort to preserve the male-based camaraderie of the workplace. Studies of police officers (Martin, 1980; Horne, 1980), steelworkers (Deaux and Ullman, 1983), prison guards (Zimmer, 1985), military enlisted personnel (Holm, 1982), and other blue-collar workers (Walshok, 1981; Schroedel, 1985) show the difficulty of women's entering the informal world of men's work groups.

A second way men's jobs take on a sexual dimension is the definition of the work itself in ways that highlight the masculinity of the job. The association of work with masculinity is seen as a reward in many male-dominated jobs with modest financial rewards and low social status. Martin has suggested that for men in blue-collar positions in particular, "working in an all-male environment reinforces the notion that they are doing 'men's work' and is a highly prized fringe benefit of a job" (1980: 89–90). Informal socializing after work is often a key way to solidify working relationships. Women are often excluded from these settings, and they are consequently hampered in obtaining information they need to do their job and especially to get ahead.

It has been argued that in male-dominated white-collar positions the work itself gives men few opportunities to display their masculinity (Pleck, 1981). In response, men make efforts to symbolize the masculinity of their jobs, taking aggressiveness, logic, and so on as masculine preserves. The presence of women doing the same work threatens these conceptions. While some men might want to work with women, preferring their presence to pinups, the motivation to preserve sex-role boundaries often outweighs this preference. Further, it only takes a minority of men with hostile attitudes to make women feel like outsiders.

In addition to the sex-role motivations for excluding women, important economic incentives exist as well. Men view the presence of women on the job as a threat to their job security and their privileged pay scale. Milkman (1987) and Summerfield (1984) argue that during the Second World War men were quite aware of the economic threat women posed. If women earning lower wages could be substituted for men, men would not regain their jobs after the war was over. And since reserving high-paying jobs helps to bolster men's place in the home, losing these jobs might diminish male power in the home as well. Thus, a complete view of the motivation for the exclusion of women from male-dominated jobs would have to combine economic and sex-role deviance motives.

The blame for the perpetuation of sex segregation should not be placed solely on male workers. As Cohn (1985) and Milkman (1987) have shown, determined management can succeed in bringing women into employment settings over the resistance of male workers. As we discuss in Chapter 8, both male resistance and management acquiescence must be explained.

Physicians: A Case Study

The movement of women into medicine should be a clear counterexample to the general thrust of our analysis. One would expect both socialization and human capital considerations to be highly operative for women physicians. Specifically, one would expect women entering medicine to be highly committed to their careers and therefore to have experienced atypical sex-role socialization. Because medicine requires extensive training, one would not expect a large number of people to move into medicine in midcareer. Further, one would expect doctors to be unlikely to change fields, given the high levels of investment in training required. Thus, both the midcareer entry and extensive field switching we have observed among women throughout the labor force should be most unlikely in medicine. If there is evidence of these patterns in the medical profession, it would constitute strong evidence of the general applicability of the model we have considered here.

Let us first consider the role of socialization in inhibiting women's entrance into medical school. Cole (1986) argues that women's internalization of their sex-role socialization experiences resulted in low rates of medical school application by women until recent years. In fact, Cole argues, medical schools have not discriminated against women for most of this century. Yet Cole claims more for his analysis than he can document. In particular, his claim that because women "internalized the societal attitudes toward sex-appropriate careers, in the past there were very few women who were interested in becoming physicians" (1986: 550) is more than his data can support. In fact, the social control model of sex segregation developed here applies to women's entrance into medicine. A careful examination of the mechanisms of social control and the timing and adaptability of women's attitudes will provide a more realistic picture of the development of career plans.

While Cole says he is not testing for the presence of discrimination either before or after medical school admission, he proposes that young women's "internalization" of values is responsible for their low rates of applying to medical school. Cole infers socialization from behavior (the low number of women applying to medical school) and has no independent measure of it, nor of the timing of its formation.

Yet there is evidence that the low application rates of women were as much a matter of obstacles placed in women's way as their internalization of a norm regarding women's place. Many young women wanted to pursue a career in medicine and had to be actively discouraged from doing so. External constraints on women's choice of a medical career included the reluctance of parents to pay for medical education for their daughters (Morantz-Sanchez, 1985), the unwillingness of banks to extend educational loans to women medical school students (Phillips, 1981), the discouragement of guidance counselors (Walsh, 1977), and the difficulty of obtaining internships and residencies for women medical school graduates (Morantz-Sanchez, 1985; Walsh, 1977). Many women who aspired to medical school as they entered college were actively discouraged from attending, and the proportion that applied was far lower than the proportion that aspired to medical careers as college freshmen. In the college class of 1961 sample discussed in Chapter 6, 432 women and 2,190 men expressed a serious interest in medicine at some point during their college careers. Yet over a third of the men—35.4 percent—entered medical school after graduation, versus only 7.4 percent of the women. The sex differences in attrition during the senior year are particularly striking. Only half—50.8 percent—of the women who said they intended to be doctors were enrolled in medical school the following year, versus three-quarters—76.5 percent—of the men. Thus, many college women aspired to medical careers during college and were "cooled out" before graduation at a much higher rate than men.[4] Women had to be discouraged from applying to medical school; indeed, the very existence of such active social control indicates that young women did not completely internalize the view that medicine was incompatible with motherhood and feminine identity. Cole's data do not allow him to distinguish whether these external constraints or the internalization of sex-role values by young women themselves was responsible for the low rate of applications.

Further, there is evidence in Cole's own data that supports the view that opportunity, not socialization, determined women's interest in medicine. In two key periods Cole's data suggest that a clear signal concerning the accessibility of medicine as a career for women dramatically increased applications. If women responded when it became clear that unfettered opportunities were available, then one must conclude that the constraints of restrictive sex-role socialization require the extra force of limited opportunities to be effective.

During the Second World War, the Johnson-Sparkman Bill, which made women physicians commissioned officers in the armed services, increased the attractiveness of medical careers to women (Morantz-Sanchez, 1985; Walsh, 1977). The shortage of male physicians also resulted in a dramatic increase in the accessibility of civilian medical internships and residencies to women. Walsh reports that in 1942, 463 internships were open to women, an increase of 440 percent over 1941, although this meant that nearly half of the nation's hospitals remained closed to women physicians. Thus, through both military and civilian avenues, the war represented an important expansion of the career prospects for women physicians. The number of women medical graduates more than doubled between 1945 and 1949. Given the four-year lag between entry and graduation, the timing of women's increased interest in medicine coincides with the increase in opportunities for women generated by the war.

The second episode is the sharp increase in women medical school applicants after the Title IX Amendments to the Higher Education Act of 1972 prohibited sex discrimination in medical school admissions. In the ensuing five years, the number of women medical applicants nearly tripled. This increase in attendance constitutes evidence that opportunity generates interest. The increases in these two periods occurred too rapidly to reflect changes in early socialization. If changes in the latter were responsible for the trends in women's applications to medical school, we would observe a much longer lag. It is incumbent on those advocating the socialization view to measure specific aspects of early socialization and to correlate changes in the socialization of young women with changes in education and career behavior. Indeed, it is much more plausible to argue that when the active discouragement of women declined, or declined in its effectiveness, as a result of the pressures brought to bear by the women's movement, women responded accordingly by increasing their applications to medical school.

Let us now turn to medical careers, with a particular focus on the specialties men and women pursue (see Lorber, 1984, for an overview of career obstacles faced by women). Internally, medicine is less segregated than the labor force as a whole. In 1982, 26.7 percent of women would have had to change specialties in order to be distributed in the same manner as men (measured across 34 specialty fields). This figure has declined gradually since 1970, when the index of dissimilarity measured across the same fields was 34.0, falling to 31.1 in 1975 and 27.5 in 1980 (calculated from data published by the American Medical Association, 1983). The number of women physicians has jumped from 25,401 in 1970 to 64,247 in 1982, and the proportion of physicians who are women rose from 6.6 percent in 1970 to 12.8 percent in 1982. Medicine is not currently experiencing a phenomenon of resegregation, a pattern evident in some other occupations (Reskin, 1987).

There is evidence of midcareer movement into medicine. In 1982, nearly 10.8 percent of women physicians who had graduated from medical school since 1970 did so at age 30 or over, compared with 7.4 percent of men. Women were thus more likely than men to enter medical school after some interruptions in their education. These statistics were calculated from individual-level data on over 400,000 physicians. The data constitute selected variables from the AMA Physician Masterfile, 1978 and 1982, provided by the American Medical Association, and were analyzed as part of a study of the career patterns of physicians. While the influx of women into medicine overwhelmingly reflects the entry of young women into the profession, midcareer mobility into medicine is nonetheless part of the story. The increased accessibility of careers as physicians for women influenced those in their twenties and thirties, despite the lengthy process of training. The delayed entrance of women into medicine bolsters the view outlined above that women respond to the availability of opportunities.

Individual-level patterns of mobility constitute even stronger support for the framework proposed here. While attrition rates of women physicians are low and have declined over time, there is a surprising degree of interspecialty mobility. Between 1978 and 1982, 18 percent of active women physicians changed the primary specialty in which they were working (see also Matteson and Smith, 1977). Given this mobility, we can examine the connection between the sex composition of initial and destination fields of specialty for women physicians who change their fields, just as we have done across occupations for women in the labor force as a whole.

The sex-type correlation of women physicians who changed fields between 1978 and 1982 was .35 ($n = 4,203$). This relationship is higher than we have observed in the labor force as a whole, but still surprisingly modest. There is movement of women from male-dominated specialties, as well as a pattern of delayed entry into such specialties. This pattern represents in the microcosm of the medical profession the same pattern of career circulation we have seen in the labor force as a whole. Given the improbability of medicine matching the general patterns we have observed, this evidence regarding individual patterns of movement is striking support for the general proposition we have outlined here. Medicine fits the model proposed here surprisingly well. The social control perspective is useful for analyzing applications to medical school, delayed entrance into the medical profession, and the changing of fields by established physicians.

Lawyers: A Case Study

Law is another high-status male-dominated profession that should serve as a counterexample to our framework. As law requires lengthy and expensive preparation, one would expect little midcareer entry and even less exit. Any evidence that the processes of social control described here exist in the legal context would lend support to the proposed framework.

As in the case of medicine, we will be looking for three developments in particular. First, as more women enter the field of law, is there evidence of internal resegregation? Second, has progress come solely from a cohort of young new entrants, or is there evidence of delayed or midcareer entrance? Third, is there evidence of continued discrimination resulting in some career shifts, especially out of male-dominated specialties?

The entry of women into law has been taken as a prominent sign of change in the status of women in society. Indeed, the efforts of women lawyers to fight discrimination throughout the labor force may be responsible for some of the occupational advancement women have experienced in recent years. Women represented 13.1 percent of lawyers in 1985, in contrast to 2.5 percent in 1951. Of lawyers under age 29 in 1985, 24.4 percent were women (Curran, 1985, 1986). By 1983, women represented over one-third of those accepted to law school. The growth of women lawyers in absolute numbers is even more striking, from less than 6,000 in 1951 to nearly 44,000 in 1980 and over 85,000 in 1985. In assessing these changes, several important facts should be kept in mind. First, this dramatic growth in women's presence is occurring in the context of a rapidly expanding legal profession. The number of lawyers has nearly tripled, from 220,000 in 1951 to 655,000 in 1985. Women are sharing disproportionately in the growth of the legal profession, but they are hardly displacing male lawyers. Second, these numbers are small relative to the size of the female labor force. The 85,000 women lawyers represents a mere 0.2 percent of the female labor force. Thus, women's rapid entry into the legal profession makes only a small dent in the overall statistics on occupational segregation by sex. Finally, on a more humbling note, as of 1986, 45 percent of male lawyers still worked in firms with no women lawyers (Reidinger, 1986).

The progress of women in the law has not yet been offset by a corresponding resegregation within the profession. Women in the law historically have been segregated from men in two ways: by location of practice and by specialty. Although data on both types of segregation are spotty, the limited evidence that is available is inconsistent with the resegregation thesis. Data on the first jobs of law school graduates in 1955–56 indicated a level of segregation across employment setting of 18.7 (data drawn from White, 1967). Recent indicators are similar in magnitude. In 1980, the women lawyers who had entered the profession prior to 1971 were mildly segregated by type of practice from their male counterparts ($D = 16.8$), while younger entrants were similarly segregated ($D = 15.8$) (Curran, 1985; categories are similar but not identical to White's). By 1985, the corresponding figures were 9.7 for the cohort over age 40 and 12.5 for the younger cohort, a decline in segregation for both younger and older women. Thus, during this recent period when the number of women lawyers nearly doubled, the segregation across settings within the profession declined for both older and younger women lawyers.

Quantitative measures of specialty, both current and historical, are also hard to come by. The earliest figures available are based on the data collected by White in 1965. Two analyses of the level of segregation evident in White's sample, based on eight and ten fields of specialization, produced indices of segregation of 14.9 and 18.4 respectively. The indices would likely have been higher if more detailed specialties were listed. Recent figures were obtained from a reanalysis of two tabulations of state bar association membership. An index of segregation calculated across 19 specialties of Michigan Bar Association affiliates using 1984 data was 21.9 (*Michigan Bar Journal*, 1984). A similarly calculated measure for 30 specialties for Illinois State Bar Association members revealed an even lower index of 16.3 (data drawn from Bruno, 1986). The current indices of segregation across specialty are roughly of the same magnitude as those found before the surge of women into the legal profession. Thus, the limited available evidence does not reveal any trend toward a resegregation of the legal profession.

The entrance of women into the law would be expected to take the form of a cohort replacement process: integration occurs as new cohorts of women enter the profession. Indeed, if there were a case we would expect to fit the cohort replacement model perfectly, it would be a high-status profession such as the law. Yet even here there is evidence of delayed and midcareer entry by women who have set new goals as a result of the recent reevaluation of women's roles stirred by the women's movement. One recent survey reported that over one-third of women entering law school were over 25, and 17 percent were over 30. Nearly one-third of the women were 30 or older when they entered the bar, compared to 15 percent of the men (Winter, 1983). Another report noted that nearly 4 percent of women entering law school were over 40, twice the number (and four times the rate) of men in this age bracket (*New York Times*, 1986).

Some of these women had raised families while others worked in female-dominated positions as teachers or social workers. Women entering law school as a second career even became typical in some law schools (Epstein, 1981). Delayed entry surely makes rising to the top of the profession more difficult, but it indicates the importance of continued social control in limiting the entry of women into male-dominated professions. Delayed entrance reveals that social control continues well into adult life; as such social control is contested, even women who grew up with a much more limited set of choices grasp the new opportunities available to them. Thus, as Epstein concludes, "The opening up of opportunities proved immediately effective in creating interest. And, contrary to popular myths, it was not necessary for women to go through long years of 'resocialization,' retraining, or reorientation to prepare for their new roles" (1981: 380).

Nor has social control during the career completely dissipated. Significant obstacles and discrimination remain in the way of women lawyers. One prominent indication of this is the continued disproportionate attrition of women from law firms. Numerous surveys have indicated that women do not attain partnership at rates comparable to their male counterparts (McNamara, 1986; Liefland, 1986; Frank, 1985; Abramson and Franklin, 1986). While some of this discrepancy is undoubtedly due to family demands, there is nonetheless significant evidence of discrimination (Simon and Gardner, 1981). Liefland (1986) reports that 11.2 percent of women reported discrimination as one of the reasons they left their first law jobs. A minority of women associates continue to report that men are given more "choice" assignments and more responsibility, leading to greater prospects for advancement (Winter, 1983). Thus, the most male-dominated and most lucrative centers of the legal profession—the large corporate firms—maintain their male dominance by inducing the selective attrition of female associates.

The continuing obstacles facing women in the law do not

come simply, or even principally, from their employers. Discriminatory treatment of women lawyers by judges, opposing counsel, courtroom staff, and administrative personnel remains common (Shrager, 1985; Frank, 1985; N.Y. State Task Force, 1986). Even male lawyers report continued sexist remarks by members of their own, and especially other, firms (Reidinger, 1986). Discrimination arises from many sources, although clear legal standards regarding discrimination, and the sensitivity of lawyers to the prospect of suits, has clearly limited certain types of discrimination. In conclusion, even in the unlikely context of the legal profession, career patterns influenced by the lifelong social control processes discussed throughout this book are evident.

Discussion

This chapter has documented a significant amount of career movement between female-dominated, sex-neutral, and male-dominated occupations. The observed levels of movement approach those that would be predicted by chance. For women occupation changers, the chances of ending up in a given sex-type category are virtually independent of the sex-type category in which the woman started. This pattern is evident for women of all age groups in the labor force; it is almost as true for men occupation changers of all age groups. It characterizes workers in a broad spectrum of occupations and from a wide variety of backgrounds. The pattern of mobility documented here parallels the sex-type mobility of young women discussed in Chapter 4. This evidence points in the same direction as that found in two recent investigations of movement between male-dominated and female-dominated occupations (Corcoran, Duncan, and Ponza, 1984; Rosenfeld, 1983).

The substantial degree of mobility between men's and women's occupations should not be misinterpreted as evidence of equal opportunity. Women work in men's occupations in limited numbers. Given these limited numbers, the chances of entry and exit are close to what one would expect by chance.

Movement between these categories is not substantially more limited than the overall distribution of men and women would predict. In other words, women occupation changers are only slightly more restricted in moving into men's occupations than women who are starting their careers.

Perhaps most striking is the mobility of women from male-dominated occupations to sex-neutral and female-dominated occupations. A large proportion of women in male-dominated occupations leave male-dominated fields altogether when they change occupations. In 1977, 50 percent of women who had been in male dominated occupations in 1967 were employed in sex-neutral or female-dominated occupations. Among women who had changed occupations in this period, over 80 percent who had been in male-dominated occupations in 1967 had left by 1977. The data suggest that employment in female-dominated occupations constitutes less of a barrier for women than might have been expected by labor market segmentation theorists. However, the data also indicate that employment in male-dominated occupations is less of a permanent achievement for women that might have been expected.

This evidence can be viewed as describing the pattern by which the sex segregation of occupations is reproduced. This pattern is one of revolving door mobility between men's and women's occupations. The low year-to-year sex-type correlations indicate that individuals are not locked into the sex-type of the occupations in which they begin their careers. For the large group of occupation changers, the sex-types of initial and subsequent occupations are only slightly related.

This finding questions the applicability of labor market segmentation explanations of occupational segregation by sex. We have seen how both the internal labor market thesis and the segregation as segmentation thesis hinge on the infrequency of mobility between male-dominated and female-dominated occupations. We have shown that the assumption these approaches make is not accurate. More detailed data on movement within firms may bolster the internal labor market thesis, but this will not completely invalidate current results. If the sex-type mobility documented here does not occur within internal labor markets, then the present data show how frequently these internal channels are circumvented.

The segmentation approach is not the only one that assumes there is little career mobility between male-dominated and female-dominated occupations. As we have seen, this assumption applies equally to the human capital and the sex-role socialization perspectives. In the language of mobility tables, the study of sex segregation to date has assumed that the sex-type mobility table was concentrated on the main diagonal; to explain the marginal distributions was to explain the career patterns as well. In other words, if the occupational system is highly segregated by sex, then the careers of individual women will inevitably be tracked into narrow sex-typed channels. The data presented here show that in fact there is a good deal of occupational mobility. Theories of sex segregation will need to take this fact into account.

A general perspective on sex segregation compatible with the data discussed here must emphasize the importance of career experiences. The interest of women in entering male-dominated occupations is not difficult to explain; the exit of women from male-dominated occupations is the counterintuitive result calling for an explanation. While discrimination in hiring undoubtedly is a major factor in restricting the access to women to male-dominated occupations, those women who succeed in obtaining such employment face a host of reminders on the job that they are less than welcome. A great deal has been written about the difficulties women face once they enter what were previously male bastions (Walshok, 1981; Meyer and Lee, 1978; Epstein, 1981; Roos and Reskin, 1984). Kanter (1977) makes a case for the role of proportions in general and token status in particular. We have seen continual pressure on women who seek to pursue male-dominated occupations, with attrition evident in the aspiration and education stages as well as on the job.

Kanter's approach is consistent with the social control framework developed here. The pressures Kanter analyzes may account for the reluctance of women to persist in male-dominated settings. While recent evidence suggests that women in male-

dominated occupations do not experience higher job turnover rates than men (Waite and Berryman, 1985), we document
a higher rate of occupation change for women in male-
dominated occupations and show that women who leave a
male-dominated occupation are unlikely to enter another male-
dominated occupation. Research following up Kanter's hypothesis has generally focused on the behavioral consequences
for minorities (Spangler, Gordon, and Pipkin, 1978; Alexander
and Thoits, 1986); the implications for attrition and mobility
patterns have not been explored. Indeed, one possible reason
for the inconsistent empirical tests of Kanter's hypothesis is
that these studies have not controlled for attrition rates (Jacobs,
1986b).

Career experiences thus may be crucial in determining the
career destinations of individual women and in perpetuating a
stable system of segregation by sex. The revolving door pattern
of movement between male-dominated and female-dominated
occupations is the final stage in a lifelong system that serves to
maintain the structure of occupational sex segregation.

It should be noted that the same circulation is evident for
men. Many men work at some point in occupations in which
women are numerically predominant. But they tend to leave
these occupations, creating room for more men to enter.
Female-dominated occupations remain so heavily dominated
by women in part because so few men enter these occupations,
and in part because those men that enter tend to leave. This
evidence suggests that there are problems inherent in holding
sex-atypical occupational roles (Jacobs and Powell, 1984). In
some ways, men in female-dominated occupations experience
the same difficulties that women in male-dominated occupations face.

For those interested in increasing women's employment in
male-dominated occupations, these results have a positive side
and a negative side. The positive side is that there is more access
for women into male-dominated occupations than one might
have otherwise thought. Women who change occupations can
and often do enter men's occupations. The negative side is that
there is more attrition of women from male-dominated oc-

cupations than one might have expected. A large proportion of women in men's occupations leave male-dominated fields entirely when they change occupations. These two processes— access and attrition—go hand in hand to produce the revolving door pattern of mobility.

These results thus support our social control / revolving door model of sex segregation. The occupational mobility patterns described here strongly resemble the patterns of mobility we observed for aspirations and college majors. Without the pressure of social controls that results in the attrition of women from male-dominated occupations, the structure of sex segregation would be collapsing much more rapidly than it has in recent years.

8

Economic Theory and

Sex Segregation

Throughout this book, we have contrasted the social control perspective with two principal alternatives: the socialization view, which emphasizes the acquisition of values early in life, and the human capital framework, which emphasizes rational self-selection of women into female-dominated occupations. We have noted a number of empirical inconsistencies between our results and the predictions of human capital theory. The instability of behavior for individuals points against human capital explanations, as does the wide age distribution of change observed in aggregate trends.

Although the human capital perspective imputes a lifelong rationality to educational decisions and early occupational choices, these choices are remarkably unstable over time. Whereas economists expect people to make decisions that maximize their expected lifetime utility, we have emphasized short-term decision making that is responsive to social pressure and the extent of available opportunities. The general instability of the sex-typing of aspirations, educational tracks, and career behavior is strong evidence against a lifetime utility-maximizing model.

The long-term stability of sex segregation cannot be attributed to the labor supply characteristics of women. Sex seg-

regation cannot be pinned on the stable attributes individuals
bring with them to the labor market, because these attributes
are less stable than assumed, both before and after labor market
entry. The short-term instability of individuals' behavior and
its responsiveness to labor force trends and the social climate
are strong evidence against this perspective. These findings
suggest that as discrimination is relaxed, women are more than
willing to move into a broad range of occupational roles from
which they had previously been excluded. This evidence suggests that it is not the lack of interest or "taste" for work
in male-dominated occupations that is the cause of women's
underrepresentation.

This reasoning is similar to the response social demographers
have made to economic models of fertility decisions. Whereas
economists assume that decisions about the timing and level
of fertility fit into an optimum lifetime framework, sociologists have emphasized the fact that these decisions are made
with reference to short-term considerations. Rindfuss, Morgan,
and Swicegood (1988) have shown that respondents are reasonably reliable informants about their fertility plans in the short
run but are quite unreliable in predicting their own fertility behavior as much as two to five years in advance. Period effects in
fertility decision making also contradict the economic model
of rational lifetime decision making, as they indicate sensitivity to contemporary values and not simply to conditions in
evidence at crucial early junctures in one's life. Our social control perspective differs from the demographic perspective in
that we emphasize coercive influences on women, and not
simply changes in values, as being responsible for the patterns
we observe.

At a number of points, our empirical findings are inconsistent with the predictions of the human capital framework. Yet
there is a need to go beyond a pure empirical critique of the human capital perspective. It is difficult if not impossible to dis-
prove this perspective with empirical evidence. The resistance
to empirical counterevidence is not solely attributable to the
resourcefulness of the advocates of this position, nor to their
ideological commitment, although undoubtedly each of these

plays a role. Rather, what is probably most fundamental is the commitment to the view that competitive markets inevitably reduce and eventually eliminate wage differentials that are unrelated to productivity. Thus, if sex segregation results in women being paid less than men, economists reason either that productivity differences are lurking in the background or that wage differentials are soon to be rectified by the unimpeded workings of the marketplace.

The question of efficiency leads us inevitably to the economics of labor markets. No matter what evidence one musters to support the presumption of nonrational (discriminatory) economic behavior, one will meet a degree of skepticism in certain quarters unless one confronts the argument that the competitive market system roots out discriminatory behavior. Yet strictly economic arguments need not arrive at the conclusion that competition will undermine discrimination. In this chapter we show that the logic of labor markets is not inconsistent with the persistence of discrimination over the long run. If one incorporates a number of longstanding findings from the sociology of work and organizations into a strict economic framework and extends the reasoning of certain recent economic models, the relatively long-term compatibility of discrimination and efficiency can be understood. The opposite assumption of most labor market economics rests on implausible assumptions about the nature of the work process. Thus, while competitive markets surely exist and exert serious constraints on the behavior of employers and employees, one can nonetheless understand the endurance of many discriminatory practices once one recognizes certain fundamental aspects of the organization of work.

Competition and Discrimination

A principal theorem in labor market economics is that competition will tend to eliminate inefficient organizational forms and workplace practices. The marketplace constantly drives producers to cut costs, and labor costs are likely to be high on

the list. Firms seek to devise and copy procedures that minimize production costs for a given level of output.

One of the implications of this view is that discrimination
will tend to be eradicated by the pressures of the market. Discrimination implies wage differentials between groups: if an
employer can hire a woman for less than a man to do the same
job, the employer will profit by doing so. Others will follow,
however, bidding up women's wages until no wage differential
remains. This view of discrimination implies that discrimination is costly to employers, that one must pay a price for in-
dulging one's "taste" for discrimination (Becker, 1957). This
view predicts the persistence of sex segregation only in those
types of work uniquely suited to one sex or the other.

But, as we have seen, sex segregation has declined quite
slowly over much of the century. The market seems slow to
promote the integration of men and women at work. Perhaps a
more conventional measure of discrimination is the gender gap
in wages. Estimates of wage discrimination indicate the persistence of this phenomenon. A recent thorough reappraisal of
this literature has concluded that while labor market theory
predicts the decline of discrimination, the empirical literature
continues to measure substantial residuals between men and
women after all measurable economically relevant attributes
of men and women are taken into account, residuals that are
typically taken as indicators of the extent of discrimination.
Madden (1985) finds studies of wage differences between men
and women typically explaining between 30 and 40 percent of
the gap, and she is critical of the methodology of those studies
that explain more than 50 percent of the gap.[1]

It is sometimes argued that the procedure of attributing residual effects to discrimination unfairly treats all measurement error, omitted variables, and model misspecification as
proof of discrimination. However, as Madden points out, much
of what is controlled for in these equations may be tapping discriminatory practices. For example, differences in experience
always explain a portion of the wage gap between men and
women. But the extent to which experience is a proxy for productivity is debatable. Surely, at the start of one's career, more

experience enhances productivity, but it is far from clear that the age-productivity profile parallels the age-earnings profile (Medoff and Abraham, 1981). Thus, one of the standard variables that accounts for a portion of the gender gap in wages is arguably a proxy for age discrimination rather than sex-related productivity differences. Some of the reasoning discussed below suggests a rational explanation for such an age-graded system, even though it interferes with the match of productivity and earnings.

In the human capital view, the explanation for differential labor market outcomes for men and women must be found on the supply side, not on the demand side. The differential socialization of women leads them to be less committed to the labor market and to train less extensively for male-dominated careers. Thus, economists assume the existence of stable social-psychological traits that lead women to choose female-dominated occupations. Our evidence has suggested that such "tastes" are not very stable and change when new opportunities arise.

A variety of economic arguments have been put forward to explain the persistence of discrimination, none of which satisfactorily explains how discrimination can persist in the face of market forces to the contrary. Economic theory has always held that discrimination on the part of employees is a possible explanation for discriminatory behavior on the part of employers. If co-workers refuse to work with members of a minority group or with women, or will do so only if offered a wage premium, then employers may minimize labor costs by discriminating. This theory is attractive to some because it absolves employers of the responsibility of discrimination. Yet it is deficient in that it still predicts the ultimate demise of discrimination.

The scenario this view implies is that, on the hiring or threat of hiring women, some men leave or threaten to leave, unless duly compensated. But if some men will work for the same amount along with women who work for less, the employer will profit despite the discriminating employees. And if the discriminating employees were to move to a firm where men's discriminatory behavior is tolerated, they would over time lose market share and eventually their jobs, as the firm's higher labor costs would cause them to become unprofitable. This case is no different from the others: discrimination costs those who discriminate.

Signaling theory proposes that employers minimize information costs by using average group characteristics to measure likely productivity: if a group is presumed to be lower on the average in education, motivation, or other relevant characteristics, employers rationally discriminate against the entire group in order to avoid the costs associated with mistakes and the information costs associated with discovering exceptions to the general pattern (Arrow, 1972; Spence, 1974). Yet employers who find inexpensive ways to identify women or minority group members who are likely to be productive would profit, thus raising the question of why employers do not devise low-cost ways of obtaining information about prospective employees rather than discriminate against them all.

Labor market segmentation theory has also been proposed as a way of explaining the persistence of labor market outcomes that are unrelated to differences in employee productivity. As we saw in Chapter 7, labor markets are held to be divided into sectors, one of large firms with a substantial degree of market power, and the other of small firms in more competitive industries. For segmentation theory as for other approaches, one must ask how noneconomic distinctions persist in the face of market conditions. In this context, one would ask why the primary-sector firms don't hire secondary-sector workers at lower wages, thus increasing their profit margins. If they did so, the line between these sectors would shift to the point at which wages reflected productivity, again eliminating discriminatory outcomes. While it is true that large firms with substantial market power are not as vulnerable as other firms, they nevertheless act vigorously to increase their profits. Indeed, there is evidence of career mobility across these sectoral boundaries (Jacobs, 1983a; Jacobs and Breiger, forthcoming).

Another radical approach to the study of discrimination holds that employers encourage discrimination and enflame ethnic and racial hostility. There is clear evidence in coal mining, steel production, and Hawaiian agriculture that such a strategy has been employed by management to inhibit unionization and to minimize labor costs (Brody, 1970; Lind, 1982; Gutman, 1977). Yet such a strategy is most effective in a monopsonist situation, where one or several large employers are dominant and employ a substantial fraction of the work force. Without such a situation, we return to the classic problem: it may be in the class interest of capital to divide and conquer workers, but it is in the individual interest of employers to minimize their wage bill. If each employer hired women or minorities at lower wages, eventually wage differentials would disappear and competitive equilibrium would be attained.

Another argument suggests that sex segregation is a form of discrimination that persists because employers, as men, have an interest in maintaining the subordination of women. Thus Strober specifically argues that "male employers are not strictly profit maximizers . . . there is a tension between patriarchy and profit maximization" (Strober, 1984: 147). While the impulse to discriminate may exist on the part of male employers, one needs to show that they are able to collectively attain this goal. In short, men may collectively want to maintain privilege, but if individual managers make more money by hiring women at lower wages, the wage gap will eventually be undermined and men's collective goal will be thwarted.

We propose three ways of employing economic arguments to predict the maintenance of discriminatory practices. The goal is to show that the logic of rational individual choice and competitive market behavior on which labor economics is based is consistent with the persistence of discriminatory behavior. We will then be free to consider the possibility of discriminatory behavior as an explanation for the career patterns of women. These arguments are (1) feedback from historical discrimination; (2) implicit contracts / efficiency wage limitations on employers' cost-minimization strategies; and (3) workplace interactions that limit the efficiency of victims of discrimination.

Home Economics and Historical Discrimination

The first argument is that feedback from past discrimination can result in its persistence over time. This argument has been made in various ways by Madden (1985), England and Farkas (1986), and others. The economic foundation for this feedback mechanism derives from the new family economics. Gary Becker (1981) has proposed a major extension of economic analysis in the area of the investment and consumption decisions within the family. The new home economics has developed formal models for investments in skills and activities within the home. This reasoning highlights the rationality of choices made by family members. Becker argues that economic analysis is likely to be fruitful in giving new insight into marriage patterns, the household division of labor, and the investment in children.

Becker argues that families will seek to maximize their returns by investing in their children in a way that will maximize total earnings potential. Thus, if sons are likely to earn more than daughters, families will invest more in their sons' educations in order to maximize the income potential in the second generation. We suggest that this reasoning incorporates the effects of current discrimination in such a way as to perpetuate discriminatory returns.

Current labor market patterns are used by individuals facing the labor market as the basis for choices. If school-age young women see that no women are currently employed in certain fields, they will avoid such areas or underinvest in the skills required to pursue such a career. In economic terms, if discrimination plays a role at time 1, labor supply will shift so that at time 2 women obtain fewer skills than would otherwise be rational. Even if there were no discrimination at time 1 but merely a different set of technology or different social values (such as a higher social priority given to women's family obligations), to the extent that this information is used as the basis for the career aspirations and educational decisions of daughters, then it will tend to persist over time. The new home economics thus gives a firm economic foundation for the role of discrimination persisting over time. In other terms, differential socialization of boys and girls may be economically rational from the family's point of view, but it has long-term deleterious consequences for women. This argument is a supply-side argument, but it demonstrates the possibility of the persistence of discrimination because it highlights present discrimination as a powerful determinant of future labor supply. Feeding information based on discriminatory market behaviors into rational family decision-making processes can enable this discrimination to persist.

How does this reasoning square with our empirical findings? As we have suggested, sex differences in career expectations by themselves appear to be insufficient to maintain occupational sex segregation because they are so unstable, but they are surely one component of an explanation. We have seen that different expectations have not led women to invest fewer years in higher education than men, but they may be related to their choice of college major. Further, the discrimintory feedback view is fully consistent with our results that suggest that when signals change, careers change, not only for new entrants but for those already in the labor market.

A public change in values can help to short-circuit this cycle. The women's movement may be credited with initiating changes in the expectations of women as well as in the attitudes of employers. We have emphasized changes in general social controls that channel women into female-dominated occupations. As we suggested in Chapter 6, some of these changes are due to the rise of the women's movement. The women's movement's highlighting of women's labor force attachment may have encouraged women to pursue additional training and may have helped persuade employers that women can be expected to be committed to their jobs. Thus, the timing of the women's movement coincides with the changes in higher education and labor force behavior we have observed (our attitudinal data do not extend far back enough to test the timing of this change).

Economists do not model such factors as the women's movement in explaining change. To the extent that they examine it, they look at the extent to which legislation that resulted from the women's movement can be linked to changes in labor market outcomes (Beller, 1982a). Yet social movements serve important informational and symbolic as well as political roles. Social movements do not only strive for political goals but also seek to raise public awareness of the grievances of a group. This emphasis is consistent with new views of contemporary social movements that stress their symbolic as well as concrete political goals (Melucci, 1985).

Implicit Contracts, Efficiency Wage Theory, and Stable Employment Conditions

The second argument is that new developments within labor economics itself, properly extended, provide a firm basis for believing in the persistence of institutional practices, including discrimination. Implicit contracts theory has been developed to explain the "stickiness" of wages in the face of economic downturns, as well as the length of employment tenures. The core idea is that a range of labor market behavior can be understood if employers and employees are assumed to make informal, implicit contracts about the length of employment (Rosen, 1985; England and Farkas, 1986).

Regarding the length of employment, the implicit contracts argument is that employers will invest in firm-specific skills only when they have reason to believe that they will be able to reap the returns on those investments. Thus it is in the interests of both the employer and the employee to develop an understanding that the term of employment will be a lengthy one, so that the long-term interests of both will benefit.

The implicit contracts approach has a number of important implications that bear on questions of discrimination. First, implicit contracts require stable employment practices on the part of firms. Why don't employers provide explicit contracts regarding the tenure of employees, rather than rely on unstated agreements? The reason, presumably, is to maintain flexibility in the face of uncertainty. Then why should employees trust the firm to continue to employ them? Clearly, the trust of employees is decisive in the implicit contracts scenario, for crucial career decisions rely on the expectations of future behavior on the part of the firm.

The only way such a trust can be established in an implicit contracts setting is by a history of consistent employment practices. To develop solid expectations on the part of employees, companies must act in a consistent manner over time. The first crucial implication of the implicit contracts framework, then, is that it limits the flexibility of the company in altering labor practices in the short run. Most important, it limits decisions regarding layoffs because of the clear and present danger such layoffs imply for those who are investing heavily in firm-specific skills. Thus, the implicit contracts framework suggests that firms cannot minimize costs in the short run because of the danger to employee confidence and, in turn, to future employee productivity-related investments.

This reasoning leads to a broadening of the implications of the implicit contracts approach. Given that the implicit contract between firm and employee depends on employee confidence, a wide range of personnel-related practices have the potential to undermine employee confidence. Thus, it is not merely the length of the contract that the employee may be counting on, but the maintenance of work conditions and pay differentials. Industrial sociologists and institutional economists have accumulated evidence for decades on the priority given by workers to such concerns. Thus, the implicit contracts framework may well constrain employers in the short run in hiring as well as in a range of personnel decision-making areas.

There is a great deal in the sociology of work literature to suggest that pay differentials are as important to workers as employment security (Berg, Freedman, and Freedman, 1978). A deliberate policy of sexual integration to reduce pay differentials between positions is likely to be resisted by male workers and viewed by them as a violation of the implicit terms of their long-term work contract. As we saw in Chapter 7, men derive symbolic as well as economic benefits from an all-male work force. The implicit contracts view can thus be extended to suggest that employers are limited in their cost-minimization efforts because of their need to maintain the good will of their employees, on which their mutually beneficial long-term contracts depend. Implicit contracts increase the power of employees to influence the conditions of employment, and the race and sex of co-workers are likely to be among the conditions they seek to influence. In short, the implicit contract may presume an all-male work force.

Not only investment in future skills but also current morale and current productivity are affected by the personnel practices of firms. For present as well as future labor productivity, consistent and reliable behavior on the part of the firm is important.

This last argument resonates with another area of economic theorizing, the recently proposed "efficiency wage" perspective. Bulow and Summers (1986) have argued that firms do not always try to minimize wages. At times, firms pay wages above the market rate so that employees will be motivated to work hard to defend their economic "rents." Wage minimization is not always consistent with maximizing return on investment because the latter depends on effectively motivating workers. The incremental wages produce more than enough extra output to pay for themselves. Essentially, workers may be paid above their replacement wage in order to encourage commitment and efficiency.

This reasoning may account for the structure of internal labor markets that has been observed by institutional economists and sociologists of the labor market for some time. This model implies that workers compete for positions that themselves influence the productivity of workers (Thurow, 1975). It can be extended to account for discrimination by employers: employers willing to pay efficiency wages will not seek employees willing to accept the lowest wages. While in a competitive labor market statistical discrimination would be under severe wage pressure, in a segmented labor market this wage pressure is less severe or nonexistent, and employers are free to choose whom they will.

This perspective suggests a sound economic basis for the maintenance of a wide range of institutional practices in industrial settings, including sex segregation (Aldrich and Buchele, 1987). Institutional economists have long criticized the simplicity of economic assumptions and their unrealistic application in the real world of work. Yet neoclassical labor theorists have been equally critical of the institutionalists, since they could not give a rational footing to the institutional practices they identified. Reasoning that directly extends the implicit contracts and efficiency wage notions provides such a basis for understanding institutional arrangements. Indeed, Block (forthcoming) has argued that such arrangements, while intended to extend the neoclassical model, in fact threaten to undermine it because a realistic appraisal of factors affecting worker commitment and effort will force economists to come to terms with more noneconomic influences than their models can incorporate. Under implicit contract conditions, maximizing behavior on the part of employers in any particular aspect of labor relations is constrained because such behavior may have associated costs for labor relations generally. Discriminatory labor policies are one such arrangement that becomes quite difficult to avoid, given the importance of maintaining labor peace and high worker morale. Change requires substantial management effort that would otherwise be devoted to other organizational goals.

Camaraderie, Teamwork, and Segregation

A third and final way to ground the long-term persistence of discrimination in economic theory is to refer to the necessity of cooperation between employees. This view integrates insights from organizational sociology with economic reasoning. The difficulty with the economists' scenario is the assumption that ability and productivity are asocial properties of labor, that workers with equal abilities are perfectly interchangeable. New, low-cost recruits cannot be successful without the acclimation to the workplace only other workers can provide.

Without cooperative workmates, they can be thwarted at every turn. If the firm is hiring women in order to reduce its wage bill, male employees have every reason to block the hiring of women. Thus, in the economists' scenario, a firm tries to hire a few women or minorities on an experimental basis, perhaps with an eye toward reducing its future wage bill. The experiment may fail, not because the new recruits are less able, but because they are harassed, ignored, and undermined by their coworkers. Kanter's analysis (1977) of women as tokens in organizations is a description of some of the ways women's performance is undermined by the organizational structure. The disappointing performance of women, real or perceived, confirms the suspicions of both managers and male employees that only men are cut out for the job. In short, the need for cooperative relations in the workplace undermines the employer's wage-reducing efforts to change the composition of the work force.

Employers may thus be stuck in a suboptimal stituation. Short of replacing a substantial group of employees, they may not be able to gradually incorporate lower-wage women or minorities into the firm. The wholesale replacement of their staff may seem a risky move that involves the loss of a great deal of accumulated experience. Wright (1987) has documented historical instances in the failure of efforts to substitute black for white workers in the South. A more limited approach is the wholesale replacement of men with women in a particular occupation. This approach may be attempted in times of labor shortage (Cohn, 1985; Milkman, 1987; Strober and Arnold, 1987). Yet more typically, employers may find a "locally optimal" situation, rather than a truly optimal one, which might be pursued only at great cost and great risk. This is a worker resistance argument, to be sure, but it differs from the one criticized above because it jettisons the assumption of the simple interchangeability of workers.

One might object to this view on the ground that it inflates the ability of male workers to enforce their preferences in the workplace. Yet male workers are likely to have more influence on keeping certain workers out than on other issues. Informal information is crucial to new workers; without it, women (or minorities) are effectively denied access.

Little of this would be new or surprising to those who experience discrimination every day in the workplace. Nor would these conclusions be surprising to institutionally oriented economists or sociologists. What is important here is the attempt to reconcile these conclusions with the classical economic views that predict discrimination will not persist.

In short, three factors—the effect of discrimination on labor supply, the inflexibility of employment arrangements, and the effectiveness of subtle employee resistance—tend to impede the economic forces against discrimination. These arguments suggest that long lags in discriminatory practices are quite possible, in part because they may not contradict employers' interest, in part because employers pursue a local costs minimum rather than a global minimum. Changes on the part of individual firms may be difficult and costly in terms of management effort. Shocks to the firm, such as government intervention or a crisis in profitability, may force a reexamination of such issues, but in the normal course of events such changes will be slow. These arguments diminish, but do not negate, the general effect of economic pressure to undermine discrimination.

Discussion

Three arguments have been advanced to account for the persistence over time of discriminatory effects. First, some of the effects economists attribute to supply should be attributed to lagged effects of discrimination. Whereas human capitalists claim that measurement error is always stacked against them in that all of the unexplained variance in wage equation models is attributed to discrimination, in fact a portion of the component they explain should itself be attributed to lagged discrimination effects.

Second, the wage-minimization goal underlying the assumption that competition undermines discrimination is not universally pursued by employers. Constrained by implicit contracts and by the desire to offer an efficiency wage, employers are relatively free to discriminate against women and minorities without feeling the pressure to reduce wages.

Third, the strategy of replacing male workers with female workers may not be effective, not because of the inability of women but because of the sabotage of women's performance by men worried about their economic position. The traditional economic models ignore the social organization of the workplace. If worker morale will decline in the process of integrating the workplace, employers may be deterred from pursuing this risky strategy.

Not only do these arguments suggest a rationale whereby competitive markets and discrimination are compatible, but they are consistent with the patterns of change we have found. If aspirations, educational decisions, and early labor market experiences are affected by lagged discrimination, a decline in the strength of discrimination is likely to produce changes in each of these contexts. This is what we have seen.

If worker resistance is the cause of the employers' reluctance to hire women workers, then we should see a pattern of some women being hired and leaving after a relatively short period of time. The evidence suggests just such a pattern. Thus, our abstract arguments presented in the language of neoclassical economics also explain the empirical behavior we have observed.

9

Conclusions

Principal Findings

We have argued for the usefulness of a social control perspective in understanding both stability and change in the sex segregation of occupations. The processes that reinforce sex segregation continue to operate throughout life. We have proposed two key tests of this thesis: first, change should be evident across different age groups, and second, high levels of instability should characterize the careers of individual women. If changes are not confined to the youngest age groups, then older groups must be susceptible to some contemporaneous influences. If instability in individual women's careers indicates that there is less continuity between life stages in sex typing than supply-oriented theories would indicate, then sex segregation must be reproduced throughout life.

The sex segregation of aspirations, college majors, and occupations has changed as much for particular cohorts as across cohorts. This evidence strongly supports the idea that sex-type attitudes and behavior remain adaptable: during the last 20 years, the decline in scx segregation in all forms considered here have been evident across a wide spectrum of those at risk of being influenced. We have found such patterns in each of the three contexts we examined: the sex typing of career aspirations, the sex typing of fields of study during college, and the sex segregation of careers. The decline in sex segregation in the last two decades has not simply been the result of the replacement of older cohorts with new, more integrated cohorts, but has been characterized by change influencing women across different age groups. In the aggregate, men have changed little in the sex composition of their career aspirations, the college majors they pursue, or the occupations they enter.

At the individual level, we find much more extensive patterns of change. The evidence indicates the prevalence of sex-type mobility for aspirations, college majors, and occupations. We have documented extensive movement from female-dominated occupations to male-dominated occupations, as well as mobility in the reverse direction. Among women changing aspirations, college majors, or occupations, there is only the weakest relationship between the sex type of the original position and the sex type of the destination position. The temporal relationship for individual men is almost as weak as it is for women. Aggregate change in recent years has been characterized by a notable change across different age groups for women, while the individual careers of both men and women may be described as following a revolving door pattern.

While social control extends throughout much of life, the evidence points against a cumulative disadvantage model. The proportion of women with male-dominated aspirations, in male-dominated college majors, and in male-dominated occupations increased as recent cohorts of young women aged, and the movement of individual women includes significant delayed entry into as well as exit from male-dominated fields. We thus find support for the revolving door model of sex segregation in each of the three contexts examined. Evidence consistent with this model is found in the case studies of women in male-dominated occupations surveyed in Chapter 7. Our examination of the legal and medical professions also provided surprising support for the social control perspective.

We have suggested that while sex-role socialization is important in beginning the dynamics of sex segregation, by itself it is not sufficient to maintain this system, since individuals move extensively after their initial choices have been formed. Further, the adaptability of sex-typed attitudes is inconsistent with an early socialization perspective; extensive change among those in their twenties and older suggests an extended period during which people's orientations may be altered.

Both the aggregate and individual changes observed are also inconsistent with an economic explanation of sex segregation. The economic emphasis on the maximization of lifetime earnings is inconsistent with the volatility of goals and educational choices and with the level of career mobility between male-dominated and female-dominated occupations. We document the prevalence of this pattern and have shown that it is not simply the result of career interruptions on the part of women. We have also argued that the net movement of women into male-dominated careers is not simply a reflection of a changing economic calculus but reflects changing values and the sensitivity of women to increased opportunities. The evidence suggests that women are highly responsive to the opportunities provided by the weakening of discriminatory barriers. Since women move into male-dominated occupations as opportunities expand, it is hard to argue that women's pursuit of female-dominated occupations represents the rational pursuit of individual self-interest over their lifetimes.

We have argued that the labor market segmentation perspective is not well suited to explain the segregation of aspirations or education, and it is ill equipped to predict patterns of change. The sex segregation of occupations is not captured by the standard structuralist categories; it needs to be understood as partly relying on discriminatory processes that include but extend beyond the point of hiring.

The social control perspective builds on the insights of these different perspectives. Social control begins during early socialization, is continued during the school years, and is continued through various discriminatory processes on the job. The values, education, and job experiences cumulate to maintain sex segregation over time. As these barriers decline for younger women, they also weaken for older women. This perspective is consistent with the patterns of change observed at both the aggregate and individual levels.

We have seen that changes in sex segregation are experienced differently by men and women. The increased college atten- dance of women and their increased labor force participation in- crease their visibility to men, even as men's visibility to women stays constant or declines. This asymmetry may account for differing evaluations of recent changes by men and women.

Finally, we argue that the discriminatory component of the social control perspective is not inconsistent with the efficient operation of labor markets. Feedback from previous discrimi- nation, the workings of internal labor markets described by im- plicit contract and efficiency wage theories, and the dynamics of work groups can account for the persistence of discrimina- tion despite the pressures of the market. While our principal concern is understanding the dynamics of women's careers, we suggest that economic reasoning is not necessarily inconsis- tent with our empirical findings.

Research Implications

Our social control framework may have more specific im- plications for research than for policy. First, studies should focus on the interplay between women's aspirations and their jobs. Rich longitudinal data are available for such studies. The present analysis indicates a great deal of instability in aspira- tions and occupations. But detailed longitudinal analysis might reveal complex links between changes in aspirations and jobs.

The weakness of the link between aspirations and jobs needs to be examined in more detail. Why do many young people pur- sue occupations other than the ones to which they recently as- pired? Is this pattern more a result of changing values or re- stricted opportunity? Such questions can be pursued in the framework of the panel data currently available.

Second, the changing educational pursuits of women need a great deal of attention. Research on sex segregation in higher education needs to develop a more dynamic approach. Rather than looking at overall distributions, the structure of change over time needs to be considered. In particular, attention to the attrition of women from male-dominated majors should be examined. Differences in the career outcomes of men and women in the same majors are also a fruitful avenue for investigation.

Third, the reasons for the dramatic movement of women out of male-dominated occupations need to be examined in more detail. Reducing the high rate at which women leave male-dominated occupations may be an important way to reduce the sex segregation of occupations. A richer understanding of this pattern is likely to require detailed case studies of particular occupational settings.

The principal thrust of these suggestions is the importance of examining women's careers in a dynamic framework. Longitudinal studies should consider the intersection of the careers of individual men and women with different dimensions of the occupational structure. Case studies ought to devote as much attention as possible to inflow and outflow aspects of occupational change.

Policy Implications

The social control perspective implies the desirability of a range of policy measures designed to combat occupational sex segregation. The social control perspective argues that the system of sex segregation rests on a multiplicity of control mechanisms that are collectively required to maintain the distinctions between male-dominated and female-dominated work. As sex-role definitions are challenged, the weakening of any of these mechanisms can serve to broaden opportunities for women. The efforts to improve opportunities for women should follow a variety of avenues, among them an attempt to broaden the career aspirations of young women.

At present, the standard that female-dominated jobs be paid at the same rate as male-dominated jobs of comparable worth does not seem likely to become law as a result of court decisions. Nonetheless, comparable worth is not dead. Comparable worth will serve as a bargaining chip for union negotiations. In particular, unions in the public sector are likely to pursue the comparable worth agenda with vigor. Comparable worth is likely to spread in public-sector negotiations and in locales such as universities, where public image is important. This may exert upward pressure on wages. Thus, comparable worth may have an important impact even if it does not become legally mandated.

One argument advanced for a comparable worth strategy is that it will lessen men's financial stake in keeping women out. The entry of women may be seen as posing a threat to men's financial position. If women's work were better paid, this threat would become less serious. Thus, while the immediate financial implications of comparable worth might be to reduce the relative attractiveness of male-dominated positions for women (Ehrenberg, 1987), the longer-term effect is likely to promote more occupational integration by sex.

While comparable worth may result in increased unemployment, the benefits will nonetheless outweigh the costs. The evidence suggests that the adoption of comparable worth in Australia did not result in significant unemployment (Gregory and Duncan, 1981). Studies of the employment consequences of comparable worth programs in the United States have also shown limited effects, partly because the comparable worth wage adjustments to date have been small (Ehrenberg, 1987). Although unemployment does result from higher wages for women, the resultant changes in technology will make women's jobs more productive, ultimately justifying the higher wages. Wright (1986) has argued that higher wages mandated by the adoption of minimum wage legislation in the 1930's were seriously disruptive for blacks in the South in the short run, but resulted in a major economic transformation and higher productivity and wages in the long run. Employers are likely to resist comparable worth, but they will no doubt be able to adapt to it.

The other principal item on the public policy agenda is the provision of child care for women. We have not emphasized work-family conflicts in this book because, in our data, marital and family responsibilities simply are not powerful factors in producing mobility from male-dominated into female-dominated occupations. Yet as women gain entrance to demanding male-dominated careers, a growing number of women will face acute difficulties in obtaining satisfactory child care. Corporate and governmental action in this area will become increasingly critical.

Less visible but equally important policy issues concern the promotion of women's educational and career opportunities. We have seen more progress for women in education than in the labor market, but barriers to women's progress remain. One important area that needs more attention is increased support for women choosing nontraditional fields, such as engineering. At work, a legacy of institutional choices needs to be eradicated. The changes that are needed include broadening women's access to apprenticeship programs and on-the-job training; gaining access for women to the informal information channels that are often so crucial in gaining access to job opportunities; eliminating job-entry criteria that are not directly related to job performance but that discriminate against women, such as height, weight, and age standards; and widening the pool of jobs that promotions are drawn from to include jobs currently filled by women (Roos and Reskin, 1984).

Equally important, feminists must fight to prevent the emergence of new institutional barriers that will be devised to restrict women's opportunities. In recent years, we have seen a decline in the force of older institutional constraints and an increasing reliance on informal mechanisms of social control. We expect that there will be attempts to institutionalize new limits on opportunities for women. Continued progress for women is not inevitable and may be contingent on political struggles, broadly conceived.

Future Trends

The informal social control system is the by-product of the lack of congruence between major social institutions, namely, the educational system and the occupational structure. The reliance on informal mechanisms to maintain sex segregation is the result of women's relatively high levels of educational attainment. The dramatic rise in women's labor force participation, especially on the part of educated women, posed a challenge to men's domination of well-paying jobs. Whereas education is the main basis for differentiating the occupational status levels among men in the labor force, women with relatively high levels of education have not been given the same access to high-status male-dominated occupations. Thus, there is a great deal of occupational segregation by sex among men and women with similar levels of educational attainment.

Recent trends suggest that this tension is being resolved in favor of greater opportunities for highly educated women. Indeed, the largest declines in sex segregation in the 1970's were found in the professions. Our country's ideological commitment to equal opportunity makes the exclusion of women from professional education difficult to justify. Once women have received professional credentials, it has proved relatively difficult to keep them out of the high-status occupations.

The revolving door pattern described here is essentially unstable. Over time, socialization, education, and occupational patterns tend to move toward greater congruence. The incongruity responsible for the career patterns we have seen is the result of large and rapid social changes. This pattern may remain in place for an extended period of time, perhaps for decades, but ultimately it is likely to be resolved in one of several ways.

One possible resolution is that women will solidify the gains they have made at work. This pattern implies a continuing trend toward convergence of career aspirations, choices of fields of study, and the occupations young women and men pursue. In the short run, the mobility of women into male-dominated occupations may increase, but over the long run the mobility in both directions may decline. The continuation of the occupational advances of the last 15 years is certainly a strong possibility. If this trend is to continue, it is likely to require the extension of child care at work and a relaxing of age-graded definitions of career lines geared to men's traditional career trajectories.

However, in stressing the effects of recent changes on different age groups, we must point out that future trends may reverse the current direction of change not only for new cohorts but for women already in the labor market as well. Who ten or fifteen years ago would have predicted the rise in the drinking age, when both the drinking and voting age were declining? Social definitions of acceptable behavior need not continue to change in the same direction. We must therefore consider other possible avenues for change.

A second possibility is the return to a pattern of women as a secondary labor supply. Strong profamily political currents are increasingly in evidence (Joffe, 1986; Luker, 1984; Mansbridge, 1986). The resurgence of family-oriented values that stress the importance of women staying at home with their children, combined with the continued inadequacy of child care, may reduce women's labor force participation, or at least stem its growth. This in turn could lead to a general acceptance of women's secondary roles at work. The informal barriers to women's career advancement may solidify into institutional channeling that more effectively constrains women's choices of careers. Just as health and safety regulations earlier in the century effectively barred women from many occupations (Lehrer, 1987), new formal structures may reappear that keep women from continuing to pursue male-dominated occupations. The entrance tests for such physically demanding occupations as fire fighters continue to be contested, and they may end up sufficiently rigid to keep women out. And the logic of restricting access for women in professional schools, due to their limited labor force participation, may reemerge, although this seems unlikely at present.

While in general, recent trends have pointed to declining occupational segregation by sex, some feminist sociologists have begun to be concerned about its resurgence. Reskin and Roos have been addressing the question of resegregation. They are considering the possibility that much of the recent trend toward integration is apparent rather than real, an interim step on the way toward resegregation (Reskin and Roos, forthcoming). Preliminary evidence suggests that such professions as medicine, law, and engineering are not resegregating at this point, but in such fields as banking and law the ability of women to enter the highest echelons remains uncertain.

A third possibility that seems increasingly likely is the deepening of divisions among women. In this scenario, one group of women will be devoted to high-status careers while another group will be more marginally connected to the labor force. High-status professions pay well enough to allow women to obtain privately funded day-care. The intrinsically rewarding work and the substantial remuneration may make it attractive for this group of women to pursue careers in the more prestigious and demanding occupations. And a growing number of self-employed women may be able to avoid the sexist environment in large law firms, investment banks, and other male-dominated corporate environments.

At the same time, women in less glamorous work roles will continue to confront the vexing tradeoffs between work and family. These women may increasingly be the victims of discrimination. Since the example of the high-status women will serve as proof that women need not take time off, those women who do interrupt their careers to raise a family may be viewed as voluntarily giving up careers. We may see a resurgence of the reasoning that sees the concentration of women in female-dominated occupations as due to women's voluntary choices, rather than as the result of the structural inadequacies of a system that fails to provide real opportunities for women. The rise of even a small group of career-committed women may increase the salience of career interruptions as an ideological justification for denying desirable career opportunities to most women. In this way, the failure to provide for the needs of families will continue the time-honored practice of blaming the victim.

Thus, in a conservative political environment, the slowly expanding options for women may increasingly polarize the career paths of women on the basis of educational differences and the patterns of career interruptions. The above alternatives stress the options women will pursue. But throughout, we have stressed that the options women pursue need to be understood in the context of available options. The question from this vantage point is whether new institutional mechanisms of discrimination will assert themselves.

We suspect that polarization is the most likely of these scenarios. Our speculation is that access for women to education may be decisive. Since education is the central means for access to high-status occupations, elite education for women will serve to maintain their jobs. And the institutional interest of colleges and universities in maintaining enrollments is likely to bolster the case for educational opportunities for women (Lasser, 1987). So, at least for the M.B.A.-toting minority of women, the future looks bright.

Without more support for child care, women in less elite careers will be less fortunate. If the high labor force participation rates of women with small children continue, women's careers are likely to continue to converge with men's. But this is far from certain, and it depends in part on the kind of jobs that open for women. At lower levels in the status hierarchy, the crafts seem likely to remain essentially closed to women. Hiring by networks, lack of co-worker support, and the threat of harassment limit women's opportunities in this area. Men may be able to block women indefinitely by relying on relatively informal mechanisms of exclusion. Sales, clerical, and service jobs will remain open for women, but most of these jobs make it difficult to maintain a middle-class lifestyle. The long-term future of women's work experiences depends on the institutionalization either of social supports that facilitate the careers of women or of institutional restrictions that form barriers against women's advancement. In the meantime, the more disorganized revolving door pattern we have described here is likely to continue.

Reference Matter

Notes

Chapter 1

1. Calculated from data in *Employment and Earnings* (U.S. Bureau of Labor Statistics, 1986).

2. These figures reflect the analysis of Current Population Survey data discussed in Chapter 7.

3. A figure of 70 percent recently received a great deal of attention, but this statistic is not comparable to the familiar time series data. See National Committee on Pay Equity (1987) for a discussion of recent data on the sex gap in wages.

4. The 30 percent figure was reported for high school graduates and those without high school degrees. The 17 percent figure was for college graduates, but if one adds the census bureau's finding of 12 percent for the sex segregation of college majors, with which we are also concerned, the total effect of sex segregation for this group is 29 percent.

5. The 43 percent figure represents Blau's estimate that 76 percent of the 57 percent discriminatory pay differential she finds is due to sex differences in job classification.

Chapter 2

1. The difficulty of obtaining an accurate account of the sexual division of labor should not be underestimated. Elizabeth Eames (pers. comm.) reports that Yoruba men say sweeping is women's work, although one frequently observes boys sweeping in both shops and

living areas. While in this case one can separate behavior from pre-
scription, not all behavior is accessible to the direct scrutiny of the
researcher.

2. The formula for D is:

$$D = \sum_{i=1}^{n} \frac{|(Wi/W) - (Mi/M)|}{2}$$

where Wi is the number of women in occupation i, W is the total
number of women, Mi is the number of men in occupation i, M is the
total number of men, and n is the number of occupations.

3. Massey and Denton (forthcoming) mention other indicators of
concentration, but C is convenient and attractive because of its analogous property to D. The formula for C for women is:

$$C = \sum_{i=1}^{n} \frac{|(Wi/W) - (1/n)|}{2}$$

where Wi, W, and n are defined as above. The formula for RC is:

$$RC = \sum_{i=1}^{n} \frac{|(Wi/W) - (1/n)|}{2} - \frac{|(Mi/M) - (1/n)|}{2}$$

where each term is defined as above.

4. The formula for P^*WM, women's probability of contact with
men, is:

$$P^*WM = \sum_{i=1}^{n} (Wi/W) - (Mi/T)$$

where T is the total number of individuals in the labor force, and each
of the other terms is defined as above.

5. Another approach to studying sex segregation is to look at
the extent of overrepresentation of men or women in particular occupational categories (Semyonov, 1980; Sokoloff, 1988; Scott and
Semyonov, 1982; Treiman and Terrell, 1975). This method is limited
because these studies compare one category to others, rather than
produce a single summary measure. Consequently, these studies
focus on a limited number of broad occupational categories, losing a
substantial degree of detail in the process. While Scott and Semyonov
make a strong case for the log odds ratio as an alternative to the index
of dissimilarity, the two views should be considered supplementary,
not contradictory, since they are designed to answer slightly different
questions. The index of dissimilarity is designed to provide a single,
summary measure of segregation; the log odds ratio and other ratio

measures are designed to indicate the degree of overrepresentation of men or women in a particular category. Scott and Semyonov's finding of increased concentration of men in certain broad categories, such as managerial and craft occupations, is in no way incompatible with a general secular decline in sex segregation. For a discussion of the indices of segregation, see Massey and Denton (forthcoming).

6. A sample from the 1970 census was assigned 1980 occupational codes. See Jacobs (1987) for a fuller discussion.

7. My figure corresponds with the figure Williams reports for 1950, which is just slightly higher than that reported by Gross. The figures presented here exclude children under 16.

8. This is not to suggest that competitive forces are absent in agriculture, but rather that the force of tradition may be stronger in agriculture than in other parts of the economy.

9. The drop in women's chances of sharing an occupation with men is reversed when the analysis is restricted to nonfarm employment; but the striking asymmetry of change—men's increased contact with women far exceeding women's decreased contact with men—remains.

Chapter 3

1. A further analysis of the 1900 public use data shows that reading and writing ability did little to influence the sex type of jobs (Jacobs, 1987).

2. The educational advantage of women in the labor force is undoubtedly due in part to the fact that working women on average have historically tended to be younger than working men. With educational attainment rising over time, younger people have generally completed more education than older ones. Thus the educational advantage of women is at least partly attributable to age.

3. As always, there is an alternative view in the human capital framework: since the opportunity costs of education for women are lower (they would make less money working instead of going to school), they stay in school longer than would otherwise be rational. One can point to institutional arrangements, such as child labor laws and compulsory attendance laws, that reduce the range and attractiveness of the alternatives to being in school. But then why do the earning differences that make it worth women's while to get so much education persist?

4. Two alternative explanations of the relatively high education of women seem less persuasive. One possibility is that men might choose educated wives in order to promote the education of their

sons. Thus, one could argue that once education becomes a corner-stone of social advancement, husbands would select educated wives in order to obtain the wife's assistance in the education of the children. Yet many cultures, including dynastic China, have emphasized the importance of education for sons without enlisting the assistance of educated wives. Alternatively, one might suspect that educational homogamy is necessary to maintain socioeconomic inequality across generations, but this too is not the case. There are many societies in which women are deprived of the opportunity to obtain more than the most rudimentary education where socioeconomic inequality is nonetheless transmitted from generation to generation. In these situations, high-status husbands marry the daughters of high-status men. Substantial dowries serve as the distinguishing feature of high-status eligible women. Indeed, it has been suggested that women's education can have symbolic value not unlike that of dowries, even when the level of education involved is low (Fricke, Syed, and Smith, 1986). Thus, educational homogamy is one of a variety of ways to maintain socioeconomic advantage through marriages, a system particularly suited to a companionate marriage system.

Chapter 4

1. This measurement bias is likely to be small, since the correlation between the sex composition in 1970 and 1980 is .9 (as measured with 1980 occupational census data and 1970 census data assigned 1980 codes).

2. In the computation of the index of segregation (D), we leave out the categories "other" and "undecided." After 1976, the ACE-CIRP occupational categories become more detailed; we report data on a set of consistent categories. We added the occupations that could not be collapsed in a manner consistent with the previous classification into the "other" category. This procedure accounts for the growth in the size of the "other" category in recent years.

3. An important methodological concern is the proper handling of nonresponse and sample attrition problems in the NLS data. Not all respondents answered the aspiration question each year, and over the course of the survey sample attrition increased. Consequently, differences between years may in part represent selection bias rather than a trend in the data. In separate analyses not reported here, we adjusted for these biases by constructing trends based on data on the same individuals over time. We did not detect significant selection bias.

4. This is not a measure of concentration across the 109 occupations in which women were represented, but across 301 occupations, whether women were represented or not.

5. The 1976 figure for men presented in Table 4.4 represents an extrapolation from 1974–75 trends. The 1976 concentration figures for men were substantially out of line with the trends in other years. They indicated a one-year decline in concentration of 7 percentage points, a rate of change wholly inconsistent with any of the data on women or men.

6. We ignore the issue of changes in educational aspirations. In this discussion, the overall differences between groups, rather than the interplay between changing educational and career goals, is our principal concern.

7. The index of dissimilarity, calculated on the ideal occupation data included in Lueptow's appendix, declined from 77.3 in 1964 to 64.6 in 1975.

8. Brito and Jusenius focus primarily on the determinants of aspirations, rather than on the aggregate trends we have taken as our primary concern here. Their brief discussion of trends is restricted to comparing college-bound women in 1968 and 1973.

Chapter 6

1. The difference between our approach and Astin's is discussed in Jacobs (1985). Essentially, the difference is that we examine change in a number of different years and focus on net flows rather than on regression coefficients.

2. The individual-level ACE-CIRP panel data were not available to us.

3. Before 1973, a number of entering students, predominantly men, indicated that their intended major was law, dentistry, or medicine. (After 1973, this was no longer an option in the CIRP survey.) Few of these students were able to major in these areas as undergraduates, since few colleges and universities offer bachelor's degrees in these areas. Consequently, the preprofessional category loses virtually all its members by graduation. Whether this pattern represents real change or is an artifact of coding is debatable. We handle this problem by presenting results that exclude the preprofessional categories before 1973 as well as results that include them.

4. We examined the effect of collapsing field-of-study categories on the observed correlation for the 1961 data. As expected, the correla-

tion declines as the units of analysis become larger. Consequently, we emphasize the similarity in the patterns of interfield mobility between the 1961 college seniors and the 1976 college seniors.

Chapter 7

1. These statistics were calculated with data from the March 1981 Current Population Survey, using the Beck-Horan-Tolbert core periphery model. See Jacobs (1983b) and Jacobs and Breiger (1988) for a more detailed examination of labor market segmentation issues.

2. This figure underrepresents the amount of occupational change in this period. It ignores exit from the labor force as well as individuals who may have changed occupations and then changed back. Analyses not reported here indicate that exit and reentry into the labor force do not change the process described here.

3. The difficulties with the NLS coding scheme were revealed in conversations with the staff of the Center for Human Resource Research at Ohio State University, which coordinates the NLS data. Coding error reduces the overall sex-type correlation but increases the correlation for the movers-only analysis by including some actual stayers as movers.

4. These totals were derived by combining those who expected medical careers at graduation, those who reported having planned on medical careers as freshmen, and those who considered medicine an alternative career. These figures were compared to the number of men and women enrolled in medical school in 1961–62, the year after graduation.

Chapter 8

1. One should note that economic theorists maintain a way out of this dilemma, namely, the hypothesis that unmeasured differences account for the gap. When confronted with data suggesting that men and women with the same education receive different levels of earnings, economists maintain that unmeasured differences in the kind of education account for the differences in wages. An initial test of this proposition, using a fixed effects model, suggests that such unmeasured differences do not explain the wage gap between men's and women's occupations (England et al., 1988). But, given a commitment to a view of markets in which discrimination cannot play a role, economists are likely to continue to search for ways of attributing sex segregation to factors other than discrimination.

Bibliography

Abrahamson, Mark, and Lee Sigelman. 1987. "Occupational Sex Segregation in Metropolitan Areas," *American Sociological Review*, 52(5): 588–97.

Abramson, Jill, and Barbara Franklin. 1986. *Where Are They Now? The Story of the Women of Harvard Law, 1984*. Garden City, N.Y.: Doubleday.

Adams, David. 1987. "Factors Related to the Retention/Attrition of First Year Women Engineering Majors." Paper presented at the Eastern Sociological Society Meetings, April, Boston.

Aldrich, Mark, and Robert Buchele. 1987. "Efficiency Wages, Women's Work, and Comparable Worth." Paper presented at the Colloquium on Comparable Worth, October, Rutgers University, New Brunswick, N.J.

Alexander, Victoria, and Peggy Thoits. 1985. "Token Achievement: An Examination of Proportional Representation and Performance Outcomes," *Social Forces*, 64(2): 332–40.

Almquist, Elizabeth. 1974. "Sex-Stereotypes in Occupational Choice: The Case of College Women," *Journal of Vocational Behavior*, 5: 13–21.

American Council on Education, Office of Research. 1966–72. *The American Freshman: National Norms. ACE Research Reports*, vols. 2–7. Washington, D.C.

American Medical Association. 1983. *Physician Characteristics and Distribution in the U.S.* (1982 edition). Chicago: Division of Survey and Data Resources, American Medical Association.

Anderson, Karen. 1981. *Wartime Women: Sex Roles, Family Relationships, and the Status of Women During World War II.* Westport, Conn.: Greenwood Press.

Aneshensel, Carol S., and Bernard C. Rosen. 1980. "Domestic Roles and Sex Differences in Occupational Expectations," *Journal of Marriage and the Family,* 42(1): 121–31.

Angle, John, and David A. Wissman. 1981. "Gender, College Major, and Earnings," *Sociology of Education,* 54: 25–33.

Angrist, Shirley S., and Elizabeth M. Almquist. 1975. *Careers and Contingencies: How College Women Juggle with Gender.* New York: Dunellen.

Arrow, Kenneth. 1972. "Models of Job Discrimination" and "Some Mathematical Models of Race in the Labor Market," in A. Pascal, ed., *Racial Discrimination in Economic Life,* pp. 83–102. Lexington, Mass.: D. C. Heath.

Astin, Alexander W. 1977. *Four Critical Years.* San Francisco: Jossey-Bass.

Astin, Alexander W., and Robert J. Panos. 1969. *The Educational and Vocational Development of American College Students.* Washington, D.C.: American Council on Education.

Astin, Alexander W., Robert J. Panos, and J. A. Creager. 1966. "A Program of Longitudinal Research on the Higher Educational System." *ACE Research Reports,* vol. 1, no. 1. Washington, D.C.: American Council on Education.

Baron, James N. 1984. "Organizational Perspectives on Stratification," *Annual Review of Sociology,* 10: 37–69.

Baron, James N., and William T. Bielby. 1980. "Bringing the Firms Back In: Stratification, Segmentation, and the Organization of Work," *American Sociological Review,* 45(5): 737–65.

Baruch, G. K., and J. Nagy. 1977. *Females and Males in the Potential Scientist Pool: A Study of the Early College Years.* Hanover, N.H.: Dartmouth College.

Bayer, A., J. Royer, and R. Webb. 1973. "Four Years After College Entry." *ACE Research Reports,* vol. 8, no. 1. Washington, D.C.: American Council on Education.

Beck, E. N., Patrick M. Horan, and Charles M. Tolbert II. 1978. "Stratification in a Dual Economy: A Sectoral Model of Earnings Determination," *American Sociological Review,* 43(5): 704–20.

Becker, Gary. 1957. *The Economics of Discrimination.* Chicago: University of Chicago Press.

———. 1981. *A Treatise on the Family.* Cambridge, Mass.: Harvard University Press.

Beller, Andrea H. 1982a. "The Impact of Equal Opportunity Policy on Sex Differentials in Earnings and Occupations," *The American Economic Review, Papers and Proceedings*, 72(2): 171–75.

———. 1982b. "Occupational Segregation by Sex: Determinants and Changes," *Journal of Human Resources*, 17(3): 371–92.

———. 1984a. "Trends in Occupational Segregation by Sex and Race, 1960–1981," in Barbara Reskin, ed., *Sex Segregation in the Workplace: Trends, Explanations, Remedies*, pp. 11–26. Washington, D.C.: National Academy of Sciences.

———. 1984b. "Higher Education Fields of Study and Professional Employment: Trends in Sex Segregation During the 1970's." Manuscript, University of Illinois at Urbana-Champaign.

Benson, Donna, and Gregg Thompson. 1982. "Sexual Harassment on a University Campus: The Confluence of Authority Relations, Sexual Interest, and Gender Stratification," *Social Problems*, 29(3): 236–51.

Berg, Ivar, ed. 1981. *Sociological Perspectives on Labor Markets*. New York: Academic Press.

Berg, Ivar, Marcia Freedman, and Michael Freedman. 1978. *Managers and Work Reform: A Limited Engagement*. New York: Free Press.

Bergmann, Barbara. 1986. *The Economic Emergence of Women*. New York: Basic Books.

Berryman, Sue R. 1983. *Who Will Do Science?* New York: Rockefeller Foundation.

Bianchi, Suzanne M., and Nancy Rytina. 1986. "The Decline in Occupational Sex Segregation During the 1970's: Census and CPS Comparisons," *Demography*, 23(1): 79–86.

Bielby, Denise V. 1978. "Career Sex-Atypicality and Career Involvement of College-Educated Women: Baseline Evidence from the 1960's," *Sociology of Education*, 51: 7–28.

Bielby, William T., and James N. Baron. 1984. "A Woman's Place is with Other Women: Sex Segregation in the Workplace," in Barbara Reskin, ed., *Sex Segregation in the Workplace: Trends, Explanations, Remedies*, pp. 27–55. Washington, D.C.: National Academy of Sciences.

———. 1986. "Men and Women at Work: Sex Segregation and Statistical Discrimination," *American Journal of Sociology*, 91(4): 759–99.

Blau, Francine. 1977. *Equal Pay in the Office*. Lexington, Mass.: D. C. Heath.

———. 1984. "Occupational Segregation and Labor Market Discrimination," in Barbara Reskin, ed., *Sex Segregation in the Workplace:*

Trends, Explanations, Remedies, pp. 117–43. Washington, D.C.: National Academy of Sciences.

Blau, Francine, and W. Hendricks. 1979. "Occupational Segregation by Sex: Trends and Prospects," *Journal of Human Resources,* 12(2): 197–210.

Blau, Peter M., and Otis D. Duncan. 1967. *The American Occupational Structure.* New York: Free Press.

Block, Fred. Forthcoming. "The Economic Sociology of Post Industrialism." Berkeley: University of California Press.

Blossfeld, Hans-Peter. 1987. "Labor-Market Entry and the Sexual Segregation of Careers in the Federal Republic of Germany," *American Journal of Sociology,* 93(1): 89–119.

Blumen, I., and P. J. McCarthy. 1955. *The Industrial Mobility of Labor as a Probability Process.* Cornell Studies in Industrial and Labor Relations, vol. 6. Ithaca, N.Y.: Cornell University.

Bose, Christine. 1985. *Jobs and Gender: A Study of Occupational Prestige.* New York: Praeger.

Boserup, Ester. 1970. *Woman's Role in Economic Development.* New York: St. Martin's.

Boulding, Elise, Shirley A. Nuff, Dorothy Lee Carson, and Michael A. Greenstein. 1976. *Handbook of International Data on Women.* New York City: Halsted.

Breiger, Ronald L. 1981. "The Social Class Structure of Occupational Mobility," *American Journal of Sociology,* 87(3): 578–611.

Bressler, M., and P. Wendell. 1980. "The Sex Composition of Selective Colleges and Gender Differences in Career Aspirations," *Journal of Higher Education,* 51(6): 651–66.

Bridges, William P. 1982. "The Sex Segregation of Occupations: Theories of Labor Stratification in Industry," *American Journal of Sociology,* 88(2): 270–95.

Brito, Patricia K., and Carol L. Jusenius. 1978. "Sex Segregation in the Labor Market: An Analysis of Young College Women's Occupational Preferences," in Frank L. Mott, ed., *Women, Work and Family,* pp. 57–76. Lexington, Mass.: D. C. Heath.

Brody, David. 1970. *Steelworkers in America: The Nonunion Era.* New York: Russell and Russell.

Bruno, Barbara. 1986. "Areas of Practice Chosen by Women Law Graduates," *Illinois Bar Journal,* 74(9): 434–35.

Bulow, Jeremy, and Lawrence H. Summers. 1986. "A Theory of Dual Labor Markets with Application to Industrial Policy, Discrimination and Keynesian Unemployment," *Journal of Labor Economics,* 4(3): 376–414.

Burriss, Val, and Amy Wharton. 1982. "Sex Segregation in the U.S. Labor Force: 1950–1979," *Review of Radical Political Economics*, 14(3): 43–56.
Cain, Pamela S., and Donald J. Treiman. 1981. "The *Dictionary of Occupational Titles* as a Source of Occupational Data," *American Sociological Review*, 46(3): 253–78.
Caldwell, J. C., P. H. Reddy, and Pat Caldwell. 1983. "The Causes of Marriage Change in South India," *Population Studies*, 37: 343–61.
———. 1985. "The Education Transition in Rural South India," *Population and Development Review*, 11(1): 29–49.
Carothers, Suzanne C., and Peggy Crull. 1984. "Contrasting Sexual Harassment in Female- and Male-Dominated Occupations," in Karin B. Sacks and Dorothy Remy, eds., *My Troubles Are Going to Have Trouble With Me*, pp. 219–28. New Brunswick, N.J.: Rutgers University Press.
Center for Human Resource Research. 1981. *National Longitudinal Surveys Handbook*. Ohio State University. Mimeo.
Cherlin, Andrew J. 1981. *Marriage, Divorce, Remarriage*. Cambridge, Mass.: Harvard University Press.
Clark, Burton R. 1960. "The 'Cooling Out' Function in Higher Education," *American Journal of Sociology*, 65(6): 569–76.
Cohn, Samuel. 1985. *The Process of Occupational Sex Typing*. Philadelphia: Temple University Press.
Cole, Stephen. 1986. "Sex Discrimination and Admission to Medical School, 1929–1984," *American Journal of Sociology*, 92(3): 549–67.
Cooperative Institutional Research Program. 1974–80. *The American Freshman: National Norms for Fall 1973–1979*. American Council on Education, University of California, Los Angeles.
Corcoran, Mary, Greg Duncan, and Michael Ponza. 1984. "Work Experience, Job Segregation and Wages," in Barbara Reskin, ed., *Sex Segregation in the Workplace: Trends, Explanations, Remedies*, pp. 171–91. Washington, D.C.: National Academy of Sciences.
Cott, Nancy F. 1977. *The Bonds of Womanhood*. New Haven, Conn.: Yale University Press.
Coverman, Shelley. 1986. "Occupational Segmentation and Sex Differences in Earnings," *Research in Social Stratification and Mobility*, 5: 139–72.
Crull, Peggy. 1982. "Stress Effects of Sexual Harassment on the Job: Implications for Counseling," *American Journal of Orthopsychiatry*, 52: 539–44.
Curran, Barbara. 1985. *The Statistical Lawyers Report: A Statistical*

Profile of the U.S. Legal Profession in the 1980's. Chicago: American Bar Foundation.

————. 1986. *Supplement to the Statistical Lawyers Report: A Statistical Profile of the U.S. Legal Profession in the 1980's.* Chicago: American Bar Foundation.

Davies, Margery. 1982. *Woman's Place is at the Typewriter: Office Work and Office Workers, 1870–1930.* Philadelphia: Temple University Press.

Davis, J. A. 1965. *Undergraduate Career Decisions.* New York: Aldine

Daymont, Thomas, and Paul Andrisani. 1984. "Job Preferences, College Major, and the Gender Gap in Earnings," *Journal of Human Resources,* 19(3): 408–28.

Daymont, Thomas, and Anne Statham. 1981. "Occupational Atypicality: Changes, Causes and Consequences," in Lois Shaw, ed., *A Decade of Change in the Lives of Women,* pp. 107–40. Vol. 5 of *Dual Careers.* Columbus: Center for Human Resource Research, Ohio State University.

Deaux, Kay. 1984. "From Individual Differences to Social Categories: Analysis of a Decade's Research on Gender," *American Psychologist,* 39: 105–16.

Deaux, Kay, and Joseph C. Ullman. 1983. *Women of Steel: Female Blue-Collar Workers in the Basic Steel Industry.* New York: Praeger.

de Cani, John, Michelle Fine, Philip Sagi, and Mark Stern. 1985. *Unwanted Attention: Report from the Committee to Survey Harassment at the University of Pennsylvania.* Philadelphia: University of Pennsylvania.

Degler, Carl. 1980. *At Odds: Women and the Family in America from the Revolution to the Present.* New York: Oxford University Press.

DiPrete, Thomas A. 1987. "The Professionalization of Administration and Equal Employment Opportunity in the U.S. Federal Government," *American Journal of Sociology,* 93(1): 119–40.

Duncan, Beverly D., and Otis D. Duncan. 1978. *Sex Typing and Social Roles: A Research Report.* New York: Academic Press.

Duncan, Gregory J. 1984. *Years of Poverty, Years of Plenty.* Ann Arbor, Mich.: Institute for Social Research.

Duncan, Gregory J., and Saul D. Hoffman. 1985. "A Reconsideration of the Economic Consequences of Marital Dissolution," *Demography,* 22(4): 485–97.

Duncan, Otis D. 1961. "A Socioeconomic Index of All Occupations," in Albert Reiss, ed., *Occupations and Social Status,* pp. 109–38. New York: Free Press.

Duncan, Otis D., and Beverly D. Duncan. 1955. "A Methodological

Analysis of Segregation Indexes," *American Sociological Review*, 20(2): 210–17.

Edwards, Richard. 1979. *Contested Terrain: The Transformation of the Workplace in the Twentieth Century.* New York: Basic Books.

Ehrenberg, Ronald G. 1987. "Econometric Analyses of the Empirical Consequences of Comparable Worth: What Have We Learned?" Paper presented at the Colloquium on Comparable Worth, October, Rutgers University, New Brunswick, N.J.

Elder, Glen, ed. 1985. *Life Course Dynamics: Trajectories and Transitions, 1968–1980.* Ithaca, N.Y.: Cornell University Press.

England, Paula. 1979. "Women and Occupational Prestige: A Case of Vacuous Sex Equality," *Signs*, 5: 252–65.

———. 1981. "Assessing Trends in Occupational Sex Segregation, 1900–1976," in Ivar Berg, ed., *Sociological Perspectives on Labor Markets*, pp. 273–294. New York: Academic Press.

———. 1982. "The Failure of Human Capital Theory to Explain Occupational Segregation by Sex," *Journal of Human Resources*, 17(3): 358–70.

England, Paula, and George Farkas. 1986. *Households, Employment, and Gender: A Social, Economic, and Demographic View.* New York: Aldine.

England, Paula, George Farkas, Barbara Kilbourne, and Thomas Dou. 1988. "Estimating the Wage Consequences of Sex Segregation: A Fixed Effects Model," *American Sociological Review*, 53(4): 544–88.

Epstein, Cynthia. 1981. *Women and the Law.* New York: Basic Books.

Evans, Mariah, and Edward Laumann. 1983. "Professional Commitment: Myth or Reality," *Research in Social Stratification and Mobility*, 2: 3–40.

Farley, Reynolds. 1984. *Blacks and Whites: Narrowing the Gap?* Cambridge, Mass.: Harvard University Press.

Feagin, Joe R., and Clairece Booher Feagin. 1986. *Discrimination American Style: Institutional Racism and Sexism* (2nd ed). Malabar, Fla.: Robert Krieger.

Feldman, K., and T. Newcomb. 1969. *The Impact of College on Students.* San Francisco: Jossey-Bass.

Fiorentine, Robert. 1987. "Men, Women and the Premed Persistence Gap: A Normative Alternatives Approach," *American Journal of Sociology*, 92(5): 1118–39.

Folger, John K., and Charles B. Nam. 1967. *Education of the American Population.* A 1960 Census Monograph. Washington, D.C.: U.S. Bureau of the Census.

Frank, Cheryl. 1985. "Law Firm Sex Bias: Mixed Bag," *American Bar Association Journal*, 71 (July): 25–26.

Freeman, Richard B. 1976. *The Overeducated American*. New York: Academic Press.

Fricke, Thomas E., Sabiha H. Syed, and Peter C. Smith. 1986. "Rural Punjabi Social Organization and Marriage Timing Strategies in Pakistan," *Demography*, 23(4): 489–508.

Friedan, Betty. 1963. *The Feminine Mystique*. New York: Dell.

Friedl, Ernestine. 1975. *Men and Women: An Anthropologist's View*. New York: Holt, Rinehart and Winston.

Furstenberg, Frank F., and Graham Spanier. 1984. *Recycling the Family: Remarriage after Divorce*. Beverly Hills, Calif.: Sage.

Garfinkel, Irwin, and Sara S. McLanahan. 1986. *Single Mothers and Their Children: A New American Dilemma*. Lanham, Md.: University Press of America.

Garrett, C., L. Ein, and L. Tremaine. 1977. "The Development of Gender Stereotyping of Adult Occupations in Elementary School Children," *Child Development*, 48(2): 507–12.

Getty, Linda D., and Arnie Cann. 1981. "Children's Perception of Occupational Sex Stereotypes," *Sex Roles*, 7(3): 301–8.

Gilligan, Carol. 1982. *In a Different Voice*. Cambridge, Mass.: Harvard University Press.

Glenn, Evelyn N., and Roslyn N. Feldberg. 1979. "Clerical Work: The Female Occupation," in Jo Freeman, ed., *Women: A Feminist Perspective* (2d ed.), pp. 313–38. Palo Alto, Calif.: Mayfield.

Goldin, Claudia. 1983. "The Changing Economic Role of Women: A Quantitative Approach," *Journal of Interdisciplinary History*, 13(4): 707–33.

Goode, William J. 1982. *The Family* (2d ed). Englewood Cliffs, N.J.: Prentice-Hall.

Goodman, Leo. 1981. "Criteria for Determining Whether Certain Categories in a Cross-Classification Table Should Be Combined, with Special Reference to Occupational Categories in an Occupational Mobility Table." *American Journal of Sociology*, 87(3): 612–50.

Graham, Steven N. 1980. *1900 Public Use Sample User's Handbook*. Seattle, Wash.: Center for Studies in Demography and Ecology.

Green, K., A. Astin, W. Korn, and P. McNamara. 1983. *The American College Student, 1982: National Norms for 1978 and 1980 College Freshmen*. American Council on Education, University of California, Los Angeles.

Greenberger, Ellen, and Laurence D. Steinberg. 1983. "Sex Differences in Early Labor Force Experience: Harbinger of Things to Come," *Social Forces*, 62(2): 467–86.

Greenwald, Maureen W. 1980. *Women, War and Work: The Impact of World War I on Women Workers in the United States*. Westport, Conn.: Greenwood.

Gregory, Robert G., and Ronald C. Duncan. 1981. "The Relevance of Segmented Labor Market Theories: The Australian Experience of the Achievement of Equal Pay for Women," *Journal of Post-Keynesian Economics*, 3: 403–28.

Gross, Edward. 1968. "Plus ça change . . . ? The Sexual Structure of Occupations over Time," *Social Problems*, 16: 198–208.

Gruber, James, and Lars Bjorn. 1982. "Blue-Collar Blues: The Sexual Harassment of Women Autoworkers," *Work and Occupations*, 9: 271–98.

Gutek, Barbara. 1985. *Sex and the Workplace*. San Francisco: Jossey-Bass.

Gutek, Barbara, and Bruce Morasch. 1982. "Sex Ratios, Sex-Role Spillover, and Sexual Harassment of Women at Work," *Journal of Social Issues*, 38(4): 55–74.

Gutek, Barbara, and Charles Namamura. 1980. "Sexuality in the Workplace," *Basic and Applied Social Psychology*, 1: 243–58.

Gutman, Herbert G. 1977. *Work, Culture and Society*. New York: Vintage.

Haber, S. 1980. "Cognitive Support for the Career Choices of College Women," *Sex Roles*, 6(1): 129–38.

Harmon, Lenore W. 1981. "The Life and Career Plans of Young Adult College Women: A Follow-Up Study," *Journal of Counseling Psychology*, 28: 416–27.

Hartmann, Heidi. 1976. "Capitalism, Patriarchy, and Job Segregation by Sex," in Martha Blaxall and Barbara Reagan, eds., *Women and the Workplace: The Implications of Occupational Segregation*, pp. 137–69. Chicago: University of Chicago Press.

Hartmann, Heidi, Patricia Roos, and Donald Treiman. 1985. "An Agenda for Basic Research on Comparable Worth," in Heidi Hartmann, ed., *Comparable Worth: New Directions for Research*, pp. 3–36. Washington, D.C.: National Academy Press.

Hartnett, R. T., and J. A. Centra. 1979. "The Effects of Academic Department on Student Learning," *Journal of Higher Education*, 48(5): 491–507.

Hearn, J. C. and S. Olzak. 1981. "The Role of College Major Departments in the Reproduction of Sexual Inequality," *Sociology of Education*, 54: 195–205.

Herzog, Regula A. 1982. "High School Seniors' Occupational Plans and Values: Trends in Sex Differences 1976 Through 1980," *Sociology of Education*, 55: 1–13.

Hesselbart, S. 1977. "Sex Role and Occupational Stereotypes: Three Studies of Impression Formation," *Sex Roles*, 3(5): 409–22.

Holm, Jeanne. 1982. *Women in the Military: An Unfinished Revolution*. Novato, Calif.: Presidio Press.

Horne, Peter. 1980. *Women in Law Enforcement* (2d ed.). Springfield, Ill.: Charles C. Thomas.

Hout, Michael. 1983. *Mobility Tables*. Beverly Hills, Calif.: Sage.

International Labor Organization. 1986. *Yearbook of Labor Statistics*. Geneva: International Labor Organization.

Jacobs, Jerry A. 1983a. "The Sex-Segregation of Occupations and Women's Career Patterns." Ph.D. diss., Department of Sociology, Harvard University.

———. 1983b. "Industrial Sector and Career Mobility Reconsidered," *American Sociological Review*, 47(3): 415–21.

———. 1985. "Sex Segregation in American Higher Education," in Lauri Larwood, Ann H. Stromberg, and Barbara Gutek, eds., *Women and Work: An Annual Review*, vol. 1, pp. 191–214. Beverly Hills, Calif.: Sage.

———. 1986a. "Trends in Contact Between Men and Women at Work, 1971–1981," *Sociology and Social Research*, 70(3): 202–6.

———. 1986b. "The Sex-Segregation of Fields of Study: Trends During the College Years," *Journal of Higher Education*, 57(2): 134–54.

———. 1987. "Long-Term Trends in Occupational Sex Segregation." Paper presented at the American Sociological Association Meetings, August, Chicago.

Jacobs, Jerry A., and Ronald L. Breiger. 1988. "Careers, Industries and Occupations: Industrial Segmentation Reconsidered," in George Farkas and Paula England, eds., *Industries, Firms and Jobs: Sociological and Economic Approaches*, pp. 43–63. New York: Plenum.

Jacobs, Jerry A., and Frank F. Furstenberg. 1986. "Changing Places: Conjugal Careers and Women's Marital Mobility," *Social Forces*, 64(3): 714–32.

Jacobs, Jerry A., and Brian Powell. 1984. "Gender Differences in the Evaluation of Prestige," *Sociological Quarterly*, 25(2): 173–90.

———. 1987. "Women's Occupational Status: A Revised Metric for Comparing Men and Women." Manuscript, University of Pennsylvania.

Jencks, Christopher S., Marshall Smith, Henry Acland, Mary Jo Bane, David Cohen, Herbert Gintis, Barbara Heyns, and Stewart Michelson. 1973. *Inequality*. New York: Harper and Row.

Jensen, Inger W., and Barbara A. Gutek. 1982. "Attributions and Assignment of Responsibility in Sexual Harassment," *Journal of Social Issues*, 38(4): 121–36.

Joffe, Carole. 1986. *The Regulation of Sexuality: Experiences of Family Planning Workers*. Philadelphia: Temple University Press.

Kanter, Rosabeth M. 1977. *Men and Women of the Corporation*. New York: Basic Books.

Karabel, Jerome. 1972. "Community Colleges and Social Stratification," *Harvard Educational Review*, 42(4): 521–62.

Kemp, Alice A., and E. M. Beck. 1981. "Female Underemployment in Urban Labor Markets," in Ivar Berg, ed., *Sociological Perspectives on Labor Markets*, pp. 251–72. New York: Academic Press.

Kent, Lori, and Nancy E. Durbin. 1986. "Educational Functions and Institutional Enrollments: Social-Structural Effects on Female Higher Educational Participation in 1900." Paper presented at the Southern Sociological Meetings, April, New Orleans.

Kessler, S., D. J. Ashenden, R. W. Connell, and G. W. Dowsett. 1985. "Gender Relations in Secondary Schooling," *Sociology of Education*, 58: 34–48.

Kessler-Harris, Alice. 1982. *Out to Work: A History of Wage-Earning Women in the United States*. New York: Oxford University Press.

Klein, Ethel. 1984. *Gender Politics: From Consciousness to Mass Politics*. Cambridge, Mass.: Harvard University Press.

Komarovsky, Mirra. 1985. *Women in College: Shaping New Feminine Identities*. New York: Basic Books.

Lasser, Carol, ed. 1987. *Educating Men and Women Together: Coeducation in a Changing World*. Urbana, Ill.: University of Illinois Press.

Lehrer, Susan. 1987. *Origins of Protective Labor Legislation for Women, 1905–1925*. Albany: State University of New York Press.

Lever, Janet. 1978. "Sex Differences in the Complexity of Children's Play and Games," *American Sociological Review*, 43(4): 471–83.

Levine, A. 1978. *Handbook on Undergraduate Curriculum*. San Francisco: Jossey-Bass.

Lieberson, Stanley. 1980. *A Piece of the Pie*. Berkeley: University of California Press.

Lieberson, Stanley, and Donna K. Carter. 1982. "Temporal Changes and Urban Differences in Residential Segregation: A Reconsideration," *American Journal of Sociology*, 88(2): 296–310.

Liefland, Linda. 1986. "Career Patterns of Male and Female Lawyers," *Buffalo Law Review*, 35(2): 601–31.

Lifschitz, S. 1983. "Male and Female Careers: Sex Roles and Occupational Stereotypes Among High School Students," *Sex Roles*, 9(6): 725.

Lind, Andrew W. 1982. "Immigration to Hawaii," *Social Process in Hawaii*, 29: 9–20.

Lloyd, Cynthia, and B. Niemi. 1979. *The Economics of Sex Differentials*. New York: Columbia University Press.

Lorber, Judith. 1984. *Women Physicians: Careers, Status and Power*. London: Tavistock.

Loy, Pamela, and Leah Stewart. 1984. "The Extent and Effects of Sexual Harassment of Working Women," *Sociological Focus*, 17: 31–43.

Lueptow, Lloyd B. 1981. "Sex Typing and Change in the Occupational Choices of High School Seniors," *Sociology of Education*, 54: 16–24.

Luker, Kristin. 1984. *Abortion and the Politics of Motherhood*. Berkeley: University of California Press.

Lyson, T. A. 1981. "The Changing Sex Composition of College Curricula: A Shift Share Approach." *American Educational Research Journal*, 18(4): 503–11.

McCaghy, M. Dawn. 1985. *Sexual Harassment: A Guide to Resources*. Boston: G. K. Hall.

McGee, Jeanne, and Jean Stockard. 1987. "From a Child's View: Children's Occupational Knowledge and Perceptions of Occupational Characteristics." Paper presented at the American Sociological Society Meetings, August, Chicago.

MacKinnon, Catharine. 1979. *Sexual Harassment of Working Women: A Case of Sex Discrimination*. New Haven, Conn.: Yale University Press.

McNamara, Paddy H. 1986. "A Follow-up on Hishon: Will the Partnership Process Change as More Women Enter Law Firms?" *Illinois Bar Journal*, 74(9): 430–34.

McPherson, J. Miller, and Lynn Smith-Lovin. 1986. "Sex Segregation in Voluntary Associations," *American Sociological Review*, 51(1): 61–79.

Madden, Janice F. 1985. "The Persistence of Pay Differentials: The Economics of Sex Discrimination," in Lauri Larwood, Ann Stromberg, and Barbara Gutek, eds., *Women and Work: An Annual Review*, vol. 1, pp. 76–115. Beverly Hills, Calif.: Sage.

Mansbridge, Jane J. 1986. *Why We Lost the ERA*. Chicago: University of Chicago Press.

Marini, Margaret M. 1978. "Sex Differences in the Determination of

Adolescent Aspirations: A Review of Research," *Sex Roles*, 4(5): 723–53.

———. 1980. "Sex Differences in the Process of Occupational Attainment: A Closer Look," *Social Science Research*, 9: 307–61.

Marini, Margaret M., and Mary C. Brinton. 1984. "Sex Typing in Occupational Socialization," in Barbara Reskin, ed., *Sex Segregation in the Workplace: Trends, Explanations, Remedies*, pp. 192–232. Washington, D.C.: National Academy of Sciences.

Martin, Susan E. 1980. *Breaking and Entering: Policewomen on Patrol*. Berkeley: University of California Press.

Massey, Douglas S., and Nancy A. Denton. Forthcoming. "The Dimensions of Residential Segregation," *Social Forces*.

Massey, Douglas S., and Brendan Mullan. 1984. "Processes of Hispanic and Black Spatial Assimilation," *American Journal of Sociology*, 89(4): 874–88.

Matteson, M. T., and S. V. Smith. 1977. "Selection of Medical Specialties: Preferences vs. Choices," *Journal of Medical Education*, 52: 548–54.

Medoff, James, and Katherine Abraham. 1981. "Are Those Paid More Really More Productive? The Case of Experience," *Journal of Human Resources*, 16(2): 186–216.

Melucci, Alberto. 1985. "The Symbolic Challenge of Contemporary Movements," *Social Research*, 52(4): 789–815.

Meyer, Herbert, and Mary D. Lee. 1978. *Women in Traditionally Male Jobs: The Experience of Ten Public Utility Companies*. U.S. Department of Labor, Employment and Training Administration R&D Monograph no. 65. Washington, D.C.: U.S. Government Printing Office.

Michigan Bar Journal. 1984. "Women in the Law." *Michigan Bar Journal*, 63(6): 450.

Milkman, Ruth. 1987. *Gender at Work: The Dymamics of Job Segregation by Sex During World War II*. Urbana, Ill.: University of Illinois Press.

Miller, Joanne, and Howard Garrison. 1982. "Sex Roles: The Division of Labor at Home and in the Workplace," *Annual Review of Sociology*, 7: 237–62.

Morantz-Sanchez, Regina Markell. 1985. *Sympathy and Science: Women Physicians in America*. New York: Oxford University Press.

Mott, Frank F., ed. 1978. *Women, Work and Family: Dimensions of Change in American Society*. Lexington, Mass.: D. C. Heath.

Murdock, George P., and Caterina Provost. 1973. "Factors in the Division of Labor by Sex: A Cross-Cultural Analysis," *Ethnology*, 12: 203–25.

National Center for Educational Statistics. 1948–80. *Earned Degrees Conferred in Higher Education*. Washington, D.C.: U.S. Government Printing Office.

———. 1971–82. *Digest of Educational Statistics*. Washington, D.C.: U.S. Government Printing Office.

———. 1976. *National Longitudinal Study of the High School Class of 1972: Tabular Summary of the Third Follow-Up Questionnaire Data*. Washington, D.C.: U.S. Government Printing Office.

National Committee on Pay Equity. 1987. "Briefing Paper on the Wage Gap." Washington, D.C. Mimeo.

New York State Task Force on Women in the Courts. 1986. "Report of the New York State Task Force on Women in the Courts," *Fordham Urban Law Journal*, 15(1): 11–98.

New York Times. 1986. "Women over 40 Choosing Law." Oct. 2, pp. C1, C6.

O'Farrell, Brigit, and Sharon Harlan. 1982. "Craftworkers and Clerks: The Effect of Male Co-Worker Hostility on Women's Satisfaction with Non-Traditional Jobs," *Social Problems*, 29(3): 252–65.

Olson, Janice Ann. 1979. *Gender Effects on Occupational Prestige*. Ph.D. diss., Cornell University.

Oppenheimer, Valerie. 1970. *The Female Labor Force in the United States*. Westport, Conn.: Greenwood.

Ott, M. D. 1978. "Retention of Men and Women Engineering Students," *Research in Higher Education*, 9: 137–50.

Parcel, Toby, and Charles Mueller. 1983. *Ascription and Labor Markets: Race and Sex Differences in Earnings*. New York: Academic Press.

Parnes, H., C. Jusenius, and R. Shortlidge. 1973. *A Longitudinal Study of the Labor Market Experience of Women*. Vol. 3 of *Dual Careers*. Washington, D.C.: U.S. Government Printing Office.

Parsons, Talcott, and Robert Bales. 1955. *Family Socialization and Interaction Process*. New York: Free Press.

Peng, S. S., and J. Jaffe. 1979. "Women Who Enter Male-Dominated Fields of Study in Higher Education," *American Educational Research Journal*, 16(3): 289–93.

Phillips, Ruth M. 1981. "Women in Medicine," in Betty Justice and Renata Pore, eds., *Toward the Second Decade*, pp. 49–56. Westport, Conn.: Greenwood.

Pleck, Joseph. 1981. *The Myth of Masculinity*. Cambridge, Mass.: MIT Press.

————. 1985. *Working Wives, Working Husbands.* Beverly Hills, Calif.: Sage.

Polachek, Solomon. 1976. "Occupational Segregation: An Alternative Hypothesis," *Journal of Contemporary Business*, 5(1): 1–12.

————. 1978. "Sex Differences in College Major," *Industrial and Labor Relations Review*, 31: 498–508.

————. 1979. "Occupational Segregation Among Women: Theory, Evidence and a Prognosis," in Cynthia B. Lloyd, Emily S. Andrews, and Curtis L. Gilroy, eds., *Women in the Labor Market*, pp. 137–57. New York: Columbia University Press.

Priebe, J., J. Heinkel, and S. Greene. 1972. *1970 Occupation and Industry Classification Systems in Terms of the 1960 Occupation and Industry Elements.* U.S. Department of Commerce Technical Paper no. 26. Washington, D.C.: U.S. Government Printing Office.

Reidinger, Paul. 1986. "The Men's Club," *American Bar Association Journal*, 72 (Nov.): 48.

Remick, Helen, ed. 1984. *Comparable Worth and Wage Discrimination: Technical Possibilities and Political Realities.* Philadelphia: Temple University Press.

Reskin, Barbara. 1987. "Bringing the Men Back in: Sex Differentiation and the Devaluation of Women's Work," *Gender and Society*, 2: 58–81.

Reskin, Barbara, ed. 1984. *Sex Segregation in the Workplace: Trends, Explanations, Remedies.* Washington, D.C.: National Academy of Sciences.

Reskin, Barbara F., and Heidi I. Hartmann. 1985. *Women's Work, Men's Work: Sex Segregation on the Job.* Washington, D.C.: National Academy of Sciences.

Reskin, Barbara F., and Patricia Roos. Forthcoming. *Gendered Work and Occupational Change.* Philadelphia: Temple University Press.

Rindfuss, Ronald, S. Philip Morgan, and Gray Swicegood. 1988. *The Transition to Parenthood.* Berkeley: University of California Press.

Rogers, Susan C. 1978. "Woman's Place: A Critical Review of Anthropological Theory," *Comparative Studies in Society and History*, 20(1): 123–62.

Roos, Patricia. 1985. *Gender and Work: A Comparative Analysis of Industrial Societies.* Albany: State University of New York Press.

Roos, Patricia, and Barbara Reskin. 1984. "Institutional Factors Contributing to Sex Segregation in the Workplace," in Barbara Reskin, ed., *Sex Segregation in the Workplace: Trends, Explanations, Remedies*, pp. 235–60. Washington, D.C.: National Academy of Sciences.

Rose, Peter I., ed. 1979. *Socialization and the Life Cycle.* New York: St. Martin's.

Rosen, Sherwin. 1985. "Implicit Contracts: A Survey," *Journal of Economic Literature,* 23: 1144–75.

Rosenbaum, James E. 1984. *Career Mobility in a Corporate Hierarchy.* New York: Academic Press.

Rosenfeld, C. 1979. "Occupational Mobility During 1977," *Monthly Labor Review,* 102: 44–48.

Rosenfeld, Rachel. 1983. "Sex Segregation and Sectors," *American Sociological Review,* 48(5): 637–56.

Rossi, Alice S., and Ann Calderwood, eds. 1973. *Academic Women on the Move.* New York: Russell Sage Foundation.

Rothman, Sheila. 1978. *Women's Proper Place.* New York: Basic Books.

Rubin, Lillian. 1983. *Intimate Strangers.* New York: Harper and Row.

Sanday, Peggy R. 1981. *Female Power and Male Dominance: On the Origins of Sexual Inequality.* Cambridge: Cambridge University Press.

Scanzoni, J., and G. L. Fox. 1980. "Sex Roles, Family and Society: The Seventies and Beyond," *Journal of Marriage and the Family,* 42(4): 743–56.

Schreiber, C. T. 1979. *Changing Places: Men and Women in Transitional Occupations.* Cambridge, Mass.: MIT Press.

Schroedel, Jean Reith. 1985. *Alone in a Crowd: Women in the Trades Tell Their Stories.* Philadelphia: Temple University Press.

Schulenberg, John E., Fred W. Vondrucek, and Ann C. Cronter. 1984. "The Influence of the Family on Vocational Development," *Journal of Marriage and the Family,* 46(1): 129–51.

Schur, Edwin M. 1984. *Labeling Women Deviant: Gender, Stigma and Social Control.* New York: Random House.

Scott, R., and M. Semyonov. 1982. "Long-Term Trends in Occupational Sex-Segregation: A Reexamination." Paper presented at the American Sociological Association Meetings, September, San Francisco.

Semyonov, Moshe. 1980. "The Social Context of Women's Labor Force Participation: A Comparative Analysis," *American Journal of Sociology,* 86(3): 534–50.

Sewell, William, Robert Hauser, and Wendy Wolf. 1980. "Sex, Schooling, and Occupational Status," *American Journal of Sociology,* 86(3): 551–83.

Shaw, Lois B. 1983. *Unplanned Careers: The Working Lives of Middle-Aged Women.* Lexington, Mass.: Lexington Books.

Shrager, Joan. 1985. "Covert, Overt Sexism Persist in Legal Profession," *Legal Times,* Jan. 21, p. 18.

Simon, Rita J., and Kathryn Gardner. 1981. "Career Patterns Among University of Illinois Women Law Graduates," *Women Lawyers Journal*, 67(4): 19–27.

Smith, James P., and Michael P. Ward. 1984. *Women's Wages and Work in the Twentieth Century*. Santa Monica, Calif.: Rand Corporation.

Smith-Rosenberg, Carroll. 1985. *Disorderly Conduct: Visions of Gender in Victorian America*. New York: Knopf.

Sokoloff, Natalie. 1988. "Evaluating Gains and Losses by Black and White Women and Men in the Professions, 1960–1980," *Social Problems*, 35(1): 36–53.

Solomon, Barbara M. 1985. *In the Company of Educated Women: A History of Women and Higher Education in America*. New Haven: Conn.: Yale University Press.

Somers, Dixie, and Alan Eck. 1977. "Occupational Mobility in the American Labor Force," *Monthly Labor Review*, 100: 3–19.

Sorensen, Elaine. 1986. "Implementing Comparable Worth: A Survey of Recent Job Evaluation Studies," *American Economic Review, Papers and Proceedings*, 76: 364–67.

————. 1987. "The Wage Effects of Occupational Sex Composition: A Review and New Findings." Paper presented at the Colloquium on Pay Equity, October, Rutgers University, New Brunswick, N.J.

Spangler, Eve, Marsha A. Gordon, and Ronald M. Pipkin. 1978. "Token Women: An Empirical Test of Kanter's Hypothesis," *American Journal of Sociology*, 84(1): 160–70.

Spence, A. Michael. 1974. *Market Signalling*. Cambridge, Mass.: Harvard University Press.

Spilerman, Seymour. 1977. "Careers, Labor-Market Structure, and Socio-Economic Achievement," *American Journal of Sociology*, 83(3): 551–93.

Spitze, Glenna. 1986. "The Division of Task Responsibility in U.S. Households: Longitudinal Adjustments to Change," *Social Forces*, 64(3): 689–701.

Stark, J. S., and B. R. Morstain. 1978. "Educational Orientations of Faculty in Liberal Arts Colleges: An Analysis of Disciplinary Differences," *Journal of Higher Education*, 49(5): 420–37.

Stone, Lawrence. 1977. *The Family, Sex and Marriage in England 1500–1800*. New York: Harper and Row.

Strange, C. C., and J. S. Rea. 1983. "Career Choice Considerations and Sex Role Self-Concept of Male and Female Undergraduates in Nontraditional Majors," *Journal of Vocational Behavior*, 23(2): 219–26.

Strober, Myra H. 1984. "A Theory of Sex Segregation," in Barbara Reskin, ed., *Sex Segregation in the Workplace: Trends, Explanations,*

Remedies, pp. 144–56. Washington, D.C.: National Academy of Sciences Press.

Strober, Myra H., and Carolyn Arnold. 1987. "The Dynamics of Occupational Segregation Among Bank Tellers," in Clair Brown and Joseph Pechman, eds., *Gender in the Workplace*, pp. 107–157. Washington, D.C.: Brookings Institute.

Strober, Myra H., and David Tyack. 1980. "Why Do Women Teach and Men Manage? A Report on Research on Schools," *Signs*, 5: 494–503.

Strong, Michael. 1988. *1910 Public Use Sample Handbook*. Philadelphia: Population Studies Center, University of Pennsylvania.

Summerfield, Penny. 1984. *Women Workers in the Second World War: Production and Patriarchy in Conflict*. London: Croom Helm.

Swidler, Ann. 1986. "Love and Adulthood in American Culture," in Arlene S. Skolnick and Jerome H. Skolnick, eds., *Family in Transition: Rethinking Marriage, Sexuality, Child Rearing, and Family Organization*, pp. 231–50. Boston: Little, Brown.

Talbert, Joan, and Christine Bose. 1977. "Wage Attainment Processes: The Retail Clerk Case," *American Journal of Sociology*, 33(2): 403–24.

Tangri, Sandra S., Martha R. Burt, and Leanor B. Johnson. 1982. "Sexual Harassment at Work: Three Explanatory Models," *Journal of Social Issues*, 38(4): 33–54.

Thomas, G. E. 1980. "Race and Sex Group Equity in Higher Education: Institutional and Major Field Enrollment Statuses," *American Educational Research Journal*, 17: 171–81.

Thurow, Lester. 1975. *Generating Inequality*. New York: Basic Books.

Tienda, Marta, Shelley A. Smith, and Vilma Ortiz. 1987. "Industrial Restructuring, Gender Segregation, and Sex Differences in Earnings," *American Sociological Review*, 52(2): 195–210.

Tolbert, Charles M. II. 1982. "Industrial Segmentation and Men's Career Mobility," *American Sociological Review*, 47(4): 457–77.

Treiman, Donald, and Heidi Hartmann, eds. 1981. *Women, Work and Wages: Equal Pay for Jobs of Equal Value*. Report of the Committee on Occupational Classification and Analysis, Assembly of Behavioral and Social Sciences. Washington, D.C.: National Academy of Sciences.

Treiman, Donald J., and Kermit Terrell. 1975. "Women, Work and Wages: Trends in the Female Occupational Structure," in Kenneth C. Land and Seymour Spilerman, eds., *Social Indicator Models*, pp. 157–99. New York: Russell Sage Foundation.

Trow, M., ed. 1977. *Aspects of American Higher Education*. New York: McGraw-Hill.

Turner, Ralph H. 1960. "Sponsored and Contest Mobility and the School System," *American Sociological Review*, 25(6): 855–67.

U.S. Bureau of the Census. 1986. "Women in the American Economy," *Current Population Reports*, P-23, no. 146. Washington, D.C.: U.S. Government Printing Office.

———. 1987. "Male-Female Differences in Work Experience, Occupation, and Earnings: 1984," *Current Population Reports*, P-70, no. 10. Washington, D.C.: U.S. Government Printing Office.

U.S. Bureau of Labor Statistics. 1976. *Concepts and Methods Used in Labor Force Statistics Derived from the Current Population Survey*. Report 463, series P-23, no. 62. Washington, D.C.: U.S. Government Printing Office.

———. 1986. *Employment and Earnings*. Washington, D.C.: U.S. Government Printing Office.

U.S. Commission on Civil Rights. 1978. *Social Indicators of Equality for Minorities and Women*. Washington, D.C.: U.S. Government Printing Office.

U.S. Department of Labor. 1975. *Handbook of Women Workers*. Washington, D.C.: U.S. Government Printing Office.

U.S. Merit Systems Protection Board. 1981. *Sexual Harassment in the Federal Workplace*. Washington, D.C.: U.S. Government Printing Office.

Waite, Linda J., and Sue E. Berryman. 1985. *Women in Nontraditional Occupations: Choice and Turnover*. Santa Monica, Calif.: Rand Corporation.

Waller, Willard. 1938. *The Family: A Dynamic Interpretation*. New York: Cordon.

Walsh, Mary Roth. 1977. *"Doctors Wanted: No Women Need Apply": Sexual Barriers in the Medical Profession, 1835–1975*. New Haven, Conn.: Yale University Press.

Walshok, M. 1981. *Blue Collar Women: Pioneers on the Male Frontier*. Garden City, N.Y.: Doubleday.

Weitzman, Lenore. 1979. *Sex Role Socialization: A Focus on Women*. Palo Alto, Calif.: Mayfield.

Westervelt, Esther M. 1975. *Barriers to Women's Participation in Post-Secondary Education*. Washington, D.C.: National Center for Educational Statistics.

Wharton, Amy S. 1985. "Blue-Collar Segregation: A Demand-Side Analysis." Ph.D. diss., University of Oregon.

———. 1986. "Industry Structure and Gender Segregation in Blue-Collar Occupations," *Social Forces*, 64(4): 1025–31.

224   *Bibliography*

White, James J. 1967. "Women in the Law," *Michigan Law Review*, 65: 1051–1122.

White, L. K., and D. B. Brinkerhoff. 1981. "The Sexual Division of Labor: Evidence from Childhood," *Social Forces*, 60(1): 170–81.

Whyte, Martin K. 1978. *The Status of Women in Preindustrial Societies.* Princeton, N.J.: Princeton University Press.

Williams, Gregory. 1979. "The Changing U.S. Labor Force and Occupational Differentiation by Sex," *Demography*, 16(1): 73–88.

Winter, Bill. 1983. "Survey: Women Lawyers Work Harder, Are Paid Less, But They're Happy," *American Bar Association Journal*, 69 (October): 1384–88.

Wright, Erik. 1979. *Class Structure and Income Determination.* New York: Academic Press.

Wright, Gavin. 1986. *Old South, New South: Revolutions in the Southern Economy Since the Civil War.* New York: Basic Books.

———. 1987. "Segregation and Racial Wage Differentials in the U.S. South Before World War II." Paper presented at the Work and Welfare Seminar, October, University of Pennsylvania, Philadelphia.

Wrong, Dennis. 1961. "The Oversocialized Conception of Man in Modern Sociology," *American Sociological Review*, 26(2): 183–93.

Zimmer, Lynn. 1985. "Sexual Integration of the Work Force: Limits and Strategies." Paper presented at the Eastern Sociological Society Meetings, March, Philadelphia.

Index

In this index an "f" after a number indicates a separate reference on the next page, and an "ff" indicates separate references on the next two pages. A continuous discussion over two or more pages is indicated by a span of page numbers, e.g., "pp. 57–58." Passim is used for a cluster of references in close but not consecutive sequence.

Library of Congress Cataloging-in-Publication Data

Jacobs, Jerry A., 1955–
    Revolving doors: sex segregation and women's careers /
Jerry A. Jacobs.
    p.   cm.
    Bibliography: p.
    Includes index.
    ISBN 0-8047-1489-4 (alk. paper)
    1. Sex discrimination in employment.   2. Sex role in the work
environment.   3. Sexual division of labor.   4. Pay equity.
I. Title.
HD6060.J33 1989   88-24986
331.4'133—dc 19   CIP